W9-CCG-125

THE DREAM MACHINE

THE DREAM MACHINE

The Golden Age of American Automobiles 1946–1965

by Jerry Flint

Quadrangle / The New York Times Book Co.

Warm regards to all the kind women who dug the pictures from the dusty files and all the writers who went before.

Photographs courtesy of:

American Motors Corporation
Chrysler Corporation
Ford Motor Company
General Motors Corporation
John A. Conde Collection
Motor Vehicle Manufacturers Association

To everyone who owned one—and was sorry to see it go.

A Norback Book

Copyright © 1976 by Quadrangle/The New York Times Book Co. All rights reserved, including the right to reproduce this book or portions thereof in any form. For information, address: Quadrangle/The New York Times Book Co., 10 East 53 Street, New York, New York 10022. Manufactured in the United States of America. Published simultaneously in Canada by Fitzhenry & Whiteside, Ltd., Toronto.
Library of Congress catalog card number: 75–13754
ISBN: 0–8129–0598–9

CONTENTS

FOREWORD

The Golden Age of American Automobiles was not in the glorious 1920s or the depressed 1930s. The Golden Age was the two decades after World War II, the years of America's great love affair with its automobiles.

It was in those years that we created an entire society around our cars, from freeways to campsites, suburbs to drive-ins. We built 116 million cars in those twenty years and put the nation on wheels. And it was in those twenty years that automobile engineering peaked. The high-compression engines, the suspension systems, the automatic and the power assists were developed, and more important, made to work. The automobile became a trustworthy machine in this Golden Age.

The art of automobile styling reached its height in these two decades, too, in beauty and in the grotesque. They will never be as good looking—or as bad—again.

Much has changed. The birth-control pill, the supersonic jet, the eight-track stereo, the nuclear power plant, and the pocket calculator. Yet if you could drive a car of the Golden Age—the first Kaiser or the Oldsmobile 88 of '49, the '55 Chevrolet or the '65 Mustang—you can handle today's car. They really have not moved forward much since then and most of the technology in the newest cars was developed in those twenty postwar years.

By 1965 the car trip was beginning to end.

But what a ride.

—Jerry Flint

There's a Ford in your future
But the one in your past
Is the one you have now
So you'd better make it last.

—A radio commercial

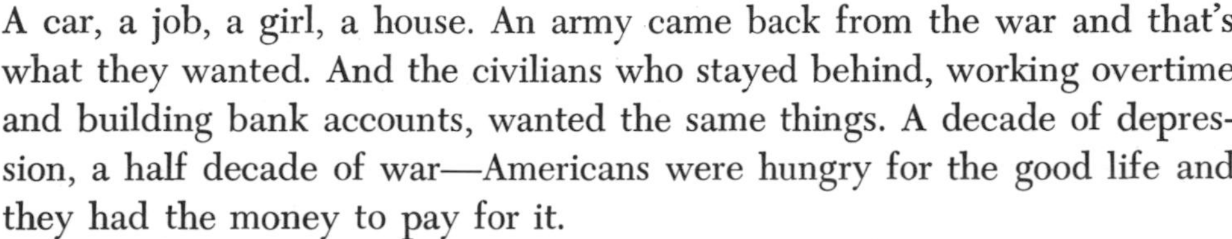

A car, a job, a girl, a house. An army came back from the war and that's what they wanted. And the civilians who stayed behind, working overtime and building bank accounts, wanted the same things. A decade of depression, a half decade of war—Americans were hungry for the good life and they had the money to pay for it.

In the end all their goals fitted together. They married and built their homes where there was room for a bit of grass, a flower bed, and a tree. The suburbs were created. The jobs, the schools, the shopping centers, and even the night life—first the drive-ins, then the bars, and then the swinging-singles apartments—followed. And the cars tied it all together.

The men who built the cars figured the machines would be different in the postwar world. Detroit finally had created a pretty good machine, one that worked, that ran, was not always breaking down, and the car engineers were breaking through with major technological improvements. In the old days the engineer ruled the auto world "often to the point of unreasonable

MacArthur purges Japanese militarists; Hirohito denies divinity. Russians loot Manchuria
Millions of GIs demobilized; GIs protest delays. Millions strike in steel, coal, autos;

insistence on having his ideas as to the design followed to the letter," a General Motors man complained. The new world would be different.

"At the close of World War II," said Alfred Sloan Jr., the boss of G.M. then, "we made the projection that for an indefinite period the principal attractions of the product would be appearance, automatic transmissions, and high-compression engines, in that order." Appearance, easy driving, and power.

It wasn't easy at the beginning. Most of the top auto men were production bosses or engineers, "wearing suspenders and belts, button shoes, with pencils in their pockets and their taste in their mouths," was the way William Mitchell, now G.M.'s styling vice-president, put it. They didn't like stylists.

"They called us 'styliths,'" recalled Richard Teague, now the top stylist at American Motors, "a cheap shot, but it hurt."

The top designer at G.M. was a giant of a man, six feet, four inches tall (which was a lot taller in 1946 than today) named Harley Earl. He was overpowering—"he just scared the hell out of you," says Teague and every stylist who ever worked for him, and practically all of them did, because Earl created the art of automobile styling for Detroit, and most of the important designers of the next two decades passed through his shop. They called him Mr. Earl. "Even his wife must have called him Mr. Earl," one said.

"My primary purpose for twenty-eight years," Mr. Earl said, "has been to lengthen and lower the American automobile, at times in reality and always at least in appearance. Why? Because my sense of proportion tells me that oblongs are more attractive than squares."

Henry Ford II, grandson of the famous Henry who still lived, drove off the line the first car for civilians, a white Ford, July 3, 1945, more than a

ationalists-Reds battle there; George Marshall peace mission fails, Chiang claims victories. Hunger, r
ical pay hike 18.5¢ an hour. average factory pay: $42.46 a week. Truman loosens wage-price controls; w

1.
Young Henry Ford II drives the first postwar Ford down the line July 3, 1943.

2.
The first postwar cars were the old prewar designs. This is a Lincoln. Note the pushbutton and the skirt length. The later "new look" dropped the hem

ioning in Europe. Col. Peron president in Argentina. Riots in Egypt, Britain to withdraw troops. Irgu
k O.P.A. extended, controls off food, prices up 18% in year. D-J industrials 206.97 in February. Senat

3.
The postwar Studebaker. The company killed this car quickly and was first in production with an all new design for 1947.

4.
The first Hudson off the line.

tern gang attack British in Palestine, British block immigration, drag refugees to Cyprus; death senten
locks fair employment law. Lynchings in Georgia, Mississippi; Supreme Court outlaws segregation on int

month before Japan surrendered on August 14 (the demobilization and swing to civilian life began before the formal end of the war). On October 26 when the '46 Fords were shown to the public, 300,000 orders were written in only two days. Chevrolet rolled its first postwar car off the line October 3 and by the 17th of that month all G.M. divisions were in production.

The cars were really prewar models with a few minor changes, such as the Buick gun-sight hood ornament, which had to be a great idea with 10 million veterans back from the war. Most of the models carried six-cylinder engines or the now almost forgotten Straight-8—with the eight cylinders lined up in a row under the long hood—although Cadillac and Ford built V-8s, with four cylinders facing each other in a V-shaped engine block (this engine came to dominate the industry). The steering wheels were enormous by today's standards, and you started the engine by turning the ignition key with one hand, pushing a starter button with the other, then hitting the clutch and shifting into first to move. The windshields were two-piece affairs, and the hoods V-shaped, since the front fenders (and the rear fenders, too) were distinct from the remainder of the body, meaning the car interior was much narrower than the total car width. A typical big car would be between 66 and 70 inches high and 200 to 210 inches long. Most of the models were what today are called notchbacks—the roofline coming down to make a distinct trunk. But there were fastbacks too, with the roof sloping all the way back, on some G.M. models; that was what passed for streamlining then. Today's designers do not like that look.

"They look like hell today," says Mitchell of G.M. The thick roofs are ugly and the sheet metal "looks as if it was hammered in a blanket." Today's fastbacks are lower, carry bigger windows and have a lower belt line that improves the look, stylists say.

s, whippings for Jewish terrorists; thousands arrested. UNO meets, Russia uses veto; NY City to be hea
state trains, buses. Talmadge elected gov. of Georgia, vows Negroes won't vote, dies before swear-in,

A third design was the mildly sloped roofline—similar to the Volkswagen Beetle—and carried by the Ford and Chrysler companys' cars.

A deluxe four-door Ford or Chevy sold at $1,325 (prices were controlled during World War II and until November 1946 to prevent runaway inflation, and the car makers complained bitterly that they were too low). A luxury model could be bought for a little more than $2,000—in theory. Anyone who got a car that first year was lucky, and possibly paid a dealer $500 or even $1,000 over the list price (there were no window stickers with the price then).

"We got a new Plymouth," one New Yorker remembers. "It had wooden bumpers." There was a shortage of steel ones. "We didn't have any radio or heater. Daddy said they were signs of softness." But you took what you could get and if you got a new car you showed it to your neighbors and drove them around the block and on Sunday you took a drive to the country on two-lane roads.

There was not much in the way of color, inside or out. "We thought it was a real breakthrough to match dark mud-colored mohair to mouse-gray mohair," said Gene Bordinat, Ford's styling vice-president.

Not many of the new cars were built. In 1945 despite unlimited demand only 83,786 cars rolled out and in 1946 only 2,155,921. A wave of material shortages and strikes erupted after World War II. If the parts makers were not struck it was the glass makers, the steel makers, or even the Detroit giants. Walter Reuther, who led the United Auto Workers at G.M., closed the plant for four months late in 1945 into 1946 in one of the postwar era's great labor versus capital confrontations.

But if it was a long strike, it was not the bloody, head-busting type strike of the 1930s, proving that attitudes were changing on both sides. In the end, the strike dragged on over one penny—a penny an hour Reuther

eds rebel. Major US policy shift: Secretary of State Byrnes warns against red agression, gets tough.
opulation 141 million. Commerce secretary Henry Wallace says give USSR A-secrets, cuts US defense; fir

5.
The Packards were handsome cars, even by today's standards, and dominated the luxury market for a time after World War II.

nada breaks red A-spy ring. Yugoslavs execute Gen. Mikhailovich, chetnik leader; shoot down US transpo
by Truman. Draft extended. GOP wins Congress; new faces: Joe McCarthy (Sen., Wis.), R.M. Nixon (Rep.

6.
The Nash Ambassador. The slope-back design is similar to the Ford.

1945

Production

Ford	37,800
General Motors	25,500
Chrysler	6,200
Nash	6,100
Hudson	4,700
Packard	2,700
Studebaker	700
Total	83,700

wanted to prove he could win more than other unions. G.M. refused to give that penny for the same reason. Reuther did not win his penny, but he won G.M.'s grudging respect, and it was a quarter-century before the U.A.W. was willing to take on G.M. again (and then, in 1970, only after Reuther had died in a plane crash months before).

The best story of that first postwar year was the struggle for the Ford Motor Company. It is almost forgotten now, but by the end of World War II Ford was not second to G.M.; Ford was third to Chrysler and fading fast.

Old Henry Ford, who had been born during the Civil War and outlived his son Edsel, was eighty-two when World War II ended, near senility and still in control of his company. But that company was disintegrating.

"The team was breaking up," said Charles "Cast Iron Charlie" Sorensen, Henry's top production genius who was fired for no apparent reason. "The

illed, apologize. German-Japanese soldiers hanged for war crimes; major trials at Nuremberg, 12 top Na

ets jam colleges. US fights famine abroad, cuts bread loaf size here, Export all canned meat. Truman

captain was a sick man, unable to call the plays. The line coaches were gone. Anyone who made a brilliant play was called out," he said.

"We found one Ford shop that was still producing propellers for Ford Tri-Motor planes," reported Robert McNamara who joined Ford after the war and was later to become Secretary of Defense in 1960. Those airplanes had been out of production for years and few were flying. "But there we were, still turning out propellers for them, and losing money, of course."

"The company was not only dying, it was already dead and rigor mortis was setting in," Jack Davis, the sales manager, said. But worst of all, the Ford family (Ford was a family-owned company then) feared old Henry would turn control over to a shadowy figure, Harry Bennett, who, when his enemies were being kind, was called a thug. Finally Ford's daughter-in-law demanded that he turn control of the company over to her son, Henry's grandson, twenty-eight-year-old Henry Ford II. She threatened to sell her stock if he refused. On September 21, 1945, old Henry gave up control to his grandson and Henry II fired Bennett immediately. What happened next was described by noted reporter Bob Considine in the Hearst newspapers.

1946

Production

General Motors	827,800
Chrysler	538,200
Ford	457,400
Nash	98,800
Hudson	90,800
Studebaker	77,600
Packard	42,100
Kaiser-Frazer	11,800
Willys	6,500
Crosley	5,000
Total	2,156,000

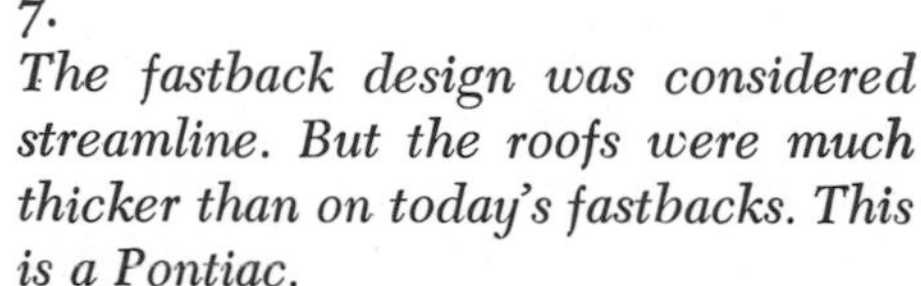

7.
The fastback design was considered streamline. But the roofs were much thicker than on today's fastbacks. This is a Pontiac.

to hang, Goering takes poison. Dutch fight rebels in East Indies. British to free India; Hindu-Mosle
aks rail, coal strikes; miners fined $3.5 million. Military unification opposed. Walter Reuther heads

8.
The DeSoto really wasn't changed in 1946, 1947 or 1948. Notice the door-openings face each other.

9.
The Chevrolet Stylemaster Sport Sedan. Noteworthy are two-piece windshield and the distinct front and rear fenders.

housands killed. French recognize, then attack Ho Chi Minh Indo-China republic. Paul Sartre emerge. J
eds. Army cast system hit, off-post saluting ends. Congress clears Roosevelt of Pearl Harbor guilt. A

10.
The Plymouth Special DeLuxe, low on styling but had a high quality reputation. The hats, though, were right in style.

John Bugas, an ex-FBI agent who had gone to work for Ford and Bennett but became an ally of young Henry, went in to see Bennett moments later.

"I walked into that long office of his and along the rug to his desk," Bugas told Considine. "Harry waited until I stood before the desk. Then suddenly he jumped up and screamed, 'you're behind all this, you son of a bitch.' He called me every name in the book, and he knew them all.

"At the height of it he tore open a desk drawer and pulled out his .45. My .38 was just inside my jacket. I was ready, if it looked like my life was involved. Then, just as abruptly, he slammed his gun down on the desk and it lay there. He cursed me until he ran out of words, and then he sank back into his chair, winded. The .45 was still on his desk."

Bugas said he told Bennett he had himself to blame, then walked out "my back to him all the way. I guess my shoulders might have been braced a bit, waiting to take a shot. Nothing happened."

That's how they did business at Ford in those days.

Louis KOs Billy Conn in 8, keeps title. Dead: Jack Johnson, Major Bows, H.G. Wells, Harry Hopkins. O
ault wins Derby. Songs: Let It Snow, It's Been a Long Long Time, Symphony, Doin' What Comes Naturally,

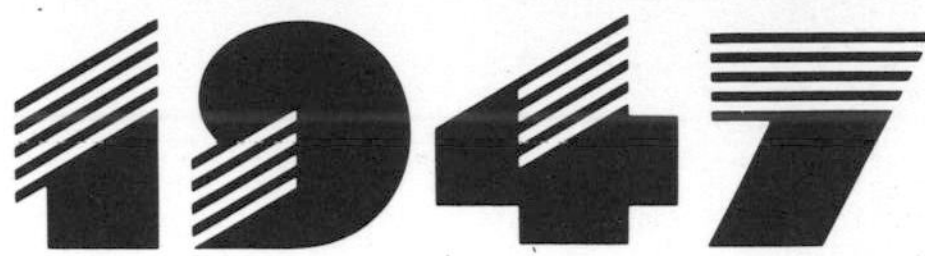

"Acres and acres of it and it's all mine."
—Joseph Frazer of Kaiser-Frazer

They were not changing models every fall after World War II, just building every car they could. Come fall and a manufacturer might just announce that anything built after November first would be called the next year's model. If anyone had a really new car they would not wait until fall; they just pushed the new model down the lines as soon as they could.

The first all-new look came on the 1947 Studebaker (which actually came out in the summer of '46). Raymond Loewy, the transplanted French designer was credited with that startling Studebaker (although one of his assistants, Virgil Exner, claimed the design credit too. Exner later headed styling for Chrysler and created the famous fins of '57). The Studebaker look was a sensation in car-hungry America, but no one was quite sure what to make of it. The prettiest model was the two-door Starlight coupe, seven inches lower than prewar models, the lowest car on America's roads, only sixty-one inches high, with the passengers moved forward, the front fenders integrated into the body, and—a real shock—the windows lapped around the rear. It may not seem funny today, but one-liners like "It's a Studebaker, but is it coming or going?" would bring a roar of laughter. Or radio comedienne Vera Vague gushing, "How do you like my new gown. It's

European coal shortage, suffering, power cuts; England nationalizes mines. Fierce fightin
Price controls off fish, fruit; poultryless Thursday ends but grain conservation asked. Po

1.
The classic Lincoln Continental.

cut low with lace in front and it's cut low with lace in back." And Bob Hope answering: "It's beautiful Miss Studebaker."

Loewy was unperturbed. "An independent, in order to succeed, must be courageous and progressive," he said. "The results may be somewhat of a shock, but it is far better than blandness."

in Palestine: Irgun-Stern Gang attack, British hang Jewish guerillas, Irgun raids Acre Prison; British
virus isolated. Georgia governor fight: Herman Talmadge with state police seizes gov. mansion; court

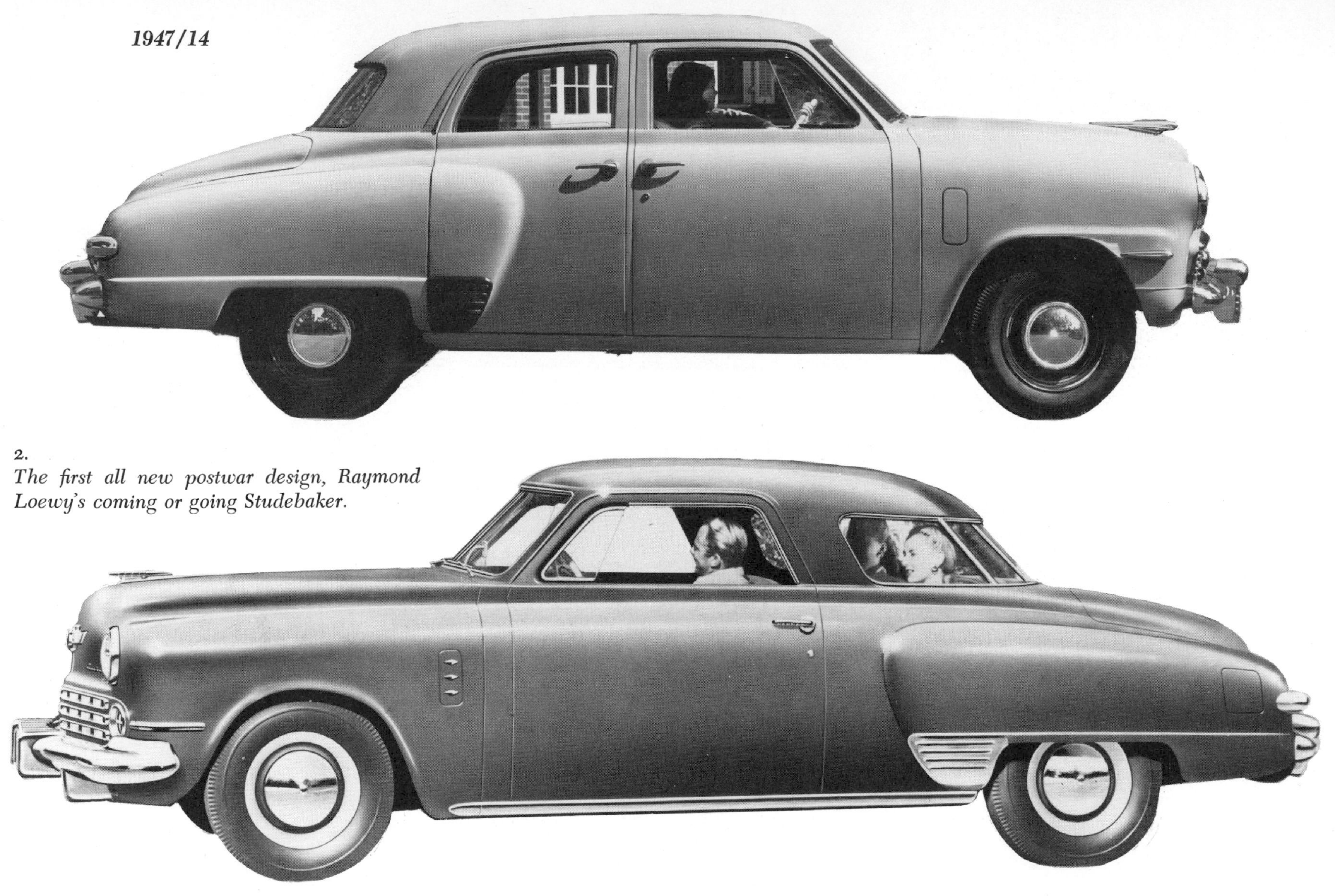

2.
The first all new postwar design, Raymond Loewy's coming or going Studebaker.

ill Jews, drag concentration camp survivors back to Germany; US-USSR back partition, UN agrees, Arabs t
rrested in Germany. Red spy Gerhard Eisler arrested in NY. NY keeps subway fare 5¢. Truman doctrine:

He was probably right. When independent car makers have succeeded, it has been with cars that were startlingly different: the '47 Studebaker, the "step-down" Hudson of '48, the "bathtub" Nash of '49 on through Dick Teague's Gremlin and his teardrop Pacer of '75 for American Motors. There's a good reason.

"They've only got to turn a certain number of people on," says Gene Bordinat, the Ford stylist. A few hundred thousand customers willing to buy a different look makes it a successful year. But the biggest companies have millions of customers to please and "have to cut more of a middle ground."

The new Studebaker models were light and low, 193 and 204 inches long, 2 feet shorter than a full-sized car of the 1970s. "Your dream car is here and in production," read the ads. The Studebaker engines didn't match the design—they were the old 80- and 94-horsepower plants—though they could give 20 miles a gallon, and there were new self-adjusting brakes.

The automobile shortage was fierce, and anything an independent built could be sold. Only 3.6 million cars were built in 1947, with the independents such as Nash, Hudson, and Studebaker each building more than 100,000 cars (not nearly as many as they wanted to produce, of course, because they were hampered by supplier strikes and steel and parts shortages, just like G.M., Chrysler, and Ford). But leading the independents in production was a newcomer—Kaiser-Frazer.

Frazer and Kaiser, a star-crossed pair. Joseph Frazer was an old-time auto man. He had worked for G.M. and Chrysler and was credited with saving Willys-Overland from the boneyard during the Depression, and just may have hung the name Jeep on the famous vehicle Willys built in the war. But when the war ended he wanted to build his own car, picked up an old-time car maker, Graham-Paige, which had been failing when the

ten war, mobilize, kill Jews in Aden, Syria; Jewish Haganah army seeks arms. British withdrawing from
0 million to fight Greek reds. NY state outlaws public employe strikes. 111 miners killed in Central

3.
The Chrysler Town and Country Woodie is almost a hardtop. Beautiful, but keep it out of the rain.

4.
The Mercury Woodie carried a price near $2,500.

5.
Even Nash had a Woodie, the Ambassador Suburban. The bodies had to be varnished yearly.

war began, and he scurried across the country looking for money. On the West Coast, while sounding out the airplane makers—unsuccessfully—he saw A. P. Giannini, head of the giant Bank of America.

"Why don't you see H.J.?" Giannini asked.

H.J. was a legend in his own time: Henry J. Kaiser, a concrete man, a road builder, a dam builder and finally the miracle ship builder who rolled his Liberty ships down the ramps faster than German U-boats could sink them (his record from start to launch was four days, fifteen hours, and twenty-six minutes). Kaiser was looking for new worlds to conquer, eager to take on Detroit with a revolutionary low-priced car. He had experimented with plastics and light metals and front-wheel drive, and built up a

parations; USSR wants $10-$15 billion; Greek reds set up mountain government; US-backed army attacks; R
s Hollywood; Dalton Trumbo, Ring Lardner, Jr., Clifford Odets called reds, contempt citations against 1

management team he felt could tackle any job. The two met July 17, 1945, and a week later they were in business.

Frazer raced back to Detroit and leased the Willow Run bomber plant, certainly the best-known factory in America. Henry Ford had envisioned building complex bombers like automobiles and created the giant factory thirty miles outside Detroit. The production men stumbled with the task, then straightened up and B-24 Liberator bombers from Willow Run darkened the skies over Europe and Asia. Now Kaiser and Frazer had it.

Richard Langworth, in his definitive book *The Last Onslaught on Detroit —Kaiser-Frazer* told how Frazer said that getting Willow Run was like being married to the circus fat lady. "Acres and acres of it and it's all mine," he said.

Howard "Dutch" Darrin, a noted custom-car designer, styled the new car. He was not happy with the changes Kaiser and Frazer made in his design. The fenders were straightened, giving it the flat slab look, the roofline raised, and the old familiar two-piece windshield popped in instead of a new curved single piece of glass—but the changes were made to ease production and cut costs. In January 1946 prototypes were displayed at the Waldorf-Astoria hotel in New York City. By June the first handful were shipped from Willow Run and by August the new company claimed one million orders in hand. Only 11,751 were built in 1946, but in 1947 production rolled with 7,000 built in January alone. Kaiser and Frazer had truly wrought a production miracle.

Along the way Kaiser abandoned his dream of a big West Coast production base, and of a radical, low-cost car. Instead, the Kaiser and Frazer were conventionally engineered, but they had, like Studebaker, a dramatic postwar look with their slab sides. All carried six-cylinder engines —bought from an outside supplier at first—and Kaiser never built an eight.

n Hungary, purges, dictatorship. Reds reject Marshall Plan; 16 nations accept. French attack Viet Min
ationing ends. Average factory pay: $50.42 a week; teachers average $2424 a year. George Marshall, se

6.
The slab-sided Kaiser put into production in the summer of 1946. The first and last serious domestic challenge to Detroit's car makers since World War II.

All were four-door models. The biggest problem was that they were overpriced. Materials were scarce, and suppliers often owed what they could ship to their older customers. Steel was a particular problem. Kaiser sent his West Coast expediters to Detroit to get the goods and speed production. The "orange juicers," as Detroit called them, did the job but at a price. The Kaisers were priced at $1,900 (a Super DeLuxe Ford four-door was only $1,440; the Ford convertible $1,740) and the look-alike but fancier Frazer was $2,100. This meant they were running against Detroit's middle-priced cars, the Oldsmobiles and Buicks, Chryslers and DeSotos (the top-

ong China border. Chinese reds advance in Manchuria; begin land reform; huge inflation in Nationalist
ary of state, proposes $17 billion to rebuild Europe; Congress debates, OKs $540 million for extra win

line Frazer, a Manhattan at $2,600, was only about $300 under a Cadillac). Kaiser and Frazer could sell all they could build in 1947, but when the shortage eased in two years they were in trouble.

There was one distinct type of car built then that has completely faded from the scene today—the woodies. These were the wood-bodied station wagons, sedans, and convertibles, as handsome a group of cars as Detroit ever built, but expensive to make (and buy) and terribly hard to take care of.

7.
The Ford Coupe. The cheaper ($1,330) Coupe had only a front seat. The 5-passenger version had a front and back seat.

Korean reunification stalls in US-USSR split; Non-red leaders arrested or flee in Poland, Hungary; red
Taft-Hartley labor law passed over Truman Veto. Food prices up 40% in year. CIO ousts officers reject

"Just as any yacht is refurbished every season, so should the beauty and luster of the wood body be maintained by periodic varnishing," read the instructions for a Chrysler Town and Country wood-bodied hardtop. (Woody owners also had to worry about keeping them out of the rain.) This Chrysler may have been the first of the hardtops, but General Motors was to flatten the roof and popularize the name and style a few years later. Chrysler built fewer than 15,000 of these hardtops and convertibles between 1946 and 1950 when they were dropped, and Ford fewer than 9,000 of its Sportsman woodies. Station wagons were not to become popular until the steel-bodied models replaced the wood a few years later.

Ironically, the two founders of the American automobile industry died in 1947 within three weeks of each other. One, of course, was Henry Ford. The other was William Crapo Durant, the creator of General Motors who was forced to give up control of G.M. in the early 1920s because of his stock market manipulations. Even the other two American companies date from Durant, because Charles Nash was a president of G.M. who quit and created Nash (today's American Motors) rather than work for Durant, and Walter Chrysler was a top G.M. executive who quit after a fight with Durant and formed Chrysler.

Only after Henry Ford had died was smoking allowed in Ford plants and offices (he disapproved strongly of the weed) but even after the formal restrictions were ended in late 1947 the ladies still were asked not to light up during business hours.

By 1947 the beginnings of the car culture could be seen, not just in the big cities but in the smaller towns. The kids might not have their own cars yet, certainly not the new postwar models, but they drove their parents' or had clunkers that survived the war. In 1947 a boy didn't have to have a car, but it helped.

1947

Production

General Motors	1,437,700
Chrysler	773,000
Ford	755,400
Kaiser-Frazer	144,500
Studebaker	123,600
Nash	113,300
Hudson	100,400
Packard	55,500
Willys	33,200
Crosley	19,300
Total	3,555,900

in Rumania; Red unions riot in France, Italy, put down after casualties. Dutch attack Indonesian rebe
non-red oath; Walter Reuther purges UAW of reds; John L. Lewis miners quit AFL. Ike to head Columbia.

8.
The prefin Cadillac. The 1947 styling was basically prewar.

"We'd drive over to Ginny's in Muttonville," recalled Jane Howes, from Richmond, Michigan, a farm town. "That was our drive-in. You could dance there a little, and there was no messing around, no fighting in the parking lot.

"But what I remember was the food. Teenagers are always eating, but the food then was real. The hamburgers weren't pre-made, and the foot-long hotdog was something new to us. The French fries were real potatoes, peeled and deep fried. There was milk and ice cream in the malts, not gelatin and powder and flavoring."

And there was the back seat. "In our town to get into the back seat was an admission a girl went all the way, so a nice girl didn't get into the back seat."

The drive-in movies were coming, but strict parents said no. "The passion pits," she recalls. "I was forbidden to go. To my mother they were as scarlet as sin."

rupp pleads not guilty at Nuremberg; even SS had protested Krupp brutality. Rose bowl: Illinois 45, UCI
orruption exposed. FBI screening White House employes. Henry Wallace to run on 3rd party left wing ti

They weren't really dragging yet in little Richmond, not formally, but they burned rubber in jackrabbit starts. "We called it peeling. Then there were the crouchees," the prehistoric ancestors of the greasers to come. "They would drive slunk way down in the seat and over to one side, with their arms hooked under the steering wheel. Crouchees didn't go steady. They went to wedding receptions and picked up people."

A crouchee would have a decal on his dash—probably a bubble dancer—and if it was his own car he would install an exhaust cut-out.

9.
The '47 Olds Dynamic 76 Cruiser. Note the split windshield and the thick roof.

.4. Supreme court OKs public funds for Catholic school busing. Songs: For Sentimental Reasons, Zip-a-
t. March, Olivia De Havilland (To Each His Own). Race: Negroes allowed in Congress Press Galleries; l

"I remember the Costanza brothers—Rico and Paul and I forget the third; they were our best crouchees. If you took Rico out of his car it was like taking a little sea creature out of his shell. He was so small and affable. But put him back in his car and there was the greasy crouchee."

There weren't any freeways out there yet, so thirty miles was a long trip, and there was no TV or rock music—the country sounds, Hillbilly it was called—was what you listened to on the car radio.

And there was something else in that small-town America, she recalls: "The great article of faith was that the Chevrolet was the greatest car ever built."

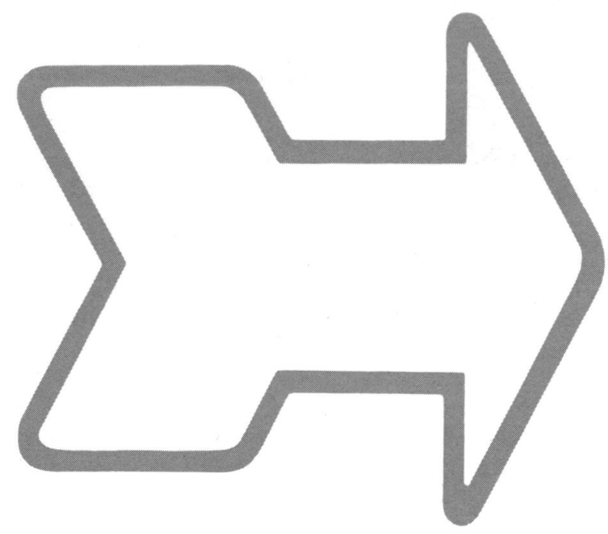

ack Benny, Fibber McGee & Molly, Walter Winchell; 18 TV stations, 150,000 sets in US. Holy Cross 58, C
vans. Divorced: Rita Hayworth-Orson Wells. Deported: Lucy Luciano. Dead: Al Capone, Harry K. Thaw, H

THE DREAMERS

"A little knowledge about cars can be dangerous"
—John Bond, publisher, *Road and Track*

If it had wheels, people were willing to buy it. They were willing to put down cash deposits if there were just a chance of getting some kind of car. Others were willing to pay cash for the right to sell an automobile, even if that auto were no more than a sketch on a piece of paper or a single hand-built prototype. And even more were willing to buy a few shares of stock in any company that said it would build a car, if the Securities and Exchange Commission investigators didn't get there first.

They had the dream of owning a miracle car, or of selling a new Model T, or of getting rich by investing in the Ford or General Motors of tomorrow. That incentive lured the inventors and the con men into the auto business after World War II.

Why shouldn't those dreams have seemed possible? There were plenty of empty war plants and machine tools around. The government was willing to sell or lease them cheaply if it could mean jobs, and people were willing to buy. And what's so hard about building a car? Thousands of backyard mechanics knew they could do it (it was before the requirements of Federal safety and antipollution regulations). After all, what was Henry Ford but a self-taught mechanic backed by a few believers? Wasn't General Motors created by a genius with a bit of con and borrowed money?

1.
The dream of dreams. Preston Tucker's super car. About 50 were built, but the car was never put into production.

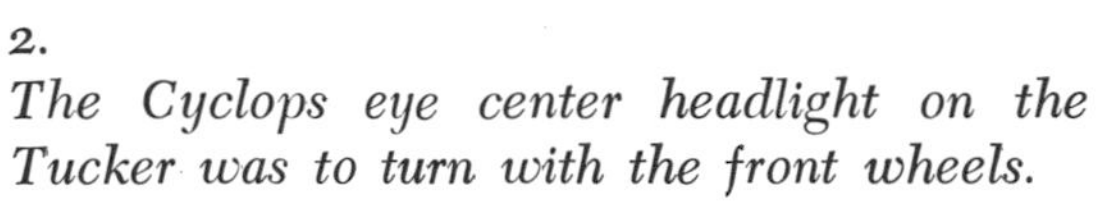
2.
The Cyclops eye center headlight on the Tucker was to turn with the front wheels.

They believed it could happen then, but don't laugh, because we're just as believing today. Let any backyard mechanic announce he has built a new miracle car, powered by steam or batteries, or let any engineer claim he has designed a flywheel that can power a car for almost nothing, and newspapers and magazines will print their claims as if they were fact, government agencies will announce they may just be the answer to the energy or pollution crises, and Congressmen will ask if Detroit is trying to destroy the new miracle cars.

Three decades after World War II, for example, a tough-talking woman announced in California that she would build a 70-m.p.g. three-wheeler made from a new space-age, indestructible plastic and the little miracle was going to cost only $1,000. Never mind that the woman was a bit strange, 6 feet tall with "fists like a prize fighter's and shoulders like a lumber jack," according to one interviewer. Never mind that three-wheelers have a built-in instability, that even a good sofa without a motor costs $1,000 or that her engineering credentials were hard to find or did not check out.

"I'm going to knock hell out of Detroit," vowed Elizabeth Carmichael, who knocked women's lib, gave off quotes like Ayn Rand and threw out her chest like Ann-Margret. The nation's press ate it up, and with the publicity potential dealers paid thousands for the right to sell her Dale car. Customers left deposits. Of course the car was a phony, and Ms. Carmichael turned out to be a Mr. and a con man with a police record. Maybe the folks after World War II could not tell a real car from a phony, but thirty years later Americans were having a hard time telling a woman from a man.

So much for progress.

By one count, thirty-two men or companies announced they would build automobiles in the years after World War II. Most of the vehicles were to be small cars, minicars, even three-wheelers, and many claimed impressive engineering innovations—on paper. Nearly all were to be sold for ridiculously low prices ($1,000 and under was common). A high proportion were to be built in sunny California.

Among the dream cars were:

The Davis, a three-wheeler, which was to be built by Gary Davis, an ex-custom car salesman from California. He took a prototype of his 500-pound car on a wild demonstration trip around America selling dealer franchises. A few dozen actually were assembled but Davis spent 18 months in jail, always complaining "I was railroaded."

There was the Playboy, a 155-inch-long model that came from Buffalo, N.Y., and collapsed after $2 million had been raised from franchise sales. There was the Scarab, a car designed by William Stout of Michigan, a radical but serious designer who had Henry J. Kaiser interested for a bit. There was the Gregory, a front-wheel-drive car to be built by Ben Gregory of Kansas City, and the Bobbi-Kar, and the Cortez. Later there was the Darrin, a bona fide two-passenger sports car built by Howard "Dutch" Darrin who designed the first Kaisers. About fifty were turned out. There was the Kurtis-Kraft of 1948 and 1949, another sports car effort—about two dozen were built—that later became the Muntz built by Earl "Madman" Muntz, a California used car dealer (and later TV set maker) who was immortalized by becoming the butt of Bob Hope's radio jokes each week. The Muntz two-seater of the early 1950s could run 0–60 m.p.h. in 12 seconds but Muntz gave up as Chevrolet was springing Corvette on the world. "We were losing about $1,000 on every car because we didn't have enough production volume," said the Madman, ending his auto hopes.

SLIPPERY
WHEN WET

4. ►
The three-wheel Davis. After World War II, anything with wheels looked possible.

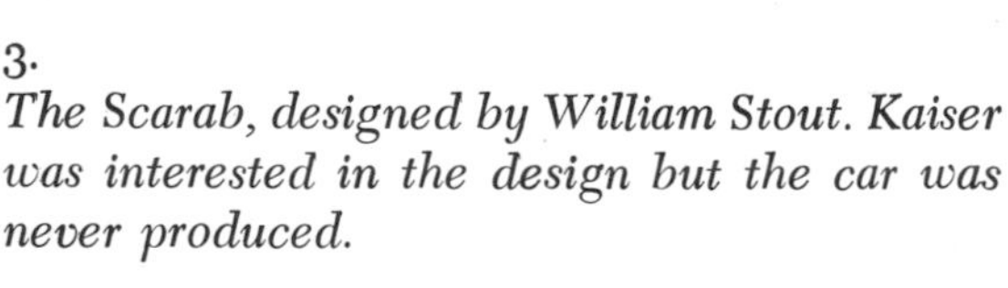
3.
The Scarab, designed by William Stout. Kaiser was interested in the design but the car was never produced.

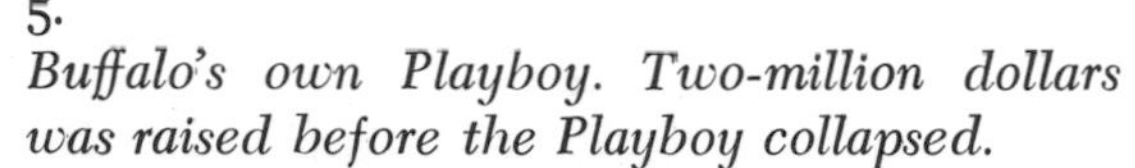
5.
Buffalo's own Playboy. Two-million dollars was raised before the Playboy collapsed.

6.
The Gregory front wheel drive from Kansas City.

There was Dale Orcutt and Claude Dry who made their dream come true in Athens, Ohio, building a little Jeep-like car called the King Midget for a dozen years, selling a few hundred a year in the factory behind the house, and earning enough to have one good Florida vacation each year. And then there was the Del Mar and the Air Way and the Keller and the Scootmobile and the Publix and the Motorette.

But the dream of dreams was the Tucker.

To this day good men will argue over the Tucker. Was it a car ahead of its time? Was it doomed by the conspiracies of a frightened Detroit or the cantankerousness of its builder? Or was Tucker just another dream car, half hope, half con, "born in a saloon" as it was said.

Ed Cole, former president of General Motors and one of the great engineers of this golden age (Cole designed the '55 Chevrolet V-8), told *Special Interest Autos*, a magazine, that the concept "was well enough conceived," that Tucker had real hope "of being able to make it work" and there were enough elements there "to make a car out of it." John Bond, the respected publisher of *Road and Track*, said the Tucker was catastrophic in many ways and called its inventor another who proved that "a little knowledge about cars can be dangerous."

Car testers such as Tom McCahill said the Tucker ran 0–60 m.p.h. in 10 seconds—magnificently fast, pre-1950—and "steers and handles better than any other American car I have driven." Automotive writer Ken Purdy said the car would do 125 m.p.h., get 26 m.p.g., and "is the safest car ever built." The United States government said it all was a fraud, but a jury said "not guilty."

7.
By one count, 32 new cars were announced after World War II, most of them small and most to sell at around $1,000. The Keller was one.

Preston Tucker was an ex-policeman, an ex-auto salesman, a race-car builder and an engineer-manufacturer from Ypsilanti, Mich. As World War II was ending he announced he had designed a new car, the Tucker Torpedo, "designed to cruise continuously at 100 m.p.h." (the Torpedo name was dropped later when he decided to emphasize safety). His car had a dramatically modern look, long and low, though the one-piece windshield was scrapped when he could not get such glass. Tucker designed a Cyclops-eye third headlight that turned with the wheels, an aluminum air-cooled engine (which did not quite work and was dropped, although later Corvair and VW used lightweight air-cooled motors), claimed a collapsing steering column (later G.M. developed such a column, a major safety advance), a padded dash and a safety compartment under the dash for a passenger to dive into when a crash appeared certain. He raised about $25 million from selling dealer franchises (at $4,000 each) and stock to the public, and when cash was scarce he sold accessories such as luggage, seat covers, and radios to potential car buyers to insure them a high place on the Tucker delivery list.

For a $25,000 check that apparently never was cashed Tucker got possession of a giant Chicago war plant in 1946. But then he had to fight off the attempt of another federal agency to take the plant and pass it out for another dream—mass-production of houses. Tucker won the fight but the mudslinging cost him precious time and prestige. Still, by mid-1947, Tucker, before thousands of dealers, reporters, and anyone else who could crowd into his plant, rolled out a Tucker car. Of course, the car had just been hammered together and in no way was a producible vehicle. But in the blare of golden trumpets, the sheen of models in strapless evening gowns, the excitement and the champagne christening, the troubles were not noticed. He flew his Tucker across the country, racing against time to raise

8.
A high percentage of these never-in-production hopes, like this Del Mar, came from California.

money to get into production before the bubble burst. Tens of thousands saw the Tucker and there were private showings for Very Important People. Col. Robert McCormick, publisher of the *Chicago Tribune*, was given a showing to enlist the powerful publisher's support. He was six feet four inches tall. When he straightened up in the seat of the sixty-inch-high Tucker "his hat came down over his ears. He left shortly without comment," according to one of Tucker's chroniclers.

When something in the original design would not work, like the air-cooled engine, he substituted.

"You guys come back with an engine in three months or we fold up," Tucker told his old racing-engineer buddies, and they went to the shop in Ypsilanti and designed a water-cooled engine for him.

Time was running out for Tucker in mid-1948. There were rumors that the Tucker was a fraud, that it could not back up (it could), that the running model was just put together from parts of other cars. He lost many of the professional car men on his team, and was attacked on the radio by Drew Pearson, the columnist and radio newscaster. The Securities and Exchange Commission demanded his records and Tucker closed his plant in a huff. He and his associates were charged and tried for fraud but found not guilty. The Tucker dream died too, like all the others.

About fifty Tuckers were built, all prototypes (some may still be seen at state fairs), and it is doubtful he could ever have gotten into production. Kaiser and Frazer, with automobile and construction know-how and solid reputations in the business community and among potential car buyers, were able to put together a production team in a year. But their car was completely conventional. Tucker was intent on putting into production innovations that read well on paper, but may have been beyond the technical know-how of the times. His boasts and tricks cost him the confidence of the public. And the $25 million Preston Tucker raised was a puny sum in Detroit's poker game. As Henry J. Kaiser, after he went down, said: "We expected to toss $50 million into the automobile pond, but we didn't expect it to disappear without a ripple."

"You wanna go?"

—The hot-rodders' challenge

The curtain went up a bit higher in 1948. The Studebakers and Kaisers and Frazers had shown some of the new look with their '47s. The big show to come from Ford, General Motors, and Nash was due with the '49s. But there were some peeks into the future with the '48s: the startling "step-down" Hudsons, the new-look Cadillacs with a strange new fishtail fin at the rear end, the Futuramic Oldsmobiles, and the new automatic transmission from Buick.

The underground auto culture was also beginning to flower. Tom Wolfe, decades later, invented a new writing style (the new journalism, it was called) in his tale "The Kandy-Kolored Tangerine Flake Stream-Line Baby." He wrote of Los Angeles, when hot-rodders ran by night: "Everybody would meet in drive-ins, the most famous of them being the Piccadilly out near Sepulveda Boulevard. It was a hell of a show, all the weird-looking roadsters and custom cars, with very loud varoom-varoom motors."

George Barris, later one of the best-known custom-car designers, told Wolfe what it was like in the late 1940s.

"We'd all be at the Piccadilly or some other place," said Barris, "and the guys would start challenging each other. You know, a guy goes up to

Gandhi assassinated for seeking India peace. Red coup in Czechoslovakia, police beat stu
Truman proposes civil rights program, antilynching, antipolltax, fair emloyment, south re

1.
The long, low and trend-setting stepdown Hudson. The sensation of 1948.

another guy's car and looks it up and down like it has gangrene or something, and he says: 'you wanna go?'. . . . as soon as a few guys had challenged each other, everybody would ride out onto this stretch of Sepulveda Boulevard or the old divided highway, in Compton, and the guys would start dragging, one car on one side of the center line, the other car on the other. Go a quarter of a mile. It was wild. Some nights there'd be a thousand kids lining the road to watch, boys and girls, all sitting on the sides of their cars with the lights shining across the highway."

The kids would block off the highway at each end, and if someone wanted to drive through, the rodders were polite, Barris told Tom Wolfe. "Well, Mister, there are going to be two cars coming down both sides of the road pretty fast in a minute, and you can go through if you want to, but you'll just have to take your best shot."

Detroit was not tuned into that scene (that came late in the 1950s and early 1960s) and some car makers were determined to look the other way. While most car makers were thinking that the postwar look would be longer, lower, and wider, Chrysler Corporation in 1948 was planning its coming line of cars as shorter, higher, and stubbier. Kaufman Thuma Keller (K. T., he was called), the engineer who headed Chrysler, explained his thinking in 1948: "There are parts of the country, containing millions of people, where both men and the ladies are in the habit of getting behind the wheel, or in the back seat, wearing hats." Chrysler cars continued without an automatic transmission—the company offered Fluid Drive, a semi-automatic system which required shifting—and the door handles were the

2.
Son of the war-time Jeep from Willys.

David Ben-Gurion premier, Arabs invade Israel, bomb Tel-Aviv, take Jerusalem, Israelis win elsewhere,
Dewey GOP nominee for president; Robert Taft, Harold Stassen beaten, Gov. Earl Warren for Veep. Democrat

old twist-down type. That does not mean Chrysler was far behind the competition, at least then. Its cars were solid. *Car and Driver* magazine found a '48 Chrysler Windsor in mint condition in 1974 and tested it.

"This big old Chrysler floats down the freeway trailing a tangible wake of dignity and peace" at a steady 55 m.p.h., reported Patrick Bedard. "You sit up straight and tall in a chair height seat facing a chrome-spoked steering wheel as wide as your shoulders." The car is quiet and the ride "as smooth and steady as Nebraska," he wrote, and the sound flows "from the 8-tube, superheterodyne, translucent pushbutton radio." There is a split windshield; a long hood covering a 251-cubic-inch displacement, 114-horsepower six; a four-speed semiautomatic transmission. The Windsor does not move off with a rush—0–60 m.p.h. in 23 seconds—and she runs up, eventually, to 85 m.p.h., "but it would take a long, long road." Braking is not good–290 feet from 70 m.p.h. (a '74 Valiant Brougham compact would stop in 220 feet). But the Chrysler gets 19 m.p.g., better than any car of its class and weight (4,000 pounds) today, and the price was $2,200.

The '48 Chrysler is happiest at 55 m.p.h., Bedard wrote, but "the tranquility melts away above 65." The body shakes when you cross a bump, yet there are no rattles and the doors close and latch with a touch. There is no crouching to get in either, no cramped feeling in the roomy interior, and "the rear seat is best of all, better than anything Detroit has offered since." And it's high. "From your lofty vantage point high above the cars around you, you can easily spot traffic snarls that may obstruct your progress."

"No doubt the Chrysler would be a fine companion as you tread the earth's surface in search of a happier life," the car tester wrote. "With its long experience, it might even show you the way."

mediator Bernadotte killed by Israeli fanatics, truce collapses, Israelis sweep Egyptians back. Anti-
ils, Truman nominated, Sen. Alvin Barkley for Veep; party split, southerners bolt over civil rights, nc

3.
The Chevrolet Stylemaster Coupe. The Chevrolet was a conservative car in styling and performance until 1955.

The most exciting new car for '48 was the Hudson, all new on the outside, long and low (only sixty inches high), with a new unitized body, and you stepped down when you got in. *Motor*, the English magazine, called the Hudson "daringly original" and "something of a sensation," low but roomy. Bill Mitchell, the G.M. stylist admitted, "it was new compared to what we were doing."

There were complaints. After all the warnings, riders learned to step down without stumbling, but practically everybody tripped stepping up to get out. One writer complained later that Hudson's trick, sinking the floorboards around the drive shaft tunnel to lower the body, "was eventually copied by the rest of the industry, to the everlasting discomfort of

ds win Italian elections. Separate states set up in Korea, north pro-red, south pro-US. White Afrikaa
nate Strom Thurmond on Dixiecrat ticket; left wing bolts to red-led Progressive party with Henry Wallac

4.
First of the fishtail fins, the Cadillac of 1948 would look good on the road today.

the middle seat passenger." *Motor Trend* said later that the design was a bit of a problem, getting in and out, "for some women and short-legged men." A car restorer said "drive it today and it's like driving a Brink's truck, and the glass was so narrow." A bigger problem was to come out later: the engine. Hudson had a grand six that was to have its moment of glory in the early 1950s, when the Hudson Hornets dominated the stock car tracks. Hudson had a straight-8 too, but that long, complicated engine could not match the simpler, more powerful V-8s that were coming, and Hudson had no V-8. Still, the step-down was the sensation of the year, and 1948 was a great year for the independents, which captured nearly 20 percent of the market. Kaiser-Frazer built nearly 200,000 cars, Studebaker with its popular new look built 165,000, Hudson and Nash better than 100,000, and even little Crosley with its midget car rolled out 28,000. Never

ontrol in South Africa. Russians blockade Berlin; airlift saves city. Stalin attacks Tito; Yugoslavia
resident. Truman attacks GOP do-nothing congress. Truman orders military, civil service desegregated.

again were the seven independent car makers (excluding G.M., Ford, and Chrysler, the Big Three) to grab such a share of the market.

Packard, too, brought out restyled flush-sided models for 1948 and outsold Cadillac that year (and in 1949). But Packard seemed to have its troubles: The luxury car maker could not get enough steel since materials still were scarce and Packard's expediters poor. Dealers complained, and when Packard's president, George "Pinchpenny" Christopher, promised to double production in 1949 to 200,000 and could not do it, the dealers were up in arms. Christopher got the nickname "Pinchpenny" by refusing to OK the repainting of the women's john in the company headquarters, and by fighting against the restyling of the '48–49 Packards, which were called

5.
Stationwagons like the Oldsmobile were still for the richer country folk in 1948.

fies USSR. Communist rebellion in Malaya. Dutch break truce, attack Indonesians. Farben-Krupp leader
red spy Elizabeth Bentley spies in government. Time editor Whittaker Chambers calls Alger Hiss a red,

6.
Pontiac, when they still carried the Indian head emblem.

the "pregnant Packards" because of their rounded sides. But Packard stayed in the black under old Pinchpenny. With all the demands to change the cars, Christopher finally got fed up and quit in 1949, returning to his farm in Ohio and saying, "farming is a damned sight easier than the auto business. You don't have so many bosses on a farm."

The big Oldsmobile and the '48 Cadillac gave a preview of G.M.'s coming change. Cadillac coupes had built-in rear bumpers, and the gasoline cap was hidden under one hinged taillight—Mr. Earl, the G.M. styling director, was always trying to hide things. The Cadillac carried a small, pretty, and

Nuremberg, jailed. W. Europe defense organization set up. Chinese reds take Manchuria, roll into nor
idence hidden in pumpkin, Hiss indicted for perjury. W. Coast dock strike lasts 3 months. Polls wrong

definitely unusual fishtail fin at the rear. Mr. Earl had taken that fin from the World War II P-38 fighter. G.M. was worried. The car maker polled viewers and half of them did not like it. A finless Cadillac was ready, but the big stylist held firm, and in a decade that little fishtail, spreading like pterodactyl wings, was to symbolize all that was wrong with the American automobile.

Buick, which built tanks during the war, brought out a new automatic transmission, its torque-converter Dynaflow (the war experience helped with the designing), giving G.M. with its Hydra-Matic two automatics to none for the remainder of the industry (although Packard was to bring out its own Ultramatic in 1949). In 1948 some 95 percent of the Cadillacs carried Hydra-Matic.

Another breakthrough came in 1948, but it was not important for another twenty years: the hatchback was born. In July of '48 Edgar Kaiser, Henry J.'s son who ran the car business, had a flash. He outlined the idea in the dust of a company car: part of the trunk lid would lift, part would drop, opening up the rear end for loading and giving a sedan some of the cargo capacity of a station wagon. Kaiser brought out several varieties of a model called the Vagabond with this feature for 1949, but it was in the 1970s that the hatchback became an important part of the design of small cars.

Kaiser also was picking a new design for his '51 models. His independent stylist, Dutch Darrin, was competing with Kaiser's own in-house designers. The story is that at the final showdown, Kaiser's men were standing in front of Darrin's model, not allowing Darrin and his car to catch the attention of the boss and Edgar. Darrin loosened his belt, called the Kaisers, and then dropped his pants. When the laughing stopped Dutch had their attention and they liked what they saw—the car, that is—and Darrin's design became the '51 Kaiser.

1948

Production

General Motors	1,565,900
Chrysler	829,200
Ford	747,500
Kaiser-Frazer	181,800
Studebaker	164,800
Hudson	143,700
Nash	118,600
Packard	98,900
Willys	32,600
Crosley	27,700
Total	3,910,700

China. US cool to Chiang's pleas, charge corruption. Britain votes-cradle-to-grave health, security
Truman elected in upset; Democrats carry congress. 3 A-bombs tested at Eniwetok. Top communists indic

One car passed away in 1948: Ford's twelve-cylinder Lincoln Continental. Today the Continental is considered a classic, but then it was just considered a money-loser. The Continentals were practically handmade, the sheet-metal work was rough, the big engine was no winner, and the price was high—about $4,700 for the coupe or the convertible. Only 5,324 Continentals had been built from beginning (1940) to end in 1948, most of them after the war.

"No one realized the impact this car would have in the future," one Ford stylist said.

7.
Nash convertible. By 1976, only one convertible, the Eldorado, was left in production.

ire a republic. Hungarian reds arrest Cardinal Mindszenty. Earthquake kills 3200 in Fukui, Japan. Mic
onspiring to overthrow government, convicted. Doctors to fight Truman medical insurance. Ronald Colema

Later Ford tried to recapture those graceful lines with its 1957 Mark II Continental, a $10,000 car, but that failed. They tried again in the late 1960s, building the new Mark off the Thunderbird body with a Rolls-Royce grille, and succeeded. That Mark was not exactly graceful, and stealing the Rolls grille, said a G.M. vice-president, was "almost sacrilegious."

But it made money and gave the Cadillac Eldorado a real run each year for the title of King of the Hill.

"The Mark is successful just because it's blatant," said one Ford designer. "After all, no one in their right mind would put an oval window in an automobile," but Ford did it on its Mark, and, he said, "they work."

gan 49-USC 0 in Rose Bowl. Court orders Oklahoma to provide equal law education for Negroes, calls ant
A Double Life). Kentucky 58, Baylor 42 for NCAA title. Citation wins Derby. Songs: Now is the Hour,

"I have had a vision. We start from scratch."
—Ernie Breech, overseer of the '49 Ford

The '49 cars were a revolution, the first full wave of postwar styling from Ford, General Motors, and Chrysler, and startling new V-8 engines from Cadillac and Oldsmobile.

At Ford, the '49 was only the fourth new car in the company's history (after the Model T, the Model A and the Ford V-8 of the Thirties) and was the work of the new team put together after Henry II seized the company in 1945. He had hired Ernest Breech, a General Motors man, in 1946 ("I was the cleanup man for G.M., but this one was really a mess," Breech said). Breech gathered a team of crack G.M. veterans to do the job. Joining up at the same time was a group of ten ex-Air Force officers who came aboard as a team. Ford's old-timers called them the "Quiz Kids" after a group of brilliant and mildly revolting children who appeared on a radio quiz show. One, Charles "Tex" Thornton, grew tired of waiting in line at Ford, quit and helped create one of the early conglomerates, Litton Industries. Another, Robert McNamara, led Ford to its victories over Chevrolet in the 1950s, became Ford president, and then quit to join President Kennedy's cabinet. Both Breech and McNamara left Ford in 1960, and without that leadership Ford drifted until Lee Iacocca's star

Israel strikes into Sinai, shoots down four RAF fighters, Egyptian ships shell Tel Aviv. Dean Acheson named secretary of state. Army bans marriages of German girls, GIs below se

1.
The 1949 model saved Ford, but nothing saved those skirts.

2.
Kaiser invented the hatchback with its Vagabond, but the idea didn't catch on for two more decades.

stern allies to form military alliance. Airlift pours supplies into Berlin. US demands Dutch leave Ir
ant. Russian Valentine Gubitchev-lover Judith Coplon arrested as spies, convicted. Pyramid clubs, cha

3.
Dodge's unusual Wayfarer 3-passenger roadster, with just a front seat and put-in and take-out windows.

rose with his Mustang and got the company rolling again. But all that was later; when Breech took over Ford was a mess and needed a car. Breech in 1946 drove Ford's projected new car, planned as a '48 model, and figured it was too big and heavy. He prayed on the way home one night.

"Show us the right way to go," Breech asked Him.

The next morning he called his Ford team together. "I have a vision. We start from scratch. We spend no time or money phonying up the old Ford, because this organization will be judged by the market on the next car it

ecognize Israel. Cardinal Mindszenty pleads guilty in Hungarian treason trial, gets life. Supporters
ad. Antifilibuster rule beaten in Senate. Rent controls extended a year. Secret FBI informant Herber

4.
The Great American bathtub: The all new and never imitated Nash Airflyte.

produces, so it had better be a new one. So we'll have a crash program, as if in war time. Any questions?"

This meant pushing back introduction a year, but Breech took a chance that G.M. would not move until 1949 either, and he was right. He brought in an outside stylist, George Walker, who had designed for Nash, and with Elwood Engel (who led the later Thunderbird team and became styling vice-president of Chrysler when it hit trouble) and Joe Oros (who did the Mustang) the heart of Ford's future styling department was created.

im he was drugged. Egypt-Israel armistice. Red Chinese sweep south. take Peiping, reject peace talks, hilbrick testifies against top US Communists, reveals plots. Armed forces told to end race discriminat

Walker's design for the new car was picked (and Ford's old styling boss quit). The car Breech thought too heavy to be the new Ford was used as the '49 Mercury. And the car originally planned as the new Mercury became the '49 Lincoln.

The '49 Ford was a stunner, 196 inches long, a half-inch shorter than the old '48 model, and 240 pounds lighter. She was narrower but with more passenger room, clean with a minimum of chrome yet with a distinctive spinner nose. More important, Ford caught up with the remainder of the industry mechanically, using new axles, springs (gone were the old-fashioned transverse springs, a fetish of Henry Ford I), shocks, and frame, but the Ford carried the same 90-horsepower six and 100-h.p. V-8.

"It provided the basic concept of our styling since then," said George Walker. "Practically all cars at that time had bulging side lines, particularly around the front and rear fenders. We smoothed those lines out and began the movement toward integration of the fenders and the body." Ford did not have the first slab side, but seemed to bring it off better than Kaiser-Frazer.

The new model was shown off in June 1948 at the Waldorf-Astoria in a six-day show (the '49 Lincolns and Mercurys were shown a couple of months earlier) and hundreds of thousands of orders were written.

Fords had their troubles, though. A friend called up Breech and said "those cars are a piece of junk." The crash program resulted in a poor body fit, meaning rattles, dust and rain leaks, but there was not much to do about it.

"We are going to have to live in sin on this shell until we get the 1952 out," Lewis Crusoe, one of Breech's division leaders, said.

The Mercury cars were not much better. "I've been through some bad cars," a Mercury official said. "These cars didn't have any major difficulty,

ENGINES

Percent of Total Production

Year	*V-8*	*Straight-8*	*Six*
1947	20	16	62
1949	24	16	60
1951	29	15	55
1953	38	11	51
1955	79	—	21
1957	83	—	17
1959	70	—	30
1961	49	—	48
1963	65	—	34
1965*	73	—	27

** Model year.*

anking, Shanghai, Canton. North Atlantic treaty signed. Clothing rationing ends in England. Nurember
tlanta bars masks in public; anti-KKK move. Kathy Fiscus, 3, dies in well as rescue fails. Hague mach

5.
One of the last of the Frazer cars, a Manhattan.

6.
The 1949 Cadillac: The new high compression V-8 engine revolutionized the American automobile.

rials end. Russians end Berlin blockade. Dutch-Indonesian ceasefire. Israel in UN. Bao Dai heads Fr
defeated in Jersey City vote. Congress OKs secret CIA operation. University of Florida rejects Negro

7.
The new high compression V-8 in the Oldsmobile made Olds king of the hill at the stock car tracks.

just a lot of little things that made it ten times worse." The big Lincolns were sluggish and hard to handle (the '49 Ford was no handling gem, either) and had no automatic transmission, though soon Lincoln and independents were buying G.M.'s Hydra-Matic.

Those problems did not stop the customers. The '49 Fords were new, bright, and pretty and made everything else look old. With that car Henry Ford II made Chevrolet the target: Beat Chevrolet. The trouble was, said Crusoe, who was to run the new Ford division, "they didn't tell me how to do it." The new Ford was neat, but Chevrolet was still an article of

ndochina regime. Allied foreign ministers deadlock on Germany. Russia calls Tito enemy; purge on in s
lger Hiss perjury trial ends, hung jury, 2nd trial ordered. US ratifies NATO pact, concedes Red victor

faith in America. Even though that series of Fords ('49–51) did not catch Chevy, they enabled Ford to catch and pass Chrysler in sales before the little tiger was retired. Ford earned $177 million profit in 1949 and the danger of collapse was over.

G.M. made history, too, with its new Cadillac V-8 engine. Three men were credited for that V-8, and two of them, Jack Gordon and Ed Cole, became G.M. presidents. The new "short-stroke" V-8 with its short piston stroke (which reduced friction) and "slipper piston" (which helped lighten the bottom of the engine) was lighter, smaller, quieter, more fuel efficient, and more powerful. The Cadillac V-8 produced a 7 percent horsepower gain with 14 percent improvement in fuel consumption. Its overhead-valve design opened the way to higher compression ratios, meaning efficiency

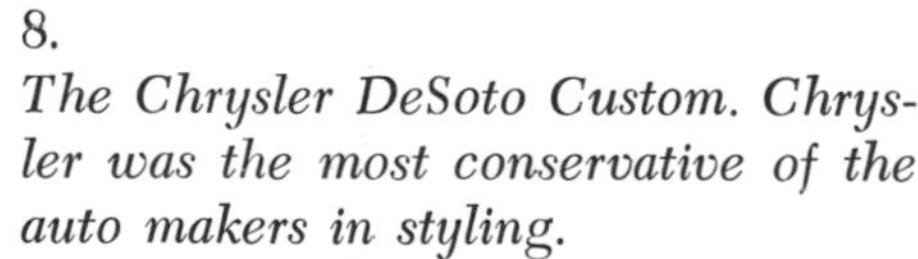

8.
The Chrysler DeSoto Custom. Chrysler was the most conservative of the auto makers in styling.

llites, Tito breaks contracts with USSR, gets $20 million US loan. Konrad Adenauer first W. German cha
n China. Unemployment at 4 million. Dow-Jones industrials at 178.04 Sept. 20. Senate investigates in

9.
The Chevrolet DeLuxe Fleetline, complete with sun visor, cigarette lighter, clock, and arm rest was $1,539.

and power could be increased as higher-octane fuel became available. The total weight saving was 221 pounds, and top speed on the Cadillac (which was *Motor Trend's* Car of the Year) went from 93 on the '48 models to 100 miles an hour (that was the report, anyway), and passengers did not have to shout at each other to be heard. Oldsmobile engineered a similar V-8 and put it in its lighter 88 model; that power in the lighter car made Olds the top of the stocks in the new National Association for Stock Car Auto Racing (N.A.S.C.A.R.) tracks in 1949 and 1950.

There was nothing particularly revolutionary about those two V-8s. But for the first time it was all put together, all the new thinking of what an

st German Red state formed. Reds test A-bomb. Free United States of Indonesia formed. Red Chinese d
ddling, Truman aide Gen. Harry Vaughan implicated, Truman defends Vaughan despite his gift taking. Fo

engine should be, and it worked. The new V-8s signaled the end of the straight-8s and even pushed the six-cylinder motors toward retirement, until the great small-car boom of the late 1950s and mid-1970s. In 1946 the V-8s were on just 19 percent of the cars built (straight-8s took another 14 percent), but 83 percent of the production in 1957.

The styling breakthrough at General Motors was the '49 Buick Riviera two-door hardtop, the car that started the hardtop trend. The flattened roof and the absence of a center pillar caught on at once, and although G.M. had a lead the competition was in quickly. The portholes were new

10.
Lincoln Cosmopolitan was the top of the line and on sale in the spring of 1948. Ford didn't have its own automatic transmission then.

nd UN seat. Allies ease control over West Germany. Chinese Nationalists flee to Formosa. Mao Tse-tun
oal strikes in year, steel workers strike, too. Minimum wage up to 75 cents an hour. 11 Communist le

on Buick that year, too: four on each side of the Roadmaster, three on the lesser models. An engineer had put them on one car and they lit up sequentially with the firing of the eight-cylinder engine. The holes were picked up as Buick's trademark, though the fireworks were left off.

The Chevrolets were new, too. Out went the old Stylemaster and Fleetmaster (for the fastbacks), and in came Special and DeLuxe. DeLuxe meant you got the right-hand sun visor, cigarette lighter, clock, and armrests as luxuries, but with all that a four-door DeLuxe was only $1,539. The options that were to run up the price by $1,000 and more were still to come—the automatic transmission, air-conditioning, power brakes and steering, bucket seats, AM-FM stereo, vinyl roof and eighteenth-century interiors. The '49 Chevrolet was fifty-five pounds lighter and a notch lower than earlier models, but the look was not startling and the basic engine was the same "stovebolt six" (Chevy was not to offer a V-8 until 1955) that had served faithfully, with modifications, since 1929.

Nash had its first postwar design, its Airflyte, better known as the "bathtub" for its long, sloped, roly-poly design. The Nash president, George Mason, a 230-pound cigar chewer, was as far-sighted an auto man as any in the business. But he had a problem on styling: "He thought the way to make a car look modern was to close the fenders," recalls Dick Teague, the American Motors stylist. Mason covered not only the rear wheels but the front wheels as well, and as long as he lived Nash stylists had to fight to show a little tire. They usually lost.

Chrysler's cars were new, too, though not style award winners. Back in the 1930s Chrysler brought out a radically styled line of cars, its Airstream models. Actually they were shaped a bit like the VW Beetle, and everyone in the 1930s called them the first word in streamlining. But they did not sell, and it was twenty years before Chrysler risked styling again.

1949

Production

General Motors	2,206,800
Chrysler	1,123,400
Ford	1,077,600
Studebaker	228,400
Nash	142,600
Hudson	142,500
Packard	104,600
Kaiser-Frazer	60,400
Willys	32,900
Crosley	8,900
Total	5,128,100

loscow. Israel makes Jerusalem capital. Adenauer offers rearmed Germany for the West. Rose Bowl: Nort
uilty of conspiracy. Pennsylvania RR ends Negro segregation going south from NY. 5 die of smog in Do

11.
The Custom 8 convertible, when the 8 was straight and a Packard was a Packard.

Engineering innovations maintained Chrysler's reputation. The '49 Plymouth station wagon was all steel. Gone was the wood body, and that opened the way for the station-wagon boom. Chrysler and Dodge introduced a key-operated ignition that marked the beginning of the end for the starter button. And Dodge offered a three-passenger (just a front seat) roadster, its Wayfarer convertible, with put-in, take-out windows (no rollup) which lasted two years.

The year 1949 turned into a disaster for Kaiser-Frazer. The Big Three had new designs while Kaiser was still building the basic car of '47. Joe Frazer, who knew something about cars, said that since their biggest competitors had new models and Kaiser-Frazer did not, production should be cut. "Every time you didn't have a new model you had to retrench," he said.

tern 20, Caliornia 14. Movies: Pinky, All the King's Men, Knock on Any Door, White Heat, She Wore a Y
, Pa. Broadway: South Pacific, Death of a Salesman, Detective Story. Ponder wins Derby. Died: Charles

12.
The portholes were new for '49 and became a Buick trademark.

"The Kaisers never retrench," answered Henry J. He wanted to build 200,000 cars in the face of the new Big Three steel. The '49s made heavy use of bright color, inside and out, which was different. There was the hatchback Vagabond and the Virginian, which was almost a hardtop, and Kaiser even offered a four-door convertible (the sedans were all four-doors). That did not help the basic problems: The competition had new cars, Kaiser had no V-8, and the cars were overpriced as the market was again becoming competitive. Production fell to only 58,000 in 1949, but the '49 models could not be sold and a sixth of them were renumbered and called 1950 models.

So much for consumer protection.

---

nos 'n' Andy, Suspense. Robert Mitchem, Lila Leeds jailed 60 days for marijuana. Books: Point of No R
larquand), Man with the Golden Arm (Algren), 1984 (Orwell), A Rage to Live (O'Hara). Oscars: Laurence

"No statue was ever erected to the man or woman who thought it best to leave well enough alone."

—George Walker, Ford styling director

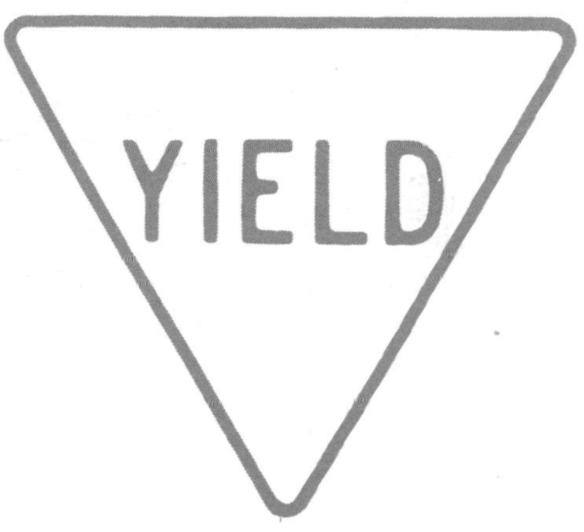

The show cars, the dream cars, the experimental cars are the fun cars of the automobile industry. They are fun to design and build; the stylists are on their own with no sales managers to complain there isn't enough room for passengers, no production men to explain that the steel just can't be tortured that way, no accountants to say just "no."

"I have a very clear picture in my mind of what the perfectly styled car would look like," George Walker, who created the '49 Ford said once. "But it will never be produced." Practicality keeps butting in.

"For example," Walker said, "my conception of the truly aesthetic automobile is one in which there are no headlights. From the design standpoint, headlights break up the continuity of the front end of the car. But it's obvious that headlights are absolutely necessary." (That explains why every so often stylists go on a binge of disappearing headlights.) If an automobile has a function, function isn't everything, a stylist would say. "How long do you think even they [the critics of style] could endure a society whose artifacts were designed solely to perform the function for which they were intended?" says Walker. "Not very long." Just because the function is the same does not mean the style should never change.

"Remember that no statue was ever erected to the man or woman who thought it best to leave well enough alone."

The experimental cars come in three classes:

Some actually are prototypes of future cars to be, perhaps not quite like the production model but with enough of a resemblance to be the clearly identifiable parent. The new idea can be tested with the show car, or it can be used to whip up excitement for the coming model. In the old days car makers might order some dream-car designs into production and for sale in limited quantities, but that is not done any more.

The bit-further-out models are design studies that might provide some ideas the stylists want to see translated from paper to full-size models, and these usually are the most exciting to the public. Some may be built with running gear, and if there is a radical engine to test (or the company wants some extra publicity) they will put it in a dream-car design. In 1963 Chrysler put fifty turbine engines in special show-car bodies and passed them out for testing around the country. They did not build the turbine or the car but reaped enormous publicity.

The third type, the "now for something completely different" or blue-sky dream cars, do not have anything to with today's or next year's or next decade's vehicles. But they get some publicity if sales are not too high, they have "an unquestioned regenerative effect on our designers," says Gene Bordinat, Ford's styling vice-president, and they let the men with the pencils get a little madness out of their systems harmlessly, like the Chrysler Turboflite which was shown after the fins had passed their peak. The blue-sky models are usually built without running gear (after all, some may be supposed to move at almost the speed of light) and they may be made of glass fiber or plaster.

1. ►
The prewar Y Job, the granddaddy of experimental cars by Harley Earl of General Motors.

2.
The LeSabre, 1950, the most famous of Earl's postwar dream cars.

The most famous of the dream cars was Harley Earl's Y Job built in 1938 for General Motors (it got the name because G.M. men just got tired of calling them X for experimental). The Y had the extended rear trunk, the grille and hood ornament that fathered Buick's, and the lines of the last prewar and first postwar cars.

G.M.'s Le Sabre dream car of 1950 (dream-car names are often put on later production models) carried the first wraparound, or "panoramic," as G.M. called it, windshield, which later became common despite the vision distortion and the knee knocking that came with it. Kaiser liked the grille of Le Sabre so much that they stole it for their last model.

3.
Hudson's Italia, a 1953 2-seater. Twenty-six were actually sold. The car looks good today.

G.M. made these show cars a feature at its Motoramas, a series of auto shows, complete with stage review, held first in the Grand Ballroom of the Waldorf-Astoria and then around the country, that went on from 1949 to 1961. The first Corvette built by Harley Earl of G.M. as a sports car prototype was put in the 1953 Motorama and caused such a stir, the story goes, that G.M. put it into production later that year.

"Harley wasn't above taking a car to a show to get some reluctant directors to part with G.M.'s money," said an ex-G.M. designer. "He knew a car in a show would draw a crowd, and he could point to that and say 'Look how they love it.' " In the 1954 Motorama Mr. Earl showed a station wagon built on the Corvette theme, called the Nomad, and in '55 Chevy and Pontiac produced a modification of the wagon. It was not much of a sales success despite the crowds it drew at the show and its good looks; most dream cars tend to be sleek two-seaters. Even the show Nomad wagon was a two-door, though wagon buyers seemed to like four-doors.

Today, of course, there are professional market-survey techniques. But when George Mason, the president of Nash and a small-car buff, wanted to test the market for a tiny two-seater, he built a show car, the NXI, and in 1950 showed it around the country. The little car drew crowds and approval, and in 1954 Mason had the look-alike Metropolitan on sale. Only 95,000 were sold before the Met was killed in 1962.

4.
Even stylists have to blow off steam once in awhile. This blue-sky design of Chrysler's was called the Turboflyte "1961."

At times the dream car loses something in its transition to production. American Motors (formed when Nash and Hudson merged in 1954) showed a sporty dream car, the Tarpon, in 1964. That model was only 180 inches long, but when a production version called the Marlin was built for 1965 it was 195 inches long, and the lean sweep to the rear lost its attractiveness on the big car—which bombed.

At times a dream-car look will hold up decades later. One such model was the Italia, a sleek two-seater designed by Frank Spring of Hudson in 1953. Twenty-six models were built in Italy and sold for about $4,600 each. Spring had planned its sleek lines for a small car of Hudson's, the Jet, but A. E. Barit, the Hudson president, liked headroom and chair-high seats—he even thought the step-down Hudsons of '48 were too low—and he vetoed Spring's sleek Jet and ordered it squared off for production.

Even if a dream-car design is rejected it can give a good hint to a market. Ford, for example, built a radical two-seater which it called the Mustang. This model with a new V-4 engine—an unusual configuration for a four-cylinder engine, with the cylinders in a V rather than a straight line—was shown to the race crowd at Watkins Glen in the fall of 1962 and made a hit. But Lee Iacocca, later Ford president and the driving force behind the 1965 Mustang, said: "All the buffs said, 'Hey, what a car. It'll be the best car ever built.' But when I looked at the guys saying it—the off-beat crowd, the real buffs, I said 'that's sure not the car we want to build because it can't be a volume car. It's too far out.' "

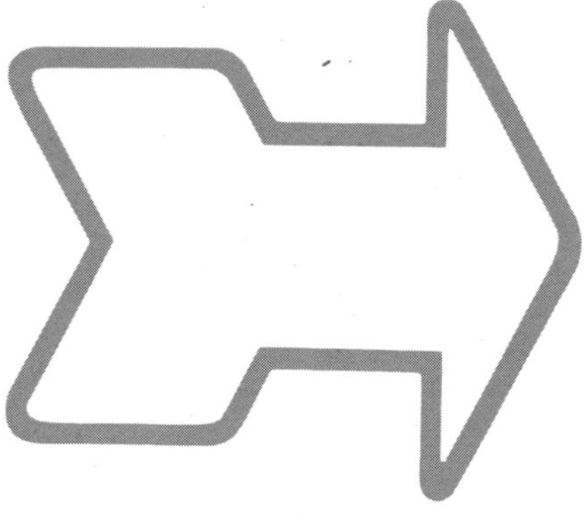

Another prototype, Mustang II, was close to the final production car, and about all that survived from the dream car was the name.

Sometime that's par for dreams.

5.
The 2-seat 1962 Mustang experimental car with Gene Bordinant, right.

6.
The Mustang II, a more advanced design study that led to Ford's Mustang car.

"I guess he figured if the seats went down, so would she."

—A comment on the bed-in-the-back Nash

George Mason, the president of Nash, was a man ahead of his time. He believed in the small car; what's more he believed Americans could like a small car for its size, and that it did not have to be cheap. This set him apart from every other small-car prophet in 1950.

For years Mason and his chief engineer experimented with small vehicles to work down to the minimum acceptable size car for Americans, and in 1950 he made his test, introducing the Nash Rambler. The Rambler carried a six-cylinder, 82-horsepower engine that gave as much as 24 miles a gallon. The car was 178 inches long, about the length of a modern subcompact such as General Motors' Vega and Ford's Pinto and about four feet shorter than a big car of the early 1970s. It was only a foot and a half shorter than a 1950 Chevrolet.

The first Rambler introduced was a convertible, the second a station wagon, and the third, for 1951, a hardtop as Mason attempted to prove that he was not aiming for a cheap-car market. The Ramblers carried as standard equipment some then-deluxe items such as radio, white walls, wheel covers, heater, and clock.

Witch hunt in East Europe: purges, spy arrests, deportations. Chinese Reds mop up mainla
Truman asks for H-bomb. Federal oleo tax repealed. February jobless at 4.5 million, pos

1.
The Hudson Pacemaker, the stepdown design and the letdown "new look" skirts.

2.
The Nash Rambler was the first attempt to prove that a small car didn't have to be cheap. Notice the unusual siderail on the convertible.

Truman says US won't defend Formosa. USSR walks out of UN for failure to oust Chiang. India a republ
ar high. Truman stops coal strike; miners settle for $14.75 a day. Major spy uproar: GOP-Dixiecrats bla

3.
The 1950 Mercury was to become a favorite of later hot rodders.

"Can't you get Mason to kill this car? It'll ruin us," one worried Nash man said to another. The Rambler did not ruin Nash. It had a good year or two and was killed after 1955 as the big-car boom exploded. Ironically, Mason's theory seemed correct despite his own failure. Volkswagen found success not by selling to the poor, but by being a darling of the upper middle class, well-to-do college students, magazine editors, psychiatrists, and the country-club set who owned Cadillacs but wanted second cars. Quality, not price, was the VW selling theme. In the compact-car boom of the early 1960s Chevrolet's Corvair found a market with its more expensive, sporty Monza, and Ford's best-selling smaller car was the Mustang. In the mid-1970s Ford

ritish A-scientist, admitted Soviet spy. Russians shoot down US plane over Baltic. France proposes Eu
epartment left wingers; CIO expels 11 unions for communism. Alger Hiss, Harry Bridges convicted of per

concluded that it could best sell its new Granada as a high-quality smaller car rather than a low-priced compact, so it styled its Granada inside and out to look like a Mercedes, loaded it with options, and priced the car at $5,000, proving the words of Ford president Lee Iacocca, who once said: "People want economy and they will pay any price to get it."

"One thing we learned was that nobody wants a car labeled cheap," Don Kidder, a Studebaker executive, said after his company had tried to sell a stripped-down model called the Scotsman during the 1958 recession.

4.
The Willys' Jeepster faded in 1950. Today, such cars have grown popular as recreation vehicles.

pean steel-coal pact. 500,000 Free German Youth march in E. Berlin; back off plan to attack W. Berlin.
ry; Judith Coplon, Russian lover convicted of espionage, overturned on no-warrant arrest. Sen. Joseph

The early Rambler probably failed because it was not that attractive an automobile. The basic style was pudgy; the convertible was an odd car with steel rails above the doors that made top-raising easy but took away some of the open-car feeling that attracted soft-top buyers. Ironically, the Rambler story did not end when the small car was killed. The Rambler name was kept and put on the larger compacts that brought success to American Motors. In the 1958 recession the small model "became the Bridey Murphy of automobiles," as Dick Teague, the American Motors stylist, put it. The old dies were brought out, dusted off, a few changes made and the small car was reintroduced as the Rambler American with great success. Perhaps the major reason the early Rambler was not the success that Mason wished was that the Standard American car had not grown to dinosaur size yet.

Still, the new Rambler and the Airflyte bathtub in its second year gave Nash a great 1950. The bathtub had become one of the most talked-about cars of its day. It wasn't just the shape, the one-piece curved windshield, the covered wheel wells (which did not help tire changing), or even the big curved rear window. It was the bed.

The seats came down in the Nash, turning the interior into a bed, and that brought a wave of Nash jokes.

"Hey, I've got a date with Lola. Can I borrow your Nash? Haw Haw."

"He has to change the upholstery on his Nash more often than the tires. Haw Haw."

But the sexual revolution really had not erupted in 1950 (today, of course, the "sin bin" van complete with bed or mirrored ceiling is a West Coast standard). Steven Spence recalled in *Motor Trend* that "as a teen-ager I remember it being controversial. For a lot of girls, it was really off limits. What father would let his daughter go to the drive-in in a car with

1950

Production

General Motors	3,048,400
Ford	1,556,700
Chrysler	1,201,800
Studebaker	268,100
Nash	189,500
Kaiser-Frazer	146,900
Hudson	143,000
Packard	72,100
Willys	38,100
Crosley	7,600
Total	6,672,200

ıvades South; UN orders fight; US sends troops, will defend Formosa. Reds take Seoul, break through Kor
ıarges 57 communists in State dept. Truman refuses Senate his loyalty files. Julius-Ethel Rosenberg arr

seats that made into a bed?" Another *Motor Trend* editor recalled that the son of a dealer had a bed-in-the-back Nash.

"This kid's girlfriend's father wouldn't let her go out in it. No way. I guess he figured if the seats went down, so would she."

The bed wasn't any Hugh Hefner pushbutton device. One now-middle-aged New Jersey man recalled his experience: "I borrowed my sister's Nash and figured that in the middle of a heavy necking session I would casually reach back and down and presto, a bed. When the moment came I pushed and pulled and shoved and kicked. The thing wouldn't fall into shape. The girl was interested in seeing it work, too, and she ended up

5.
The Ford Crestliner was in the forefront of some future styling trends like the wild two-tone and the covered roof.

ans; US troops flee, abandon weapons, wounded; ordered to stand or die around Pusan, stop Reds. Marines
sted as A-spies, Congress passes communist registration act over veto; red aliens deported; California d

6.
Remember the plastic covered steering wheel hub with the planet and the stars against a blue background? The Olds 88 Futuramic.

standing up outside the car while I struggled, without luck. Uncool? I was so embarrassed by my failure to get it down that I never tried that car bed again. To top it off my untrusting sister inspected her car the next day and found a bobby pin in the back seat and there was hell to pay."

The bathtub's instruments were gathered together in a single pod above the steering wheel, the "Uniscope," which was interesting but with all the instruments jammed together changing a speedometer cable, it was said, was enough to make strong men cry. Maneuverability was not the bathtub's

---

nd at Inchon behind N. Koreans; attack from Pusan, Reds broken, Seoul retaken. W. Europeans agree on
yalty oath from profs, 157 refuse, fired; Hollywood Ten to jail; networks blacklist accused leftists.

---

strong point but the car was roomy—gave the feeling of space—which is not found in today's cars. Looking back toward that far-away rear window, Spence said, was "like looking down a long tunnel to where the light is."

With the bed, as with the small car, Mason was touching a coming trend: the coming boom in travel and camping, though he would have been better off producing a camper. He offered seat belts as an option on the bathtub; the belts were aimed more at holding a rider dozing in the reclining seats than as a basic safety device.

That far-sighted executive was to make another move that was to influence the destiny of Detroit: He hired George Romney, who a few years later was to take the dead Mason's ideas and combine them with his own evangelistic fury and lead a shattered and almost bankrupt American Motors to its great moment of glory.

7.
The Chevrolet in 1950. Not much on power, not much on looks, but something to believe in.

bined army, Eisenhower in command; Germans demand equality, more freedom for troops. US arms to Indoc
groes integrated in combat units; courts OK Negro ban at NYC Stuyvesant Town, but order southern colle

Studebaker restyled in 1950, putting a spinner nose on, not one of Loewy's better ideas. Robert Bourke, one of Studebaker's stylists, recalled the nose.

"I remember Mr. Loewy to this day with his French accent saying 'Now Bob, eet has to look like ze aeroplane.'" And Bourke told *Special Interest Autos*, a magazine: "At that time, Lord help me, I said 'Yes sir, Mr. Loewy.'"

G.M. restyled its big Cadillac and the biggest Buicks and Oldsmobiles. The Buick carried a long chrome spear along its sides and Buick's success—the big medium priced car almost caught Plymouth for third place in the industry—helped incite a ten-year chrome war. The smaller Oldsmobile, the 88 with its powerful V-8, was king of the stocks. *Motor Trend* called the '50 Olds 88 the first stock car it had tested that could come from the factory without any doctoring and top 90 m.p.h. (Top speeds are usually controversial, as different testers get different results, but the Olds was fast for its day.)

Chevrolet made two significant moves for 1950. The first was the introduction of the Bel Air hardtop just a year after Buick put its Riviera on sale. Chevy was the first low-priced car to offer the pillarless body style. The second move was Chevy's offering of an automatic transmission, again the first automatic in the low-priced three, as Chevy, Ford, and Plymouth were called. For the first time a low-priced car was moving to offer the type of features that made the medium-priced cars distinctive. The ingredients that Sloan of G.M. had predicted would be important after the war were at work to shape the cars of the '50s: style with the hardtops and chrome; high-compression engines with the new V-8s, and automatic transmissions.

One car faded in 1950, one that is probably more missed by buffs today that it was at the time. Willys, which won fame as the best-known pro-

HARDTOPS

Year	*Number*	*Percent of Total Production*
1949	10,000	negligible
1951	480,000	9
1953	860,000	14
1955	1,720,000	24
1957	2,030,000	33
1959	1,560,000	28
1961	1,190,000	22
1963	2,230,000	30
1965	3,960,000	44

Chi Minh troops attack. UN pushes past old 38th parallel border; China warns of intervention; MacArth
mit some Negroes. Southern RR removes curtains hiding Negroes in dining cars. 108 killed in 2 Long Is

8.
With its portholes and gunsight hood ornament, Buick was to replace Plymouth as the third best selling car in America.

ducer of the Jeep in World War II, had been creeping back into the car business. After the war it kept making Jeeps but had not built an ordinary passenger car. In 1948 Willys began production of a six-cylinder Jeep-like station wagon and convertible called the Jeepster, and in 1949 began producing a new four-wheel drive all-steel station wagon as part of its Jeep series. But it was the Jeepster, which really was an open car—no real roof—that scores high on the nostalgia scale. Willys made 19,000 of them in 1948, 1949, and 1950, but then gave it up.

In June of 1950 the Korean War began, and with it came production and financing restrictions. But even the war could not stop the revolution in automobiles that was under way, or the social changes that the automobile was bringing.

9.
The 1950 Chrysler. There are millions of Americans, the company insisted, that want to sit in cars with their hats on.

Whatever the faults the cars of 1950 may have had, they are part of a simpler era that is still remembered by adult Americans.

"We had an Olds 88, a green four-door," remembers Dollie Katz, a Detroit newspaper reporter who was seven years old then. "We lived in Cleveland, in the inner city, in an apartment with real rats and a real newsman on the corner. It really was rotten [good housing was scarcer then than now, for the great suburbs were just being built]. But on Sundays my father would take us for a long drive in the country in that Oldsmobile. Sometimes I'd sit in front and I'll never forget that steering wheel. There

sea, saved; US army digs in at 38th parallel. Matthew Ridgway takes command. Europe arming. Sugar Bo
ll Truman. GOP wins Congress election, Nixon to Senate. Draft upped, $17 extra billion for arms. Bost

was a plastic covered hub, with a planet inside and stars against a blue background. The planet and the stars were always in that steering wheel. And the back seat was such a nice place to sleep, except my sister used to drive me bananas. The top of the back of the front seat was covered with some material, silky, like the inside of a purse, and she'd run her fingernails against it. I still get the shivers when I think of it. We finally traded it in for a pink car with just two doors. It wasn't the same."

10.
The Pontiac Silver Streak.

: Oklahoma 35, LSU 0. Sweetwater Clifton joins NY Knicks, 1st NBA Negro. Songs: Rag Mop, Chattanoogie
Brinks robbed of $1 million. City College of NY beats Bradley twice for NCAA, NIT titles. Ingrid Ber

"They didn't have vinyl then."
—A remembrance of a 1951 interior

The great horsepower race dates to the 1951 models. In that year Chrysler introduced its new V-8. Engines have names, too, and the Chrysler engine, because of its unique hemispherical combustion chamber, was called the hemihead V-8, and it was a challenge to the short-stroke V-8 G.M. brought forth in 1949. The Chrysler engine incorporated the G.M. advances: more powerful, designed for higher compression ratios and higher-octane fuel, meaning a more efficient engine. But it was not a copy; this new powerful Chrysler V-8 was rated at 180 horsepower to Cadillac's 160. Cadillac would not be second, and in 1952 its engine was stepped up to 190 h.p. By 1954 the Chrysler was at 235 h.p.; by 1958 the big Lincoln and Mercury models were at 400 h.p. Horsepower also climbed on the Chevrolets, Fords, and Plymouths. While the bigger cars had higher horsepower numbers, the lighter weight of the low-priced three meant they were as fast or faster than their bigger brothers—and eventually even these cars were run up to 425 horsepower. When smaller cars became popular in the early 1960s, Pontiac hit on the idea of jamming a big V-8 into its compact Tempest model (and called it GTO) and the supercar era was born. Even today Detroit can't resist the temptation of putting big engines in little cars. When the energy

Reds take Seoul, UN asks Korean truce, Chinese reject. Ike takes over Atlantic Pact defe
Atomic testing ground established in Nevada. Air Force calls up 158,000 reservists. Wag

1.
"Eet has to look like zee aeroplane," the pointie-nosed Studebaker.

crisis of the early 1970s struck, a wave of smaller cars appeared, such as General Motors' Chevrolet Monza 2+2 (no relation to the original Monza) and Ford's smaller Mustang II (no relation to the original Mustang). But the weight saving and good fuel economy was quickly curbed as V-8s were jammed under the hoods. What a squeeze. Chevy planned a radical and powerful rotary engine for its Monza 2+2 but canceled this engine and pushed in the V-8 to make the small car a dragster. Of course, the engine compartment was so small that you couldn't change the rear spark plug without pulling the engine, but that was not going to stop Chevy from climbing on board the small-car horsepower express.

e. French stop Vietminh drive near Hanoi; more US aid to French. Germans jail Ilse Koch for life; US r
price freeze. 83 killed in New Jersey commuter train crash. 22nd Amendment limits presidents to 2 term

2.
Chrysler's new V-8 outpowered this Cadillac in '51, beginning the horsepower race.

Those horsepower figures of the 1950s and 1960s were called "advertised" horsepower, which meant they were not quite real. The power was not tested in a car; instead the engine was placed on a test stand, unconnected to any of the equipment it was used to run, and then the figure was puffed up a bit. In the 1970s Detroit used a more honest rating system to avoid environmental criticism—the engines were just as big and powerful but the figures came out lower.

Chrysler's hemihead of 1951 could not stand the pace of the race and was dropped in 1958, reappeared in the 1964 supercar era to give Chrysler its stock-car victories, then killed again in 1971. It wasn't that the engine

ationalizes steel industry. Allies dig in; halt Reds, retake Seoul, push past 38th parallel. Ho Chi M
yndicates, Frank Costello, crooked politicians. 10% ceiling put on year's wage boosts. Rosenbergs gui

was inadequate; the hemi was a great engine, but unlike the G.M. V-8, Chrysler's was heavy and expensive to build. The use of the hemi in the 1950s, one writer said, "marked a triumph of engineering over cost accounting."

The horsepower race that Chrysler and Cadillac began was to spill over into public controversy and eventually helped to put the automobile business under government regulation.

3.
The new Kaiser was the independent's last gamble for success. It was a handsome car, but still overpriced and without a V-8.

. orders long guerilla war in Indochina. 5,000 more US troops to Europe. Britain-Iran dispute over oil
- in A-spy trial, death sentence. Basketball gambling scandal; City College of NY, Long Island U playe

Chrysler recaptured its position as number two car maker behind General Motors in 1951. It was not because its styling or engines caught the public fancy. Rather, the Korean War brought production restrictions to save material, and Chrysler, having outsold Ford in the years after World War II, got a higher allocation, thus crimping Ford's big expansion program.

Chrysler introduced another major engineering feature on its '51s—power steering. The purists have never forgiven the company.

"An abomination in its earliest forms," said John Jerome, once the managing editor of *Car and Driver* magazine and author of *The Death of the Automobile*. The complaint is that power steering insulates the driver from the feel of the road. "There is no estimating how many drivers went off roads because they could no longer feel the delicate sensory transition from a condition of steering control to that of front-wheel skid." That is basically the buff's argument, and the buffs have decried every comfort change, or any change that made driving simpler, from automatic transmissions to roll-up windows. Despite their talk of the improved safety of foreign cars because of better handling (not to knock better handling), death rates in American cars on American roads are lower than European rates on European roads. There is even some indication the rates are lower for American cars than for imported vehicles on the same American roads, although the larger size of the American cars could be the most important factor. It was galling to the buff to see more of the art needed to master a car built into the vehicle itself and taken from the driver; a five-foot, three-inch mother of teenagers could wheel around the corners in an American auto and make the supermarket run just as fast as a gymkhana veteran (and then beat him into the parking space) despite his years of training mastering the stick shift, wheel swing, and brakes. Making it easy took some of the sport from driving.

POWER STEERING

Year	*Number*	*Percent of Total Production*
1952	200,000	5
1953	700,000	12
1955	1,800,000	23
1957	2,300,000	38
1959	2,200,000	40
1961	2,200,000	40
1963	3,800,000	50
1965*	5,300,000	60

* *Model year.*

ıreats, riots. British diplomats Burgess, Maclean defect to Russians, were spies. UN troops retake Py
ibes. Truman recalls MacArthur; General addresses Congress, old soldiers never die, they just fade a

4.
Chrysler with cars like this DeSoto Custom and the generous production allowance from the government, outproduced Ford in 1951.

Chrysler's styling still was on the plain side despite its engineering achievements. *Motor Trend*, for example, called the '51 Dodge "a safe, sane, stylish car," which is about as damning with faint praise as an auto magazine can get.

Chrysler and Ford brought out low-priced hardtops with the 1951 lines —the Plymouth Belvedere and the Ford Victoria—to catch up with Chevy's 1950 Bel Air, and the hardtop was on its way. Some 10,000 hardtops were built in 1949 when Buick introduced the Riviera, 268,000 in calendar 1950, and 478,000—9 percent of production—in 1951. In 1955 four-door hardtops were added and 1.7 million built in that year's model run—24 percent of production. By the 1963 model year they were accounting for 2.2 million or 30 percent of production.

yang. Cease fire talks in Korea open, stall. Jordan's King Abdullah assassinated. Egypt defies UN, w
speech hailed; Congress investigates war conduct. Congress bars aid to nations selling war goods to C

The hardtops were an issue that Ralph Nader used against the car makers in his 1965 book *Unsafe at Any Speed.* They were less safe in rollover accidents, he said, quoting an unnamed General Motors executive as admitting they were "on the borderline" of safety.

"But who knows what the borderline is?" asked Nader. By the mid-1970s the safety movement had driven the hardtop from the auto world, and Detroit did not fight for it. Following a styling trend set by Thunderbird, the rcar or "C" pillar (the "A" pillar is at the windshield, the "B" at

5.
The 1951 Dodge Coronet, dependable was its reputation.

uez Canal blockade. Japanese peace treaty signed. USSR explodes 2nd A-bomb. Fighting hard in Korea,
upreme Court upholds Communist convictions; FBI arrests more Red leaders. Race riot in Cicero, Ill., N

6.
Packard was new for 1951, but didn't sell. When the great bird on the hood dipped its wings, Packard began to die.

the center door post, and the "C" at the rear) had widened enormously, giving more support to the roof on two-doors. With most cars air-conditioned and the windows always rolled up, the unbroken sweep of the four-door hardtop vanished anyway.

With the coming of the hardtop in 1951 the old streamline or fastback style began to disappear. Chevrolet started building its fastbacks as usual for the '51 run but stopped early in the run, and Pontiac killed its models in 1952. It was about fifteen years before the fastback returned on cars such as Plymouth's 1965 Barracuda, American Motors' Marlin, a Mustang fast-back, and the Dodge Charger.

truce talks at Panmunjom. Conservatives win English vote; Churchill prime minister. US agrees to sup
nal Guard called in. 90 West Point cadets expelled for cheating. Navy orders A-sub. George Marshall

7.
Chevrolet had no V-8s in 1951.

Cadillac went to a one-piece curved windshield in 1951, which was the coming thing—this was not the wraparound—and Oldsmobile dropped its six-cylinder engine, offering only the V-8.

For independent auto makers 1951 was a key year, more so than for the Big Three. Hudson, Packard, and Kaiser brought out '51s aimed at challenging the Big Three, and the failure of those cars to give their creators a permanent lift was a major factor in their demise.

For Hudson it was the Hornet, the King of the Road it was called, a shortened descendant of the famous '48 step-down model with a new 308-cubic-inch displacement, 145-h.p. six, the last of the big sixes. With that engine Hudson went racing.

.o Yugoslavia. British-Egyptians clash over Suez, Sudan. Pope opposes rhythm birth control. US Army
ıs defense secretary. Post card stamp price doubled to 2¢. Senate investigates loss of China to Reds.

"It was the hottest stock car in the business," said Bill France, the founder of N.A.S.C.A.R. Hudson was third in the stock car rating in 1951 and first in 1952 and 1953. A from-the-factory Hudson tested by *Motor Trend* hit 97 m.p.h., but it was a V-8 world that was coming because the powerful, quiet V-8 engine was better able to carry weight and accessories, and Hudson's big six wasn't enough. Production was only 93,000 in 1951. By 1953 output was down to 76,000, and the next year Hudson saw the handwriting on the wall and disappeared into Nash. Hudson was quite a car, but in the biblical words, *Mene Mene Tekel*, it was weighed in the balance and found wanting.

8.
This was the last year for the Fords descended from the famous '49 model.

rms Reds murdered prisoners in Korea; UN-Reds exchange prisoner lists; 70,000 UN missing not on list.
arthy accuses 26 in State Dept. of disloyalty. 119 killed in W. Franfort, Ill., mine disaster. Major

Packard had a new model for 1951 too, a car that George "Pinchpenny" Christopher had not wanted to build. Most everybody agreed that the new Packard was handsome, modern looking and up-to-date with two tones. But it did not sell well and in 1952 Packard hired a new go-go president from the appliance business with a lot of fire and spending ideas, and with that went the last of Packard's money. *Mene Mene Tekel* you too, Packard.

Kaiser also gave the dice their last big roll with the '51s. There was a new full-size Kaiser, now in two- and four-door models, with its distinctive widow's-peak split windshield and a low beltline. That model still is considered a pretty car.

"We had a great amount of respect for that Kaiser," said Dick Teague, the American Motors stylist.

"The future has caught up with us," a Kaiser official told his dealers. "If you don't grab it now you never will have another chance like this." There was even a brougham model, the Golden Dragon, with the cloth-covered roof that was to prove so popular in the 1960s. The Frazer was about finished, however, and the 1951 models were leftover '50s dolled up with new trim—strangely, the rehash seemed popular—so that when the leftover bodies ran out the car was killed.

Henry J. Kaiser had one more ace for 1951, a small car. He ran a nationwide name-the-car contest and—shades of Edsel—the winning entry was Henry J. The little bird got about 25 miles to the gallon but had cheap written all over it: no trunk lid, no glove compartment, and a plain interior. There was a 68-h.p., four-cylinder engine or an 80-h.p. six, but the six at $1,350 was only about $50 under the price of the low-end Chevrolet. Kaiser spent his last big money on the Henry J and while they sold moderately well at first, by spring of 1951, with the war having slowed buying, thousands of Kaiser cars were piled up around the fat lady of a

1951

Production

General Motors	2,255,500
Chrysler	1,233,300
Ford	1,165,000
Studebaker	222,000
Nash	161,200
Kaiser-Frazer	99,300
Hudson	93,300
Packard	76,100
Willys	28,200
Crosley	4,800
Total	5,338,700

ecomes independent. Truce talks stall. Rose Bowl: Michigan 14, California 6. New York City bans nudi
RS officers fired, Truman pledges cleanup. Taylor-Nicky Hilton, Frank-Nancy Sinatra, Judy Garland-Vinc

9.
The 1951 Lincoln and clothes to match.

plant, Willow Run, and before the year was over Kaiser was renumbering the '51s as '52s.

What went wrong? There never was a V-8. The cars were overpriced, the dealer organization weak, and the union and workers never seemed to realize that Kaiser could not give as much—or more—than the richer Big Three. And the Orange Juicers from the West Coast (as Kaiser's team was called) never got along with the Detroit team. The Detroiters "weren't able to weld in," said a West Coaster. The Detroiters joked about the Orange Juicer who said (a fiction, but symbolic) upon seeing the spare tire in the trunk, "You've got the life preserver on the port instead of the starboard side."

Joe Frazer, who saw his chance for greatness go down, said, "If we just

gazines from newsstands. Plays: I Am a Camera, King & I, The Rose Tattoo, Stalag 17, Gigi. Army disba
Minnelli. Court Turf wins Derby. Oscars to: All About Eve, Judy Holiday (Born Yesterday), Jose Ferrar

10.
The Oldsmobile 98 Holiday hardtop. The one piece, curved windshield was new and Olds dropped its 6 cylinder in '51.

didn't want to go too fast, we could have had our place in the sun." But that wasn't Henry J.'s way, so *Mene Mene Tekel* you too, Kaiser.

One thing everyone remembers about all the '51s was the interior, so different from today's cars. "They were made up of that prickly gray upholstery," said Kathy Warbelow, a Detroiter, who used to fight her brother for the right to sleep on the back seat on Sunday drives—loser gets the transmission hump.

"They didn't have vinyl then," she said.

Here to Eternity (Jones), The Caine Mutiny (Wouk), The Cruel Sea (Monsarrat), Catcher in the Rye (Salin
Sea Around Us (Carson). Married: Frank Sinatra-Ava Gardner. Died: Sinclair Lewis, Eddy Duchin, Fannie

THE SMALL CAR

"If this doesn't crash the American small car market, there is no such market."
—Don Macdonald, a car expert, on the tiny Nash Metropolitan

Despite myths to the contrary, American car makers were continually planning or building small cars in the first decade after World War II. Not one of these cars was a rousing success. Yet Volkswagen and later other importers found hundreds of thousands, then a million and then close to 2 million small-car customers a year. Even when the American manufacturers found the small-car market with their compacts of 1960, they lost it again—then found it again with the Mustang-size cars of 1965, and promptly lost it a second time. They're still trying, and the four-cylinder, 40-m.p.g. (on the highway) Chevy Chevette of 1976 is proof of the effort.

What was this Lorelei luring so many to failure, yet always there, beckoning?

As World War II ended, Detroit believed there would be a tremendous demand for a new generation of small, light cars, a new group of Model Ts to put car-hungry America back on wheels. In 1944 young Henry Ford II said his company would build "a lower-priced car than has been offered the public since the days of my grandfather's famous Model A." Before long the rumors were spreading that Ford was planning a $500 car.

1.
The Crosley wagon. Crosley just wasn't enough car for the United States and folded after 1952. About 75,000 were built.

Ford was serious. A special light-car division was set up with orders to have the car ready for introduction by October 1947. General Motors did not sit still, planning a new plant in Cleveland for its little car; and Chrysler promised that if the others moved, "Chrysler will be ready with something competitive."

Yet in September of 1946 G.M. canceled its plans and Ford followed. (The G.M. car later was built in Australia and the Ford car in France.) Both companies learned, as Harlow Curtis, G.M. president in the 1950s, said, "you can take the value out so much more rapidly than you can take the cost out."

The projected small cars would not have come in more than $100 or $200 under the prewar models Detroit was building (a '47 Ford coupe had a price tag of only $1,410). With strikes and material shortages, the car makers were having enough trouble just building the old models, and they were discovering that Americans did not need a new model to excite them. They were bidding for anything that rolled off the assembly line.

In later years both G.M. and Ford pulled out their small-car plans, looked at them, then shoved them back in the drawer. "To the average American our present car and its size represents an outward symbol of prestige and well-being," said Ford in the early 1950s. "It seems reasonable

2.
The Nash Metropolitan, built in England from 1954 to 1962.

to ask—if we need a smaller car, do we need a smaller refrigerator or a smaller washing machine?"

Even when VW sales began to grow after 1955, Detroit categorized the buyers as professors and that type, left-wingers, intellectuals, critics who were somehow trying to undermine America. One Ford product planner called them "a bunch of creeps." Of course, that was before Ford brought out its Falcon in 1960. Then the same executive smiled and called them "our customers." It makes a difference.

Besides which, stylists who were wielding power in the 1950s did not care for small cars. "It's hard to do a small car," admits Bill Mitchell, the G.M. styling vice-president. "It's like tailoring for a dwarf."

Boiled down, their hearts were not in it. Did the customers want it?

Chrysler, preparing for the Ford and G.M. minicars that never came, offered a cheaper, shortened version of its Plymouth and Dodge models in 1949. They came only as two-doors, the wheelbase was eight inches shorter than the standard car—a real chop—and they were duds, killed in 1952. And Chrysler's "shorter on the outside" line of 1953 was a sales disaster.

"It's one thing for a small company, a marginal firm, to pioneer a new concept like that and really push it," said George Romney, the compact car prophet. "But it's another thing for people who already have a big slice to begin pushing something that undercuts their basic market."

And the independents' efforts?

Powell Crosley found a fortune by putting shelves on the inside doors of refrigerators (the Crosley Shelvador) and owning the Cincinnati Reds. Despite his six-foot, four-inch frame, he was a small-car believer.

"Why buy a battleship to cross a river when a rowboat will get you there just as well?" he said, and in 1946 he was building his car. The Crosley was not quite twelve feet long, had room for four people (almost), and had a two-cylinder engine. Later a more proper four-cylinder job ran "at speeds closer to 45 m.p.h. than the 60 that was advertised" and got mileage of around 35 m.p.g., although up to 50 was claimed, according to Iver Peterson, a *New York Times* reporter and Crosley buff. There was a sedan, a wagon, and a two-seat sports car, the Hot Shot.

While the Crosley still has its supporters, it was not much of a car by American standards. "Drivers got accustomed to the little knacks of moving the car, like the coordination of left foot and right arm to shift the unsynchronized gears, or the little dip-and-twist necessary for anyone more than six feet tall to look back while backing up," said Peterson. Crosley

3. *Kaiser's Henry J, probably the best known of the small car failures of the postwar era.*

built 75,000 cars between 1946 and 1952 (the best year was 1948, with 28,000 assembled), when the car folded.

George Mason was a believer, too. He put his established Nash company behind the small-car dream with his '50 Ramblers. The Rambler convertibles, wagons, and hardtops were not stripped or cheap. They were priced within a few dollars of bigger competing cars, though better equipped, with deluxe interiors, radios, and the like. They were killed in 1955, though brought back to life later.

Mason also tested the market by showing a tiny dream car, the NXI, and after a warm reception ordered the Metropolitan into production for 1954 (the Met was built in England for the U.S. market). The Met was cute, came as convertible or hardtop (and later carried a snappy continental tire kit), had a 42-h.p. engine (upped to 52 h.p. in 1956) and claimed up to 40 m.p.g.

"If this doesn't crash the American small-car market, there is no such market," wrote Don Macdonald, the McGraw-Hill auto expert. After 95,000 sales the Met, no rousing success, was killed in 1962.

Henry Kaiser abandoned his plans for a revolutionary small car when the war ended but in 1951 gambled that America was ready. Out came the Henry J. Sears, Roebuck & Co. even tried to sell the car in its stores as the Allstate (Sears sold a grand total of 2,363 in two years and decided to stick to parts). Romney said the Henry J "was identified as a car basically for poor people. The result was that poor people didn't want it either."

Richard Langworth, in his book on Kaiser-Frazer, *The Last Onslaught on Detroit*, told how a Georgia farmer described the Henry J to Joe Frazer. The little car was "like an unsavory gal ah once knew," he said. "She was really pretty great—but ah wouldn't associate mahself in public with 'er." In all, 127,000 were sold.

4.
The small Nash Rambler was killed, then brought back successfully as this American Motors Rambler American in 1958.

Then there was the Willys Aero, introduced in 1952—Willys's first and last un-Jeep car. The Aero was designed by Clyde Paton, who had worked on a small-car package for Ford right after the war. The Aero had good-looking, clean lines, with four- or six-cylinder engines offered, 25–30 m.p.g. and 87 m.p.h. top speed. But Willys had no real sales organization. Only a couple of dozen dealers were more than truck sellers or gasoline-station operators. Willys sold 31,000 in 1952, 42,000 in 1953—and thenKaiser bought Willys, and under that old magic Kaiser touch, the Willys car died.

In 1953 Hudson brought out another small car, the Jet, 181 inches long, 2,700 pounds (1,000 pounds lighter than an Oldsmobile, 500 pounds lighter than a Chevy) and with a 104-h.p. six. The styling was conservative—

5.
Hudson tried to crack the small car market with its Jet, but the Jet died when Hudson merged into Nash in 1954.

the sleek lines of the Italia dream car were not allowed on the Jet—and the Jet died when Hudson and Nash merged.

Why?

Except for the tiny Crosley and the two-passenger Metropolitan, all were about the size of an American subcompact—about 180 inches long. The standard-sized car up to the middle of the 1950s was about 200 inches long, or about the size of a typical compact car today. Thus the ordinary-size car was not gross—it was about the size that is considered just right now.

The prices of the smaller cars were not much different from the low-priced series of the Fords, Chevys, and Plymouths. They had no exceptional reputation for quality—sometimes, as in the case of the Henry J, just the opposite. When Volkswagen sold well in this country its reputation for quality was a major factor. And with gasoline at 25 cents a gallon, a few more miles did not save much money (at 25 cents a gallon, and 10,000 miles driving a year, a 25-m.p.g. auto eats up $100 in fuel, and a 15-m.p.g. car eats only $67 more in a year).

The economies of mass production may be part of Detroit's problem. To build a profitable low-priced car of good quality, high volume is needed. In 1959 Chevrolet's new Corvair was priced above the VW. "Let me build a million cars a year, all alike, and see what my price will be," said Ed Cole, who then headed Chevrolet. VW and the big Japanese makers produced in high volume, lowering cost, but figuring on dumping off a large share of their output on the American market. Detroit could build only for its home market (trade restrictions kept American cars out of Europe and Japan), a few hundred thousand cars at most for each company. Even when Detroit built compacts and then subcompacts, the dealers and factories encouraged loading. Power steering and brakes, automatic transmissions, luxury interiors, air conditioning, even V-8 engines raised profits but eliminated the price advantage and much of the fuel advantage of a smaller car. A typical G.M. 1975 small car—its Chevy Monza 2+2 and sister models from Oldsmobile and Buick—could cost $5,000. And an American dealer was likely to be interested in trading any small car buyer up into a larger-size car.

Style might have been a factor. The Volkswagen, at least, looked distinctive. Year after year, model change after model change, the VW would have what Detroit stylists sought: instant recognition. The American Motors Gremlin and Pacer have those qualities. Even after they have been in production for years they are fresh looking, because nothing on the road looks like them.

When Stuart Perkins, who heads American Volkswagen, saw G.M.'s new 1971 Vega minicar, he told a reporter he was not worried. The Vega looked fresh then, he said, but in three years it would just look like an old 1971, while the Beetle still would be different.

The Lorelei beckons still.

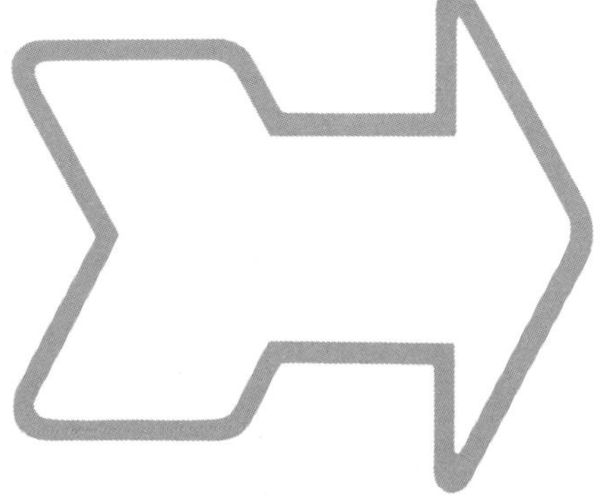

"Chrome is my favorite color."

—A Detroit secretary

There is no exact moment marking the beginning of the chrome revolution, although the long spear on the side of the '50 Buick was a spark. Certainly by 1952 the great chrome war that was to rage for a decade had been declared. Chrome was god and Harley Earl was its prophet.

A Ford stylist admitted that by the late 1950s, "God help us, we were measuring the number of square inches of chrome" on the competition's cars to make sure Ford had enough.

A stylist working on the '52 Oldsmobile told of the two separate chrome proposals the designers had for Mr. Earl. "We expected him to take one or the other," the spade—chrome along the rear with a spade-like splotch by the rear fender—or the spear. "He came in, looked hard and said 'great, fellows. Put them both on the car.' You just couldn't do too much chrome to offend him—even if it was in poor taste."

There was the story of the Detroit secretary, who when asked about her choice in hue, said "Chrome is my favorite color."

Certainly the plated steel did look good, though enough never seemed to be enough. Chrome became associated with the deluxe, higher-priced models, and it was the age of aspiration.

Truman-Churchill meet in Washington. Korean truce talks stall; Reds charge germ warfare; Truman orders reform of scandal ridden IRS, bans political appointments. Ike says he'd ac

"The more chrome, the more money," said Bill Mitchell, G.M.'s top designer today. That was the gospel of the sales department. The peak came in the late 1950s. "On those '58s we laid the chrome on with a trowel." The break came in the early 1960s and Pontiac proved a car could look good without a silver finish. Pontiac wanted a Riviera-Thunderbird type car and created the Grand Prix, a fancy version of its regular car but with less chrome, not more. Nothing in the mid-1960s was prettier than a black GP.

How did the artists of the styling department succumb to chrome madness? Certainly the push from sales could not be ignored, but they also

1.
The Rambler Country Club hardtop. A small car but not a cheap car.

sks for US troops there, rejected; coup in Egypt, King Farouk out, Gen. Mohammed Naguib rules. UN vote
osenbergs appeal death sentence, lose. Supreme court OKs ban of subversive teachers; state loyalty oat

2.
The Allstate, a version of the Henry J sold exclusively in Sears Roebuck stores. One experience was enough for Sears. They never tried selling a car again.

wanted to make cars look longer and lower, and when they could not change the size, the chrome spears and two-tones (which later turned to three and four tones) helped. Then, as Mitchell put it, there was the problem "of falling in love with your own Rembrandts."

"And if you don't like it, you'd better like it because everybody else does," he says.

By 1952 another trend was well under way: the push to automatic transmissions. Chrysler still did not have a full automatic, but they were offered on all G.M. models. Ford and Studebaker were buying automatics from Borg-Warner, Packard had its own (showing that Packard had a reservoir of engineering talent, because an automatic was a challenge), and G.M. would sell Hydra-Matic to any car maker wanting it.

$250 million for Palestinian refugees. George VI dies, Elizabeth II queen of England. Britain tests A
outlawed in California, Oklahoma. Attorney McGrath fires corruption investigator, Truman fires McGrat

Chevy's move to offer automatics on its 1950s was the breakthrough. In 1947 just 1.3 million cars or 25 percent of the total production carried automatic transmissions. By 1952 the figure was 2.1 million or 47 percent. By 1957 it was 4.9 million or 80 percent, and in 1975 about 90 percent of the cars built in the United States carried automatics. When the sporty-car boom began with the Corvair Monza and then Mustang, Detroit discovered it could get more money through the console approach, putting an automatic on the floor, imitating at extra cost the four-on-the-floor of the sports car. The small imports handle best with four-speed manual shifters because they would lose some of their not-too-plentiful power with an automatic, as well as cut down gasoline mileage. In 1975 G.M. offered a five-speed manual shifter to improve fuel economy on one model, which could start a trend since G.M. charges extra for it and Detroit favors anything that can be sold as extras.

The early automatics had their problems: they were balky, plagued with service problems, ate up gasoline and crippled performance. The perfection over the years of the automatic transmission was a major achievement.

Purists did not like them. The automatic, for example, was one of the reasons that Ken Purdy, a noted automobile writer, labeled the '49 Buicks "turgid, jelly-bodied clunkers." Yet by 1952 some 85 percent of the Buicks carried the Dynaflow automatic. John Jerome in *The Death of the Automobile* said: "The automatic transmission removed us, as operators, from the category of engineers and mechanics, boosted us to that social class which doesn't have to know about things like gears and clutches. We no longer had to accrue any skills in order to manage our own private transportation."

No one had to be an expert to drive, and anyone might beat you away from the stoplight, even a grandmother. That did not help machismo.

AUTOMATIC TRANSMISSIONS

Year	*Number*	*Percent of Total Production*
1949	1,300,000	25
1951	2,400,000	45
1953	3,100,000	49
1955	5,000,000	70
1957	4,900,000	80
1959	4,000,000	72
1961	4,100,000	74
1963	5,800,000	76
1965*	7,200,000	81
1975*	6,200,000	92

* *Model year.*

TO approves European army. Fulgencio Batista overthrows Cuban government. French attack in Indochina, w attorney general slows corruption probes. Truman seizes steel industry to block strike, court calls

3.
The Hudson Hornet, with its big 6, was king of the stocks.

The year was not the biggest for change, but interiors were becoming brighter. Buick added a colored steering wheel and Nash had a self-winding clock. More important, Ford brought out a new body, finally eliminating the leak problems caused by the poor fit on the '49s. The look of the new Fords was not as exciting as the '49s, but they finally got one-piece windshields. A two-door all-steel station wagon, the Ranch Wagon, was introduced, and the four-door Country Squire used wood just as a veneer trim. There was a new six-cylinder engine which was needed for the new Ford car, rated at 101 horsepower, and the power on the V-8 was boosted to 110 h.p. In 1952 Ford nailed down second place behind G.M. permanently and began its domination of the wagon market.

ietminh overrun northwest Indochina, French claim victory. US-Japan peace treaty. US weapons to Yugos
izure illegal. Major teacher shortage in US. Tough McCarran-Walter immigration bill passed over Truma

4.
The Olds 98 Holiday Coupe with the spear in front and the spade along the side. You couldn't have too much chrome for Mr. Earl.

1952

Production

General Motors	1,801,500
Ford	1,004,800
Chrysler	952,600
Studebaker	161,500
Nash	152,100
Hudson	76,300
Kaiser-Frazer	75,300
Packard	63,000
Willys	48,800
Crosley	1,500
Total	4,337,400

The heady air of success caused Ford to begin thinking of new worlds to conquer: a new high-priced car, a replacement for the old Continental killed in 1948. Age had improved the reputation of that car. The debate popped up again on challenging G.M. in the medium-priced market, although no decision to go ahead was given until 1955, and that was the Edsel. And there was talk of a sports car. The year before, while tramping through the Paris auto show, Ford executive Lewis Crusoe pointed to the flashy sports cars and said to George Walker, his stylist: "Why couldn't we have something like that?" Walker, not one to be caught with his sketches down, told Crusoe that his boys had a sports car in the works, then found a phone, called Detroit, and told them to design a two-seater. When Ford learned G.M. was working on a sports car, activity increased and in 1954 the two-passenger Thunderbird rolled out.

st German military buildup. Premier Mossadegh gets dictatorial powers in Iran, orders land reform, qua
curbs travel to Soviet bloc. Ike wins GOP nomination; Richard Nixon for Veep, Nixon fund revealed, Ch

Chevrolet had a face-lifting for 1952. The grille got the toothy smile but Chevy still carried its Blue Flame six, now up to 105 h.p. and accelerating from 0 to 60 in a long, long 19 seconds. Unlike Ford, Chevy did not have a V-8. They did have an old six that was a dead reliable, easy-to-repair, gasoline-stingy engine, although it has been said by the performance buffs that the Chevy six "made a better anchor than auto engine." As for looks, one critic said the '52 Chevys looked as if they "had been designed by Herbert Hoover's haberdasher," and the debate was over whose cars looked stodgiest, Chevrolet's or those of the Chrysler Corporation.

5.
The Plymouth Belvedere hardtop. Still a split windshield and no fully automatic transmission. Not exactly the style king.

els with West over oil; Iran-Britain break relations. Germans to pay Jews $822 million reparations. M
kers speech on TV wins public, Ike's support. Adlai Stevenson Democratic nominee, Sen. Sparkman for Ve

This would lead to trouble because Ford was beginning to have the cars to challenge Chevy for number one. But change was coming as Edward Cole, a brilliant engineer who helped develop the famous 1949 Cadillac V-8 shifted to Chevrolet and began designing a new engine.

For the independents, 1952 was another ride down. Crosley ended production and one slice of the car buyer's choice was gone forever. Packard got a new president, James Nance, who had revitalized the appliance business of General Electric. He came on with a rush to do the same for Packard.

6.
The '52 Chevy with the Blue Flame 6. Dead reliable but 0 to 60 in 19 seconds.

rror increases in Kenya. 240 die in 4-day London fog. Purges in East Europe, leaders arrested in Alba
nounces Dems for Korea, Communism, corruption, carries 39 states. First US H-bomb tested. Owen Lattim

7.
The Nash Statesman. Nash still hid the front wheels.

"The company has just been lulled to sleep," he said, and told his executives that "any guy who loses good doesn't go on my team." A Nance motto was "make no little plans."

The styling department was expanded, but told to listen carefully to the sales department. The Clipper would be revived and turned into a competitor in the medium-priced market, which was growing. (Packard still used the straight-8 engine, though, and a V-8 would come too late.) Nance began looking around for some way of making Packard a full-line auto maker—that is, having low- as well as medium- and high-priced models to sell, just as G.M., Ford, and Chrysler had.

Unfortunately, he found the way and Packard was out of business a few years later. Some say the drive into the growing medium-priced market

a, Bulgaria, Hungary, many Jews; Trials in Czechoslovakia, 11 leaders hanged for treason. USSR ousts (
-e indicted for perjury on red issue: Charlie Chaplin denied re-entry to US. George Meany heads AFL, W

8.
The Lincoln Cosmopolitan.

9.
Ford's '52 was all new and had cleared up the leak problem of the previous models.

ambassador. Riots in French Morocco. John Foster Dulles new secretary of state. Sugar Bowl: Marylanc
ads CIO; Ike visits Korea. Dock corruption revealed in NY. Jambalaya, Blue Tango, Cry, Littel White Cl

10.
Remember the side vent? All the cars like this Mercury Custom hardtop had them.

caused Packard to lose the allegiance of its high-dollar customers. After all, Rolls-Royce stayed with the high roller and survived; Mercedes did the same, and Cadillac scrupulously avoids any idea that it makes any kind of cheaper car. When it brought out its smaller Cadillac Seville model in 1975 the smaller car was priced above the larger Cadillac to drive home that point.

Then there's the legend of the cormorant, the great bird of the hood ornament on the glorious Packards, its wings spread wide. In 1952 Packard dipped the wings of its silver bird on the hood. It's said that when the cormorant folded its wings Packard began to die.

Nash abandoned its bathtub design in 1952. The noted Italian designer

28, Tenn. 13. Books: Diary of Anne Frank, Witness (Chambers), Old Man and the Sea (Hemingway), Giant (
d That Cried, Kiss of Fire, I'll Walk Alone. Hill Gail wins Derby. SS United States crosses Atlantic

11.
The Pontiac: Notice the chrome and fender skirts and the deep front wheel opening, a Harley Earl trademark.

Pinin Farina was credited with the new look, which is now called a notchback. But even Farina could not get George Mason of Nash to expose the wheels—full fender skirts front and back still looked streamlined to him.

Kaiser was sinking fast with no money and no new cars (although a two-seat sports car would be offered at the end). Willys brought out its Aero small car for 1953 with moderate success but like the other small cars of the time, could not make it. The Aero was priced above Chevrolet. Willys was a one-man company and the man was Ward Canaday, who liked to prove the point. When a stylist discarded a hood ornament for the Aero, Canaday saw it in a waste basket, pulled it out and said, "I run this company and I like it"—and slapped it on the Willys. A year later he sold out to Kaiser, which proved that two could go out of the automobile business as fast as one.

heavily; Red prisoners riot, 52 killed; UN vows no forced prisoner repatriation. Riots in Suez, Chur
Sen. McCarthy attacks State Dept. loyalty programs; Truman attacks McCarthy. Spy Judith Coplon wins n

"Bigger on the inside, shorter on the outside"
—The motto of the '53s from Chrysler

Chrysler struck back in 1953. While most of Detroit was planning longer, lower, and wider for the future, Chrysler brought out a completely new line on all its cars from Plymouth to Chrysler. They were the kind of car a man could wear his hat in, could put in his garage with ease, boxy, but dependable. The new Plymouths and Dodges were five to seven inches shorter than the old models. They were well-built cars—Chrysler was still an engineers' company.

If that was not enough, there were those singing radio commercials:

Higher on the inside
Lower on the outside
Bigger on the inside
Shorter on the outside

They were a disaster.

"We put on intensive advertising campaigns," said Lester Lum Colbert, who was to head Chrysler and lead it into the fin era. "We did all the talk we could that people needed shorter cars to go into their garages, the

Red antisemitism. Doctors Plot in Russia; Jews arrested in satellites; USSR breaks with
Rosenbergs ask Ike for clemency, denied; executed. Reds, aliens, teachers arrested, depo

1.
Raymond Loewy and his famous Studebaker coupe. This car is considered one of the handsomest ever designed in this country..

parking facilities were crowded. We used every argument known to man to impress on the American public they needed a smaller car rather than larger cars.

"We had been running those cars from October 1952, about six months, and finally," Colbert said, "after we tried everything else, we tried price reductions." The price cuts ran from $14 to $274, averaging $100 a car, and Chrysler announced "we were reducing the price to increase volume." Perhaps customers get a bit suspicious when a car maker cuts prices, for it has not been a sure-fire way to get sales. Chrysler tried it again early in 1975, when sales fell, with about the same results. After the 1953 disaster Chrysler went the styling route, hiring Virgil Exner who had worked for Raymond Loewy and claimed credit with Loewy for the radical '47 Studebaker (which brought about a split with Loewy, but Studebaker hired Exner

u-mau terror in Kenya; Jomo Kenyatta gets 7 years as M/M. Guatemala expropriates United Fruit land; go
unches mass attacks on: Mrs. Roosevelt, reds in schools, books in US libraries, State dept., Voice of A

immediately). Exner triggered a fin war with his 1957 line for Chrysler, which succeeded at first and then turned cold. Chrysler then replaced Exner with Elwood Engel, a Ford stylist, who swung Chrysler to a modern but conservative styling approach (they copied G.M.).

There were other problems in 1953: a general slump throughout the industry and a cat fight between Ford and G.M. for what business there was, which meant Chrysler and everyone else was caught in the middle. While Chrysler finally brought out a fully automatic transmission in mid-year, not all the Chrysler-built models had it. The '53s were part of the heritage of the Chrysler Airstream failure of the 1930s. "They just didn't

2.
The Buick Skylark convertible. The American car makers tried to catch the flare of the foreign Jaguar and Mercedes with expensive, low volume models like this.

g red, U.S. says. W. Germany to pay $822 million to Jews, Israel. Exchange wounded POWs. US learns c
rica, Adlai, Harvard, press, church ministers, Dulles, Ike, GOP. Aides Roy Cohn, Gerald Schine tour Eu

3.
The Willys' Aero, aimed at the small car market that never quite materialized. The car also cost as much as its larger competitors.

dare take any chances," said a stylist of those shorter-on-the-outside lines. "They hadn't taken their nerve pills yet."

Raymond Loewy, though, was taking chances. He designed the 1953 Studebaker line, and even today the '53 Starliner coupe is considered one of the loveliest cars ever built. *Fortune* magazine, in a list of history's best-designed products, put the '53 Starliner coupe as number four (Ford's two-passenger Thunderbird of '55 was number forty-one) and there are those today who will put a silhouette of the '65 Mustang against the '53 Starliner and claim a copy. The Starliner was only fifty-six inches high and if the trunk wasn't much the V-8 could push it to 97 m.p.h.

Yet the Starliner failed too. The Loewy team had a weakness: They produced the sweetest coupes in the world—the '47 Starlight, the '53, and

arch, atrocities, forced confessions. Stalin dies; Georgi Malenkov premier. General thaw. USSR calls
ies. Hundreds resign, fired at State, VOA. McCarthy attacks signal corps, army. Ike attacks book bu

later the Avanti are the evidence—but those same designs did not look so good translated into sedans and four-door models, the bread and butter of an auto company. Even worse, Studebaker had trouble getting the beautiful coupe into production, and when they reached the dealers months after the announcement and the heavy advertising, many of the orders had been canceled and a general slump set in. Studebaker's labor costs were abnormally high, too (this was true of many independents, since they felt they could not afford strikes and gave in more readily to union demands) which means the cars were not as competitive as they should have been.

4.
The Dodge Coronet: Bigger on the inside, shorter on the outside and nobody cared.

ctors Plot a frameup; secret police boss Beria arrested, executed. Queen Elizabeth II enthroned. Ever
rs (McCarthy), cuts air force budget $5 billion, stiffens loyalty standards. Treasury bonds sell for 3

5.
The Kaiser with the widow's peak windshield was old hat by 1953. This is the lower priced Carolina model, but Kaisers were always overpriced.

The Starliner struggled on for a decade, was later called the Hawk, but was never a major success. Still, Loewy never gave up his ideas of lightweight, slim cars. "How many times have we heard the dear [sales] boys say to us, what the public wants is a big package, and we know that a big package means a great deal of weight and a lot of money," he said. "Weight is the enemy." Regardless, bigger and heavier cars were to come in the next few years.

The sales slump triggered an unexpected problem. Ford was still chasing Chevrolet and decided to push hard for sales during the '53 slump, to "blitz" instead of falling back and cutting production. General Motors pushed right back. Cars were forced upon dealers whether they wanted them or not. There were price cuts, sales-incentive contests, pressure to make dealers move cars. The dealers pushed with lowballs (offering to sell a car

y Edmond Hillary, Tensing Norkay. Truce talks on; quarrel over anti-red POWs; S. Korea frees 25,000 N.
ate since '33. Jonas Salk claims vaccine againsta polio, mass tests planned. States voted control of

at a low, low figure, then after the customer is about committed, finding there was a "mistake"). They pushed with highballs (an unreal figure for the trade in) and phony come-ons (the handbill under the windshield saying "would you take $1,200 for this '49 Hudson on a new Ford? See Harry at . . ."). There was price packing (no price stickers on cars, so the dealers could put a few dollars extra on every item on the car), fictitious prices and bootlegging. The dealer would dump off, or bootleg, unwanted new models on nonfranchised car dealers who might sell them at cutrate prices but offered no service, making it hard for an honest dealer to earn a living. The automobile companies encouraged these practices with their own pressure on the dealers, and between 1954 and 1960 there were at least eight Congressional investigations.

If the independents did not have enough trouble already, they and their dealers were sliced to bits in the Big Three crossfire. In 1948 seven independent car makers accounted for 19 percent of the industry's production; in 1953 the share fell to 9 percent, with only six companies left. Kaiser bought Willys in 1953 and Edgar Kaiser said bravely, "We aren't, by a long shot, through yet." Later that year General Motors bought the big Willow Run plant outside Detroit, Kaiser's first home. Kaiser transferred production to the Willys base in Toledo, Ohio. The '54 Kaiser still carried only a six-cylinder engine, and although it could be supercharged for more power, just 6,101 were built that year. Only 11,865 Willys cars were assembled. Unsold '54s were renumbered again as '55s. Dutch Darrin designed a plastic-bodied two-seat sports car for Kaiser and production started in December 1953, but no more than 500 were built before it faded in the Kaiser death throes. In spring 1955, the best year Detroit ever had to that time, Kaiser ended its American car production.

1953

Production

General Motors	2,799,600
Ford	1,546,500
Chrysler	1,246,600
Studebaker	186,500
Nash	135,400
Packard	81,300
Hudson	76,300
Willys	40,600
Kaiser	21,700
Total	6,134,500

ean POWs, threaten to quit talks. Anti-red riots in E. Berlin put down by Russian tanks; strikes in E.
shore oil. 1st atomic cannon tested. AEC develops breeder reactor. Gov. Earl Warren signs California

There was a restyled Chevrolet for 1953 with a one-piece curved windshield, but somehow the new Chevy did not look much different from the old one. Chevrolet also introduced the Corvette in 1953, the first American-made sports car (excluding a few other, half-hearted efforts) of the postwar era. The first Corvettes had Chevy's six-cylinder engine—Chevy still had no V-8—and all carried automatic transmissions. If it was not the world's finest sports car in 1953 Chevrolet just kept working at it until it was. "That was an exciting car, even with a six," said a competitor. "You just can't wait to get to work on a car like that."

6.
The Corvette and the regular Chevrolet. The Chevy was redesigned but still looked like its predecessors. Note the new one piece windshield.

mre Nagy premier in Hungary; promises reform, frees prisoners. Korean truce June 27. US casualties 1
anning Communist Party. Tornadoes kill 242, Flint, Mich., area hit. Harry Bridges conviction upset.

7.
The Nash Ambassador. Independents like Nash were caught in the crossfire of the Ford-Chevrolet sales war of 1953.

Nash introduced a closed hardtop version of its English-built Nash Healy sports car in 1953, but the entire Nash Healy run, from December 1951 through August 1954, when Nash quit the sports-car business, was only 506. Nash also came up with a Petty Girl hood ornament (the Petty girls were the best-known pin-up drawings until Playboy came along with its own brand of reality).

Ford had twelve single-tone colors for its lineup and fourteen two-tones, along with six interior color options, because color ruled the road. Twelve-volt batteries came on to replace six-volt systems. Hudson brought out a squarish, small model called the Jet, which was killed after Hudson merged into Nash in 1954. For the first time the number of eight-cylinder engines installed in cars topped the six-cylinder total, and the horsepower race continued as Cadillac went up to 210 h.p. and would climb to 230 in 1954.

0 (33,629 U.S. KIA, 20,616 other dead). Russians test H-bomb. Army overthrows Mossadegh in Iran, Sha
t holds racial covenants unenforceable. Warren named Chief Justice; Court weighs school segregation.

8.
Ford: There were 12 single-tone colors and 14 two-tones available.

The production restrictions of the Korean War ended February 13, and on March 5 price controls ended. No one but Chrysler formally cut prices in 1953, though discounting was heavy, and in the fall of that year prices were up about 3 percent on the '54s (although about half of this was offset when the car makers stopped putting phony transportation charges on cars). The increases continued over the next few years—5 to 5.5 percent in 1955, 7 percent in 1956, and another 3.4 percent in 1957. Of course, these increases were on list prices; as competition sharpened, discounts climbed, and this held costs down. Customers were taking more extra-cost options, meaning they were getting more in their car by paying for it. The '53s were possibly the last of the low-cost cars—a Ford convertible still

rench seize Dienbienphu, reject red peace feelers; get $385 million more in U.S. aid. USC 7-Wis. 0 in
rders civilian desegregation at southern bases, army, air force resist. (High Noon), Shirley Booth (Co

listed at $2,230, a four-door Country Squire Wagon at $2,410, and a plain Mainline two-door was only $1,720. By 1960 the car makers would have to bring out their new compacts to get a car close to $2,000 again.

Nineteen fifty-three was a good year for specialty convertibles as well as low prices. Packard offered its Caribbean convertible. Cadillac introduced the Eldorado as a convertible, and while only a few hundred of the special model (it had a wraparound windshield, as did the first Corvette) were sold, it was the beginning of the high-priced Eldo that exists today. "According to legend, Eldorado was a South American Indian figure whose body was sprinkled with gold dust and periodically washed off in a lake," said Cadillac explaining the name.

9.
Even the conservative luxury cars like this Imperial got a bit of two-toning.

bowl. Charles Chaplin rejects U.S., stays abroad. Plays: The Crucible, Tea & Sympathy, Can-Can, Kisme
ck Little Sheba), Greatest Show on Earth. Harvester works in Memphis strike when Negro promoted. Kins

10.
Don't ever fall on the hood ornament of a 1953 Pontiac.

Bright among the '53 specialty cars, straight from the era of Elvis and Pat Boone, of excitement with gadgets and the soft ride, was the Buick Skylark convertible. The Skylark carried Buick's new 188-h.p. V-8 (the low-priced Buicks still had straight-8s for '53), power steering, power brakes, power seats, power windows, air conditioning, a foot-button control for the radio, and the new automatic transmission Buick introduced that year. There were no portholes on the '53 Skylark and the top of the windshield was chopped to give it a lower look (you had to hang on to your hair), the wheel cutouts were raised, wire wheels and two-tone leather were included, and the owner's signature was imbedded in plastic in the steering wheel emblem. The Skylark lasted only two years—2,500 sales all together—and the '53 was the prime model.

Not too surprisingly, Jaguar owners were unimpressed, but it was about as American as baseball, hot dogs, apple pie, and Chevrolet.

rael. Air-ground fighting in Korea; truce talks hinted. Coal-steel common market starts. South Afric

ed or fired if Communists. Allen Dulles heads CIA. LA school board bans UNESCO school program. McCar

CORVETTE & THUNDERBIRD

"Beauty is a good ten-day sales report."
—A Ford vice-president

Of all the automobiles launched in the 1950s two that still exist stand out as the peak and the valley of Detroit's aspiration level: Corvette and Thunderbird.

The creators of both had a similar vision: a moderately low-priced car, which they would call a sports car or personal car, that would perform and handle exquisitely and look the part. They would be more than just transportation. These cars would take you away from all your cares and woes, flying low.

Both Corvette and T-Bird abandoned those aims. First written off was the idea that a fun car could have a low price tag. Today the Vette and Bird go to the ordinary buyer with $9,000 to spend on wheels and about a king's ransom for insurance each year. Ironically, it was General Motors, which brags about wearing its heart in a money clip, that tried hardest to stay with the idea of a sports car, a buff's car. In the end the handling and performance were accomplished by brute force—the biggest engines in the lightest bodies, burning fuel and rubber. Ford quickly decided there was more money to be made if grace and charm were ignored. "Beauty," a Ford vice-president said, "is a good ten-day sales report," and that rule is the basis for all Thunderbird decisions today.

These cars were conceived in the early 1950s when sports cars were in the air. The English Jaguars and MGs were on the road, and a few Americans tried to get into the act: Nash imported the Nash Healy, Hudson sold a few Italias, there was the Kurtis, later called the Muntz, and Crosley's Hot Shot, while Kaiser's last gasp was the two-seat Darrin sports car. Packard, Cadillac, and Buick all tried to catch a bit of the swing with their

1.
The first Corvette off the assembly line, June 30, 1953.

2.
A 1956 Vet with the top attached. Chevrolet still wasn't sure where to go with the sports car, but it had given up trying to sell them to bankers and the like.

Caribbean, Eldorado, and Skylark convertibles, which were not quite what sports cars were about.

Harley Earl, the styling boss of General Motors, moved first, deciding it was time to build something for young folks, a two-seat sports car that would sell for around $1,850. The G.M. engineers had been using glass fiber in their experimental cars and were interested in trying it as a production material. Ed Cole had moved to the chief engineer's slot at Chevrolet and eager to do anything to spruce up Chevy's image, pushed the project.

Mr. Earl put his little experimental sports car in G.M.'s 1953 Motorama, and it is said that the stir it caused encouraged Chevy to put the Vette into production that same year. For sports cars, the first Corvettes of '53 were strange. All carried the Chevrolet six—there were no V-8s, and the six was no prize-winner—and carried automatic transmissions. All were

3.
By 1960, with big engines, manual transmissions and race track victories, the Corvette had become accepted as a high performance machine.

Polo White with red interiors. There were no roll-up windows; just plastic side curtains. Not quite a sports car and not quite a rich man's toy.

Chevy had decided that the Corvette would be sold only to Very Important People, bankers, retired generals, and the like, on the apparent assumption that in every man there is some boy and that V.I.P.s could afford the then $3,500 price tag. They could afford it, but they didn't want it. They were not, for example, the type of customer who appreciated side curtains and leaks. Chevrolet's conception, wrote Don Macdonald, an auto tester, "is that no owner will be caught in the rain without a spare Cadillac."

In 1953 only 314 were built. Production went to 3,265 in 1954 and down to 700 in 1955 as the bankers and retired generals stayed away. Some at

G.M. wanted to kill the car. "We really didn't know what we wanted," said Cole in Karl Ludvigsen's book on the Corvette. "We had no real feeling of the market. Was Corvette for the boulevard driver or the sports car tiger? We weren't quite sure. But we loved that car. We weren't going to let it go."

An engineer with European racing experience, Zora Arkus-Duntov, was put in charge of the Corvette program. In 1956 there was a new body, a V-8 engine, a three-speed manual transmission, then victory at Sebring, fuel injection (a measured amount of fuel is fed into the cylinder, eliminating the carburetor where air and gasoline are mixed before injection—

4.
The 1961 Corvette.

5.
Perhaps the most sensational of the Vets was this 1963 Sting Ray.

increasing power and sometimes economy), big power, and four-speed transmissions—constant improvement. The Vette men fought off Cole's suggestion that it be made into a four-seater. In 1963 G.M. brought out the Sting Ray Vette and today, even in the worst sales year, Vette business is strong. Even the 55-m.p.h. speed limit has not hurt sales. "A person who drives a Corvette doesn't drive it for its high speed potential but because he likes driving a finely tuned machine," said David McLellan, the Corvette chief engineer in 1975—not very truthfully, but what can you say with a 55-m.p.h. speed limit? There's no doubt the Vette is as good a machine as G.M. can make.

"There were 130,000 miles on my Corvette," recalls Marty Schemer of New York. "In all the years I owned it, the only trouble I had was one disc-brake cylinder. You'd drive around the country in your Corvette and it was kinda friendly. People in other Corvettes would beep their horn and wave to you. Now in New York it was different. If you were stopped at a light and another Vette came up the guy would roll down his window and say 'You want to run, you f– – – ?' "

The Thunderbird story is quite different although it began in much the same way. Lewis Crusoe, who ran the Ford division, asked for a sports car when he saw the foreign models in a Paris auto show; work began in earnest when Ford learned of Chevrolet's Corvette plans. Ford aimed to use as many parts common to its ordinary Ford car as possible, thus keeping costs down and giving the Bird the Ford look. They had a V-8 engine which gave the Bird an early power advantage over Chevrolet, but Ford never built—or even tried to build—into the Thunderbird the handling qualities that would make it a sports car in the European fashion.

Like Chevy, Ford was unsure what the Bird was. They quickly decided it was not a true sports car, but one that looked like a sports car, a "boulevard" sports car as it was to be called. Wally Wyss wrote in *Motor Trend* that the Bird was for "the kind of guys who wore those Ben Hogan caps and baggy Perry Como sweaters." The two-passenger Thunderbird was put into production in 1954 as a '55 model. The name, Ford said, symbolized "power, swiftness, and prosperity," but it wasn't a bad name anyway. Unlike the Corvette, it was an instant sales success, and outsold Corvette two or three to one until 1958, when Ford really found the road to the bank.

A continental tire kit was added to the two-seater's later models, and the portholes were put in because Crusoe discovered that the wide rear

CORVETTE & THUNDERBIRD

	Production	
Year	*Corvette*	*Thunderbird*
1953	314	—
1954	3,265	3,546
1955	700	15,660
1956	4,987	18,517
1958	9,298	53,407
1960	12,508	87,218
1962	15,726	75,536
1964	19,892	90,239
1965	27,700	75,710
1975	45,900	37,800

6.
The two pasenger T Bird of 1955 wasn't a sports car, but it is considered one of the prettiest designs of the postwar era.

pillar blocked side rear vision. The detachable top was standard, and the convertible cloth top an extra-price option. The car was immediately hailed as a major styling achievement, and it is still considered a modern classic until the '58 model when—to the purists—Ford committed the act that to this day is unforgivable, junking the little Bird and going to the four-passenger Thunderbird (the last two-seater rolled down the line December 13, 1957, and a worker wrote "Bye Bye, Baby" on the hood in soap).

The hate shows through almost every test of a modern Thunderbird by the buff magazines. Even their more pleasant comments are barbed. *Car and Driver* admitted that the motoring press would look at the Thunderbird "and by reflex register shock that Ford would have the effrontery to market such a vehicle," noting that it is "a massive assault in achieving all that is frivolous and Mittyesque in a motor car." The magazine also noted that once a driver "resolves that he won't try anything smart in the way

7.
The purpose of the porthole on the 1957 Thunderbird attached top was to eliminate the blind spot behind the driver.

8.
Car lovers have never forgiven Ford for junking the 2-seat Bird and bringing out the big model for 1958.

9.
If the afficianados didn't like the big Birds like this 1961 model, they were really horrified by the 1967 four door.

of turning corners or changing speed, riding in a 1964 Thunderbird can be fun." If you like that kind of thing, of course.

If Ford had anything new, like sequential taillights, the Bird was sure to get it, and the taillight systems became so big and bright that one writer said the car "had the look of a city burning down behind you." There were always some nice words. *Consumer Reports* in its test of the '59 Bird said it was quiet, steers well, handles "outstandingly," and called it "a downright pleasure to drive." The tester counted 10.6 seconds for 0–60 m.p.h., with 13.6 miles a gallon.

In 1967 Ford heaped on another horror by offering a four-door T-Bird. What angered the purists probably was not what the Thunderbird had

10.
Despite criticism, the big Birds like this 1965 model outsold Corvette three to one.

become, but their feeling of loss for the little Bird and their vision of what it might have become. Even at Ford the big Bird draws some laughs. Of course, when the Thunderbird went four-passenger with the '58s, sales soared to 48,000 and the car outsold Corvette five to one. By 1960 it was selling 80,000. And that four-door Thunderbird was the basic body upon which Ford built its highly profitable Continental Mark III in 1968.

They still get letters at Ford asking for a return of the two-seat Thunderbird, but it will never come back. "You can't breathe life into these things," says Gene Bordinat, the Ford styling vice-president.

The question remains: What would Corvette and Thunderbird be and how many customers would there be had they stayed with their early dreams—a simple, sporty, lower-priced, two-passenger machine in the tradition of the British two-seaters instead of, on one hand, a mighty brute fit for the race track, and on the other hand a wheeled jukebox?

Maybe not much. It was H. L. Mencken who said "No one ever went broke underestimating the taste of the American public."

"This time I think Cadillac has really gone too far."
—An auto industry executive talking about the Dagmar Bumper

Everything was coming together—the engines, the automatics, the gimmicks, the options, and most important, the styling—and 1954 was the last year of the old order; 1955 was to explode as the best car year in history. The styling and horsepower wars would escalate.

It was a nightmare year for Chrysler, which was still selling its smaller-on-the-outside line. Of 5.5 million cars built in 1954 Chrysler built only 723,000. When the line was obviously failing, Virgil Exner, the stylist, was shown the proposed '55 models, which were just a facelift, and asked if he could help. "I don't think there's anything you can do with this car," Exner told K. T. Keller, the Chrysler boss, "you need a whole new skin on it," and Chrysler began its crash program that ended in its Forward Look of '55 and the Great Fin War a few years later.

Just because a car was setting no sales records did not mean it was unloved. The slow-selling Chrysler was as powerful a car as any on the road in 1954, with the biggest engine—235 horsepower—in the New Yorker Deluxe and Imperial models, and it had its admirers.

USSR warm to atomic energy talks. Chinese POWs go to Formosa. Dulles rejects talks with
Dulles warns of new US strategy: massive, instant retaliation. First atomic sub Nautilus

1.
Convertibles were the prestige cars of the decade. Notice that Packard's Cormorant had dipped its wings.

"If it's possible to love a car, I was in love with that car. I worshiped that car," reminisces Judy Klemesrud, a New York writer. The car was her parent's black New Yorker; the place, Thompson, Iowa. She never gave the car a name, "but it was a person," and twice a week she scrubbed the dust of Iowa from it. "There were gold letters saying NEW YORKER on the rear fenders and a gold star on the hubcaps, and I polished them until they gleamed."

Thompson was too small to have a drive-in of its own. "We'd go fourteen miles to Forest City where they had an A&W. We'd roll in with that gleaming Chrysler and the car hops would whisper 'whose car is that?' "

d China. Gen. Naguib ousted in Egypt; Gamal Nasser new premier. US arms to Pakistan, India irked, re
unched. Army dependent schools ordered desegregated by '55. Ike says 2,200 Federal employes dropped a

She is convinced that the night Paul Larsen took the car (with Judy and everyone else in it) that he ran it up to 140 m.p.h. on those empty Iowa roads. That is really impossible, even for that big hemihead—well, unlikely at least—but it's the stuff memories are made of. One day the black beauty was traded and another day Judy shook the dust off and left, too. For years, she said, "when I was out in California, I'd see a '54 black Chrysler ahead of me, and I'd follow it and pull up, thinking—" but it never was. Teenagers should not be allowed to drive such a car, she insists today. "It gives you ideas of grandeur you shouldn't have. I've never loved a car since."

Chrysler found another lover that year: Prudential Insurance Co., which loaned it $250 million for 100 years. That gave Chrysler enough money to

2.
Ford's Crestline with its see-thru plastic roof, an idea whose time never came.

econd Comet jet crash. US sending French $250-$350 million for Indochina war, training plane mechanics;
ina experts out at State Dept. Maurice Chevalier kept out of US. McCarthy attacks army, insults gener

3.
The Hudson Super Wasp, one of the last real Hudsons.

ready the '55s and gave the nation's financial institutions such a stake in Chrysler that they could not afford to let it go down later. They were always around with more rescue money when things were tough. In contrast, when American Motors was successful and almost caught up with Chrysler in sales, George Romney, a Mormon, paid off his loans instead of making more when the borrowing was easy. When things went bad for American Motors, the banks, without any bad money already in to throw good money after, always held back.

The independents were squeezed again in 1954. Hudson built only 32,000 cars, Nash only 63,000, and the two merged, forming American Motors, which was really the end of the Hudson car. Detroit's Hudson plant was closed, and with all the production at the Nash Wisconsin plants, the cars

ke vows to get technicians out; Vietminh attack Dienbienphu, French ask help, intervention considered,
, calls Army Secretary Stevens a dupe; Nixon attacks McCarthy; McCarthy aide Roy Cohn accused of threat

given Hudson nameplates were rather grotesque versions of the Nash. The saving grace of the merger was that after Romney left American Motors for politics (governor of Michigan and a presidential contender) and the company went back against the wall, it was an ex-Hudson man, Roy Chapin, Jr., son of the founder of Hudson, who calmly pulled that once-again shattered company together and led it to success.

Packard, with only 28,000 cars built in 1954, merged into Studebaker which built only 85,000. Studebaker's output, low as it was, was tops for the independents. The Kaiser-Willys merged company built only 17,000 cars in its fadeout year. The goal of James Nance, who headed Packard and pushed for the combination, was to create a full-line manufacturer, and he was readying all-new models for '55. The '55s on which Packard counted failed with the customers, and the Studebaker acquisition was in trouble. Neither side had spent much time examining each other's books; after the merger was effected Packard discovered that Studebaker's costs were out of line and they could not compete with the low-priced Fords and Chevrolets. There were too many workers and executives.

"Studebaker kept telling their workers that they were craftsmen [even the advertising stressed this] and the trouble was that they began to believe it," said Dan Cordtz, who was a *Wall Street Journal* reporter in Detroit during Studebaker's troubles. Packard went down first. A couple of years after the merger its Detroit plants were closed or sold, the famous Packard nameplate put on Studebakers, and Nance's grand plans for super luxury cars washed out. It was a long time ago, but the men who tied their fortunes to Packard still feel the pain. "When they put my [Packard] Clipper taillights on the rear of that tired '58 Studebaker," said Dick Teague, one of the veterans, "it was enough to make a maggot vomit."

1954

Production

General Motors	2,874,300
Ford	1,687,200
Chrysler	723,300
Studebaker	85,300
Nash	62,900
Hudson	32,300
Packard	27,600
Willys	10,900
Kaiser	5,800
Total	5,509,600

enbienphu falls; Pierre Mendes-France new French premier; Geneva peacetalks. Red state under Ho Chi M
my to get deals for drafted buddy G. David Schine; Senate investigates McCarthy, McCarthy censured, his

4.
In 1954, Dodge finally had a fully automatic transmission, but styling was still plain and sales low.

Ford launched an all-out assault on Chevrolet in 1954, continuing the blitz drive of 1953. There was a new Ford V-8 with 130 h.p., the biggest engine in the low-priced field, to go with Ford's new six of '53. Chevrolet had little styling change and kept its old six with 115 and 125 h.p. (its most popular model that year was the Bel Air four-door sedan at $1,884). It was a race. Ford claimed its first sales victory over Chevrolet, but when the final figures were in Ford showed 1.4 million car registrations and trailed Chevrolet by 17,000. Chevrolet was in trouble, but help was coming as Ed Cole readied a new engine and body design that would sweep all before it in 1955.

Among the other changes on the '54s: Tubeless tires became standard

set up in North, free states in South, Laos, Cambodia. Ngo Dinh Diem pro-West premier in South Viet N
olitical power crippled. Puerto Rican terrorists shoot five Congressmen on House floor. US tests H-Bo

before the year was over. Buick went completely V-8, leaving Packard with the last of the straight-8s. Nash brought out its 150-inch, two-seat Metropolitan, which lasted until 1962.

General Motors began putting wraparound windshields on the Cadillacs and the big Buicks (most popular Buick in 1954 was the Super Riviera Coupe, a two-door hardtop listing at $2,626 and weighing 4,035 pounds). Eventually most American-made cars carried the wraparound windshield, which brought on a generation of sore knees because it was natural to bang your knee against the door post getting out of such a car. They really did not help vision either: The windshield post was pushed back to a point where it hurt the side vision, and the wrapped corner glass usually distorted vision.

Gimmicks became more common. Cadillac had automatic windshield

5.
The Cadillac with the Dagmar bumpers. Automatic windshield washers became standard on the luxury car that year.

verthrow pro-Reds in Guatemala. Yugoslav VP Milovan Djilas attacks Red Party, loses job. Britain ends
bert Oppenheimer security risk. Production of Salk polio vaccine begins. Building of St. Lawrence Se

6.
Chrysler's New Yorker, the big 235 horsepower engine made this car one of the fastest on the road.

washers as standard (actually a good idea)—push the button and it would squirt and wipe, then make six more wipes automatically. There was the "autronic eye" headlight dimmer that would automatically dim the brights for an oncoming car. In a later year Chrysler brought out an electronic rear-view mirror that went from night to day (with the terrible sound of tearing metal) when light hit it. The trouble was that the mirror switched not only when someone with brights came up from the rear but every time the car passed under a streetlight (that was like the marvelous electric door locker Ford invented later that locked the doors automatically when the car went faster than 7 m.p.h. Passed every test and then was put into production—and killed after the first proud owners took their cars to the car wash, got out, saw them pulled through the wash at more than 7 m.p.h., and then could not get into their locked cars). Cadillac carried hooded headlights (almost everyone would soon have the metal visors over the lights). And then there were the Dagmar bumpers.

Dagmar was a TV actress whose assets were entirely visible. Her name became the semiofficial designation for G.M.'s new bumper mounts, big,

od rationing. 200,000 refugees flee to South Viet Nam. W. German secret service boss defects to East.
approved. Supreme Court rules school segregation unconstitutional, overturns separate but equal doct

7.
Buick went all V-8 in 1954. Note the wire wheel knock-off hubs, an effort to imitate the foreign sports cars.

full, pointed protuberances in the front of the car—terribly sexy to the designers but a pain in the rear end to any car in front. To run into those Dagmars was to get a dent. When a competitor saw them on the '54 Cadillac, according to *Fortune* magazine, he said, "This time I think Cadillac has really gone too far." Cadillac hadn't. Later, when the complaints about the dents grew, Cadillac put a black rubber tip on the Dagmar, which gave it a black-lace bra look.

Nothing was too much—not Dagmars and not weight. The 1954 Cadillac 62 model weighed 5,100 pounds, up from 4,200 pounds for the '49. The weight increases were to become common to all the cars in the next few years, but two vehicles that would buck this trend made news in 1954.

Nash brought out a new-size Rambler, 193 inches long, 8 inches longer than the Rambler descended from 1950 (both the bigger and smaller Ramblers were built for 1954). That 8 inches was the difference between a small car and what George Romney later called a compact. That compact a few years later would drive the dinosaur from the highway.

And in January, 1954, Will van de Kamp, an ex-Luftwaffe fighter pilot, arrived in the United States to sell Volkswagens. Until then no more than a few hundred were sold each year. Van de Kamp immediately began building a distributor and dealer network that would later give VW a half-million sales a year in this country. He believed in VW as only Germans can believe. He also believed that reliable service (something Detroit had written off in the blitz sales efforts) was the key to success.

8.
The Oldsmoblie Super 88.

in 20,000 troops. Kenya drives against Mau-Mau. French reject European Defense Community, Germany as
tate attorney general arrested, martial law in sin city. Congress passes Communist Control act; party

9.
The Lincoln Capri hardtop: 1954 was the last of quiet styling. Note the dagger-like hood ornament.

10.
The Imperial was not a separate car line then, but the most luxurious Chrysler. The Imperial name-plate has since been killed.

earm, full sovereignty; France OKs German rearmament. Orange Bowl: Oklahoma 7, Maryland 0. Songs: O Me
llegal. Dr. Sam Sheppard convicted of wife's murder. Oscars to Audrey Hepburn (Roman Holiday), Williar

VW men tell about the day he saw a disabled VW on a turnpike (in the days when there were not many VWs or many turnpikes). He stopped, found a lady with a flat, and then he and the VW executives with him changed the tire. She asked if she could pay them something. Van de Kamp, in his homburg and immaculately tailored British suit, clicked his heels together, bowed, and whipped out a card for her, identifying himself as head of American Volkswagen. "A pleasure, madam," he said. "Just typical of Volkswagen service, nothing more."

In his first year VW sales here moved up to 6,600. By 1958 VW sales here were 100,000. They fired him that year.

Guderian, the panzer leader, used to have the same trouble with his boss back at headquarters.

11.
The Mercury Monterey, a fairly clean, simple design. In a few years, wrap-around windshields and the notorious dogleg would produce driver's knee.

Papa, Changing Partners, That's Amore, Young at Heart, Sh-Boom, Heart of My Heart. Married: Joe DiMagg
lden (Stalag 17), From Here to Eternity. Books: Sayonara (Michener) Sweet Thursday (Steinbeck), I'll C

"Today if you wanted to take the same sort of risk at Chevrolet, you'd promptly be fired."
—Ed Cole, former general manager of Chevrolet

For wine 1961 was a great year. For witchcraft you would have to go a bit to beat 1692. For Chevrolet it was 1955. If we build automobiles for a thousand years we will still remember 1955 as Chevrolet's finest hour. That '55 Chevy opened the path to the crest of the Golden Age.

"The stodgy car died in 1955," wrote John Jerome in *The Death of the Automobile*. "All our clinging Calvinistic sensibilities of practicality, economy, simplicity, and the cramped guidelines of American Gothic were junked." A decade later the '55 Chevy and the '56 and '57 that came from the same womb were to teenagers what the Model A was to a generation of kids in the 1930s. Twenty years later you could run a '55 against a similar size '75 Nova which still carried the same basic engine as that '55 and find the 1955 Chevy faster, roomier, and stingier on fuel.

This was the year Detroit began, as one writer put it, "a six-G dive into Hedonism." The '55 Chevy made Ed Cole head of Chevrolet, and in that role he pushed through the Corvair. The Corvair was the rock upon which Ralph Nader built his protest, and that protest helped curb innovation. So it all came home again.

US gives $29 million to S. Vietnam for refugees. Chou En-lai promises Formosa conquest; 3,000 fired in year as security risks, Civil Service says. Job bias ended on Washington

1.
Basic black and beads and the 1955 Chevrolet. The Chevy with its new V-8, flashy styling and lowness was a landmark.

The heart of the Chevy was its new engine, Chevy's long-awaited V-8 designed by Cole (as Chevrolet chief engineer) and Harry Barr, two of the team that created the industry-rocking Cadillac V-8 of 1949.

"Eddie, anything you can design, we can build," the manufacturing manager told Cole who took the challenge. The Cadillac engine was now too heavy and costly, he decided, and started with what Detroit calls "a clean sheet of paper." The key to the new engine was the precision-casting technique the Chevy team developed for closer tolerances and lighter weight. At 506 pounds this engine was 200 pounds lighter than the Ford V-8 and 40 pounds lighter than Chevy's own six-cylinder engine. The engine carried one of the lightest weight-to-power output ratios ever, and was easy for owners to work on. It was infinitely expandable, starting in 1955 with a 265-cubic-inch displacement and a 162-horsepower rating.

leet reinforced; fighting for Quemoy-Matsu. Georgi Malenkov ousted in USSR, Nikita Khrushchev in powe
s-streetcars. Congress OKs any Formosa straits fight; ratifies defense pact with Chiang. Anti-Red wi

2.
Packard tried to move into the big medium priced market with its Clipper model, but failed. Note the weird two-tone.

Over the years it moved up to 283 cubic inches, then 302, 307, 327, 350, 400. When the energy crisis struck, Chevy ran it down in 1975 to 262 cubic inches and used it as the economy V-8.

With that engine went a new car—new frame, new ball-joint front suspension, 12-volt electrical system, and brand-new body. Of Chevy's 4,506 component parts that year, 3,825 were entirely new and wouldn't interchange with the '54 Chevy. There was just a trace of a Cadillac look about the car, which was to increase in future years.

Cole, in the magazine *Special Interest Autos*, said: "Today if you wanted to take the same sort of risk at Chevrolet, you'd promptly be fired." The styling was clean and simple. When Mr. Earl offered Cole a body "only" sixty-one inches high, Cole reportedly retorted: "Hell, I wouldn't want to make one over sixty inches." (The hardtop came out at sixty and one-half

outh Africa begins resettling blacks outside cities. Red China refuses UN peace moves, demands Chiang
ying in court. High school segregation ended in St. Louis. AFL-CIO to merge under George Meany. US g

inches high.) For once the front-end designers abandoned the great teeth and bars that were taking over the grille-work; Mr. Earl had one of his inspired moments and put a Ferrari grille on the '55.

How good was it? First, remember that Chevrolet had a reputation as an old man's car, reliable but yecky. "Can you imagine a Chevy outdigging every '54 but a Cadillac and a Buick Century, and being able to stay with a Chrysler, Lincoln, and Oldsmobile?" raved *Motor Trend* after an early

3.
Last of the Kaisers. There never was enough money or a V-8 engine, but it was a pretty car.

xpelled. USSR proposes arms freeze but no inspections. Ngo Dinh Diem whips sect armies in S. Vietnam,
al, 342 officers to train S. Vietnam army; $200 million in arms, too. Ike plans 40,000 mile interstate

test. It was "neither too large nor too small, too light or too heavy" and was to become the classic among "street rodders, drag racers, and restorers alike. There's never been another car like it," said *Special Interest Autos*.

"It was my first car. I was the hit of my high school in Queens. They asked me out for dates. I'd buy one again if I could," recalls Agis Salpukas, chief of *The New York Times* bureau in Detroit.

4.
Ford's Crown Victoria, the car with the carrying handle across the roof and some snappy two-toning.

pull out. Churchill retires, Anthony Eden prime minister. Armed, sovereign W. Germany approved. Pro-
system. Edwin Teller given H-bomb credit. Stock market booms. Ike cools talk of China war. Polio se

5.
Chrysler took its style pill in 1955, chrome, spears, two-toning, the works, as exemplified on the DeSoto Fireflite.

There is no reason he should not be willing to buy one today. One car magazine ran a '55 Chevy sport coupe (the hardtop) 265-cubic-inch V-8, 3,470 pounds, against a '75 Nova LN coupe with 262 c.i.d. and 3,510 pounds. The '55 blew 0–60 m.p.h. in 12.3 seconds (one tester in '55 ran it in 9.7) against 16 seconds for the Nova (though one LN with a big 350 c.i.d. V-8 ran it in 8.7). At a steady 65 m.p.h. the '55 swallowed a gallon in 20 miles, the '75 gulped one in 18. And while they were both within an inch of 196 inches long, the '55 was voted the roomier. The '75 did have better seats, was almost 8 inches lower, and had a clear advantage in steering. The 1955 could be had for under $3,000; the '75 would start at $4,000 and run $5,000 and up with normal equipment.

Chevrolet was not alone with new steel in 1955. Everyone came on strong. Chrysler junked its stodgy approach and moved into the Forward Look,

ans purged in China. Peace treaty with Austria; a major East-West achievement. B & K visit Tito, part
alled success after massive tests. Auto workers seek guaranteed annual wage; win 26 weeks 60% layoff p

6.
The Plymouth, at 204″ long was the biggest of the low priced three, and helped Chrysler rebound.

1955

Production

General Motors	3,990,000
Ford	2,240,700
Chrysler	1,361,800
Studebaker-Packard	182,100
American Motors	161,800
Kaiser-Willys	5,800
Total	7,942,200

leaning heavily on two-tones (so did everyone, of course) with all models finally available with V-8 and automatic transmission. The '53 shorter-on-the-outside Plymouth had been 189 inches long and carried a 100-h.p. six. The '55 Plymouth was 204 inches long, noticeably longer than Ford or Chevy (Ford was 198.5 and Chevy 195.6 inches long), and a 167-h.p. V-8 was available. Dodges were 212 inches long (the Oldsmobile 88 was 203 inches) and DeSotos were 2 to 12 inches longer than the Buicks. There was the Chrysler 300 (for 300 h.p. that first year of the 300 series), a New Yorker hardtop with an Imperial dash and grille and a stiffened suspension. The 300 carried enough brute force to circle the ovals at 140 m.p.h. with the handling to match, a package the buffs have never forgotten.

There was also La Femme—something for everybody. "Completely pink.

make up. Chinese release downed US fliers, ease tensions. Nehru visits Moscow, Khruschev compliments
Steelworkers win 15 cent hike to $2.44 an hour. Richard Daley elected Chicago mayor. Court orders all

7.
Nash tried wild two-toning and even three- and four-toning, but never quite knew how to do it, as the paint job on this Statesman Country Club shows.

8.
Last of the Willys, the Ace Deluxe Kaiser, who bought Willys, finally folded car production.

Reds thaw to West. B & K tour Asia, attack colonialism. Hungary releases Cardinal Mindzenty from pri
.berate speed in school desegregation. Ike has heart attack; Dow-Jones industrials off 31.89 in one da

9.
The Dodge Royal Lancer, another example of Chrysler's swing to high styling. Notice the chromed headlight hoods.

It was all pink," Frank Wylie of Dodge recalls. "The stylists thought it would be just right for the ladies. There was even a pink umbrella to go with the car and a special place to put it and a special purse hook." But women did not like La Femme. "You couldn't wear anything with the car but black or white and look good," Wylie said. "But we sold some. No self-respecting pimp or homosexual could be without one. They used to fly into Detroit from all over the country to pick them up."

With a lineup like that Chrysler rebounded, building nearly 1.4 million cars in 1955, almost double the 1954 production. It was the best year in Detroit's history—if you were GM, Ford, or Chrysler. Some 7.9 million cars rolled down the lines, a total unmatched until the 9.3 million built in 1965, the last year of the Golden Age.

There were other highlights. Ford had its two-passenger Thunderbird,

ulgaria shoots down Israeli airliner, 58 dead, Bulgaria sorry. 1,000 killed in anti-French attacks in
lacklist revealed in radio-TV. 121 killed in midwest tornados; army discharges soldiers, denies commis

and the regular Ford line was one of its prettiest: A full-length chrome bar started at the rear a foot or so below the window level, dipped into a sharp V by the front vent window, and then twisted up along the top of the fender edge. There was Ford's Crown Victoria hardtop (which was not really a hardtop at all) with the wide chrome band stretching across the roof, the Ford with the carrying handle. The top-line, option-loaded Fords carried the new Fairlane designation. Fairlane is the name of the old Ford family estate in Dearborn, Mich., just west of Detroit, where the company headquarters and the giant River Rouge plants are concentrated. The low-priced Mainline series "is practically unsaleable. People do not want it,"

10.
The Mercury Monterey. This one had the wraparound windshield and the dogleg. Ouch, my knee!

eria, Morocco. Peron-Church split in Argentina, Peron overthrown. USSR tests H-Bomb. Border fighting
ns because of Red relatives, admits error after exposure. New Pow code of conduct. Negro Emmitt Till,

said Lewis Crusoe, the Ford executive. Ford sales did not challenge Chevy in 1955 as they had in 1954. Still, the year was so good that Ford nailed down the decision to build a new medium-priced car for 1958 because a goodly part of the added sales in 1955 were in the medium-priced range.

Buick and Oldsmobile introduced the four-door hardtop and the hardtop helped push Buick to third place in the industry—Chevrolet, Ford, Buick—with three-quarters of a million Buicks built that year. It was to be the last good year for Buick and its red-hot mammas. Harlow Curtis, then G.M. president, had run Buick and pushed for the soft ride, power, and flashy styling. (All the tricks that Cadillac was afraid to try went to Buick, though the hooded headlights introduced on the '54 Cadillacs spread throughout the industry.) The '55 Century was rated at 110 m.p.h., and emphasized low-priced models to lure customers. The trouble was Buick could not build three-quarters of a million good cars; when those push-'em-out '55s began to fall apart, Buick's reputation was gone (and it took a decade to repair it). The low-priced cars also were getting bigger, more powerful, and fancier, challenging the mediums (Chevy's V-8 was bigger than the Buick Special engine in 1955).

Nash finally got a V-8, its first, and so did Packard. (Nash bought the Packard engine that year.) Packard had a new body and suspension to go with that engine. This was the car Packard and James Nance, its president, counted on so much for the comeback. Though the Packard was credited with the best ride in the industry its big new engine did not match Cadillac for acceleration and top speed, the two tones just did not look right on the Packards, and the new engine and suspension acquired a reputation for trouble. All new cars have some troubles—even those new Chevrolets had some—but the rumors hurt Packard and only 70,000 were built in 1955, the industry's record year. The gamble had failed.

srael; Egypt-Syria form joint military command against Israeli; US-Britain to finance Aswan dam. Sugar
n Mississippi, accused whites acquitted. Court bans bias in places of public recreation. Waterfront,

11.
Buick's best year was 1955 with 750,000 built and the Century rated at 110 miles an hour.

Kaiser and Willys folded car production during the year after turning out just 6,000 automobiles. The company continued making Jeeps.

Volkswagen moved from 6,600 registrations in 1954 to 31,000 in 1955 and made a decision which haunts the German giant to this day. In 1955 VW bought a Studebaker plant in New Brunswick, N.J. Six months later VW sold the plant, canceling a plan to build cars in the United States. The excuse was that American parts suppliers had raised their prices after looking at VW's tough specifications. More likely, however, is that Willy van

l: Navy 21, Mississippi 0. Books: Bonjour Tristesse (Sagan), Auntie Mame (Dennis), Sincerely Willis Wa
e Kelly (The Country Girl). San Francisco 77, LaSalle 63 for NCAA title. A billion comic books sold

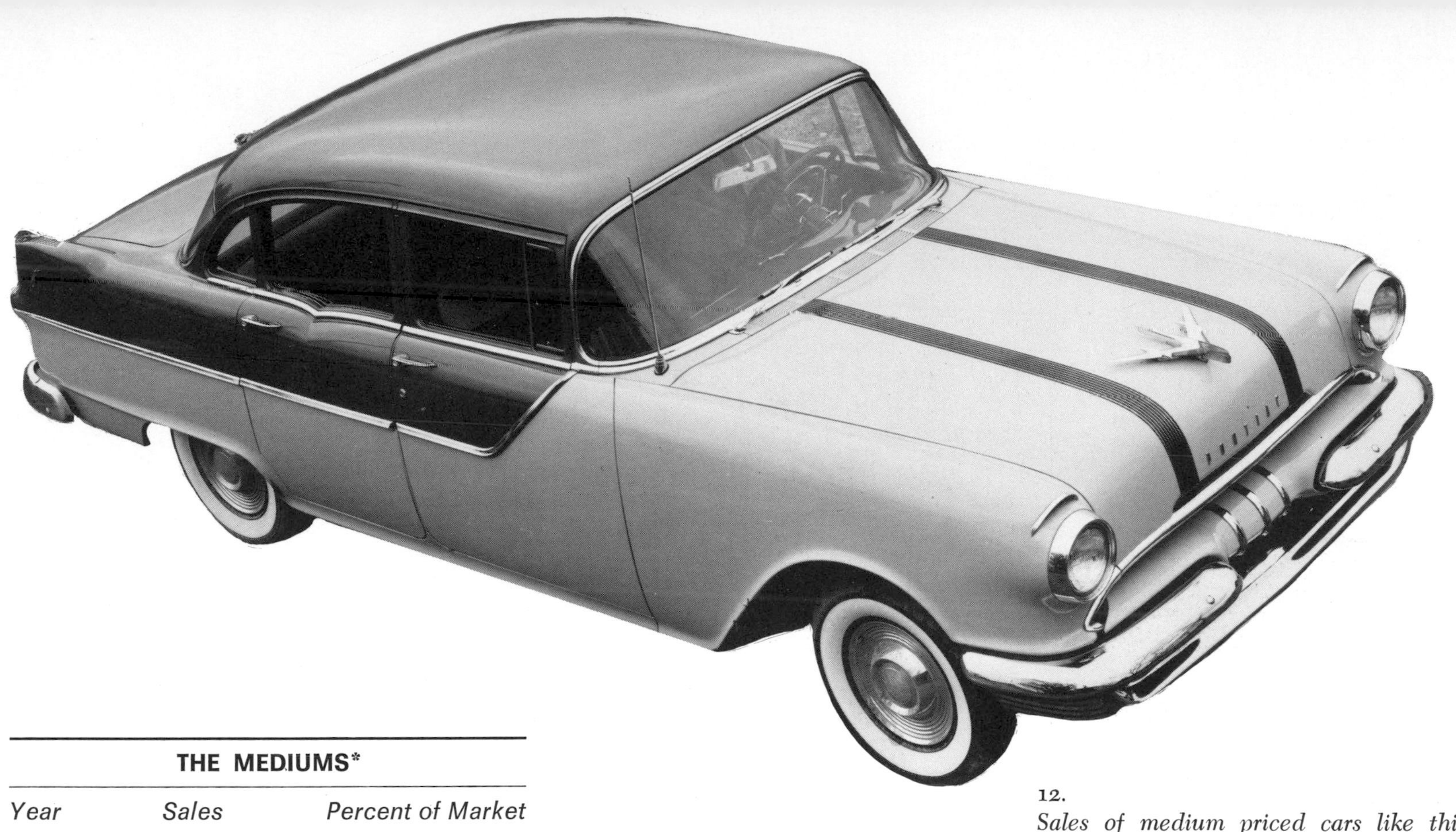

THE MEDIUMS*		
Year	*Sales*	*Percent of Market*
1954	1,909,000	34
1955	2,788,000	39
1956	2,028,000	34
1957	1,841,000	31
1958	1,217,000	26

** The medium nameplates include Pontiac, Oldsmobile, Buick, Mercury, Edsel, Chrysler, Dodge, and DeSoto*

12.
Sales of medium priced cars like this Pontiac fueled the sales boom.

anda. Princeton hires first Negro instructor. Songs: Rock Around the Clock, Davy Crocket, Mr. Sandman
, Inherit the Wind, Damn Yankees, Diary of Anne Frank, Silk Stockings. Post office bans Lysistrata, t

de Kamp's enthusiasm for VW's potential sold the bosses on production here, but when they were alone back in Germany they figured they had been hypnotized and would never sell as many cars as their American agent predicted. Had they started in the 1950s they might have avoided the trauma of the mid-1970s, when VW management knew it needed an American plant but VW directors from labor unions and local governments, fearful of losing jobs, were set against it.

Eat your heart out, VW.

They are not the only ones who misjudged the VW market. In 1948 Heinz Nordhoff, an ex-General Motors of Germany official who built up VW after World War II, was called to a meeting with Henry Ford II, Ernie Breech (Ford's right hand), and a colonel of the British occupying army. There has been some dispute about the meeting. Breech insists he was not there. Henry Ford does not remember it quite the way Nordhoff did. As the Germans recalled, the British were trying to give the VW plant to Ford, free, and Henry asked Breech what he thought.

"Mr. Ford," he said (again, according to the Germans, not Breech), "I don't think what we are being offered here is worth a damn."

Eat your heart out, Ford.

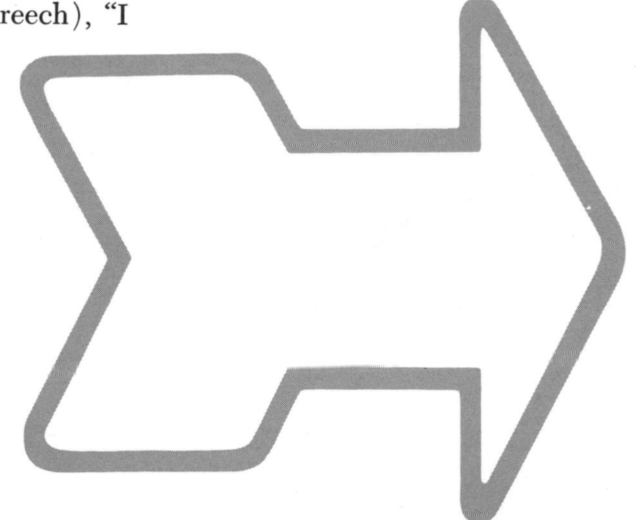

: Tons, Yellow Rose of Texas. Estimated 60,000 narcotics addicts in US. Plays: Bus Stop, Cat on a Hot
revokes ban. Movies: Bad Day at Black Rock, Bridge of Toko-Ri, Blackboard Jungle, Marty, East of Eden

"It looks like a guy with his eyes in his mouth."
—A description of the '57 Hudson grille

Like the pyramids of Egypt, the mystery of the Bermuda Triangle, and the Temples of Angkor Wat, it is easy to believe that the grilles of American automobiles are more than just things. If anyone goes to that much trouble to design and build them, it is reasonable to believe they have some meaning. Are they subconscious sex symbols built into the cars to turn us on without our knowledge? Are they there just so the consumer will be forced to spend millions of dollars each year repairing them (thus enriching the auto companies that sell the replacement parts)? Or are they part of a Communist conspiracy to use up our stockpile of vital chrome ore?

In the first place, the grille was put on the automobile to hide the radiator: it's that simple. The radiator usually is in the front of the car with the engine and holds coolant—formerly water mixed with a bit of cheap alcohol to keep it from freezing in winter, now a special nine-dollar-a-gallon compound—which keeps the engine from overheating. Most auto engines are water-cooled even if the coolant is not really water. Air-cooled engines do not need radiators, and a few cars such as the Volkswagen Beetle and the Chevy Corvair have been air-cooled, but water cooling usually seems to work better.

In the early days the radiator was right out in front of the car with a

1.
At first, grilles were simple, an ornamented and decorative cover for the radiator as on this 1947 Ford.

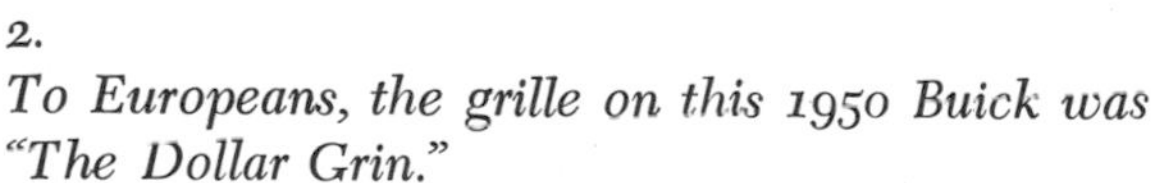

2.
To Europeans, the grille on this 1950 Buick was "The Dollar Grin."

3.
The pointed nose on the 1951 Studebaker was an effort to make an automobile look like an airplane.

bit of screening to keep stones from bouncing up and damaging it. With the urge to hide and decorate parts of the car, that screening became today's grille. At first there had to be openings in the grille to allow air flow into the car, although now the air enters in other ways, so this function is less important.

Grilles just do not have any significance or meaning. They are on cars because it's traditional to have something decorative and bright at the front of the car. And they tend to be ostentatious because designers want to impress their bosses, and since the cars are usually seen for just a few moments in a closed room, they want something that will knock their bosses' eyes out immediately.

The cars had to change each year and stylists had to struggle to come up with a noticeably different look every twelve months.

Even designers themselves make fun of grilles. Raymond Loewy said the big toothy grille common to American cars of the '50s was called "the dollar grin" in Europe (that's the same Loewy who put the pointed

4.
The 1954 Pontiac: "The Chinese Obstetrician," quipped one stylist.

5.
The 1958 Edsel: They wanted a readily recognizable grille and ended up with the famous Edsel horsecollar.

spinner on the Studebakers so the front would look like "ze aeroplane"). Another stylist looked at the Pontiac front end and quipped, "its the Chinese Obstetrician." Ernie Breech, who was chairman of Ford Motor Company, said the grille of the Edsel had the misfortune to be compared in looks to a toilet seat. The 1956 and 1957 Hudsons had their headlights inside of the grille instead of outside and one styling vice-president said, "it looks like a guy with his eyes in his mouth."

When Chevrolet brought out its air-cooled, rear-engined Corvair there was no need for a grille in the front, but eventually chrome was put in the front because Detroiters just could not bear an unadorned front.

Cadillac changes its grille very slowly, sticking to the same basic bars, sometimes thicker, sometimes thinner, and the grille became a trademark for the car. When that happened other makes began putting copies of the Cadillac grille on their models in the late 1960s. Ford copied the famous

Rolls-Royce grille for its Continental Mark IV and the car has been a success. The grille of the '55 Chevrolet was a simple waffle taken from Ferrari (and considered quite daring since the typical American car grille was much more ornate), but as one General Motors body designer noted, Chevrolet "chickened out in 1956 and went back to a full-width grille and jazzed up the taillights."

Today Detroit tries to copy the grille of the German Mercedes car in the hopes that some of Mercedes' quality image will rub off. When Ford was designing a new luxury compact for 1975 they designed their body, grille, and interior to make the vehicle resemble the Mercedes. Then they sought a German-like name, some name familiar to Americans yet symbolizing strength and power. They gave the problem to the computer and the

6.
The great Chrome Fence school of design on the angle-eyed '58 Lincoln.

7.
The symbolism of the 1956 Mercury grille can't be explained today. Note the hooded headlights.

8.
Free standing headlights appeared for the first time in a quarter century on a 1961 Imperial. They haven't been seen since.

machine popped back one candidate: Bismarck. Ford named the car Granada instead.

The regular grille change that took place was part of Dynamic Obsolescence. The idea was that Americans would buy cars regularly, not keep them forever, and trade them in for new ones, if the new vehicles changed regularly. They might lose prestige if seen in a readily identifiable old car. Since it is a lot easier and cheaper to change a front end than to design and tool for a new engine or new body, the big effort has been to keep changing fronts. At G.M., for example, headlights have been the target for change. Their cars have two headlights, four headlights, vertical headlights, horizontal headlights, round headlights, and square headlights. Why is all

9.
The horizontal grille dominated the American front end in the '50s and '60s as exemplified on this 1963 Thunderbird.

that money spent to change the shape of a headlight? So a customer can readily tell if a car is old or new by the shape of the headlight. And the theory is, a president of General Motors said, that a buyer is more likely to want a new car if he—and his friends—can tell the new from the old.

Loewy once tried to explain how grilles got the way they are. He said there was "The Great Chrome Cataract School" of design that starts "with a tiny chrome leak at the top of the hood" that spreads right and left. Another was "The Great Chrome Fence School" of front ends. "It all started with a little waffle-like grille, then it extended up, down, and sideways, until we reach the monumental chrome-plated banner."

The banner or horizontal grille has been the major front-end theme throughout the Golden Age. There were a few deviations: the first postwar Packards, the Pontiac nose of the 1960s, and the famous Edsel horsecollar. The idea was to make the Edsel readily recognizable. Since all other

10.
The Cadillac grille has been recognizable as a Cadillac grille since the end of World War II. This is a 1953 limousine. Notice the Dagmars.

medium-priced cars had horizontal grilles, the vertical look would make the new car stand out and be a throwback to the famous Packards.

"I always had a soft spot for a narrow nose," said Gene Bordinat, today's Ford styling vice-president. He says the first proposals for a vertical nose were "very clean, simple, spectacular, but the car was committed to death." The result was the horsecollar.

The emphasis on the rear ends of cars was an effort to build in some identification in the back as the grilles had done in the front. (Unfortunately, when a rear end is recognizable it's fairly awful; the '59 gull-wing Chevrolet was the best example of that.) This explains the eagerness to put on fins or wall-to-wall taillights, or gigantic bullseyes.

When Jack Gordon, the G.M. executive, was worried about the fins on the Cadillac rear, Alfred Sloan, the chairman explained: "Jack, now you've got a Cadillac in the back as well as the front." But rear-end styling faded in importance and always will be subservient to the front. "Your identity is out front," said Bordinat, in "a good nose."

"Safety Doesn't Sell"

—**Industry scuttlebutt**

Everything slid a bit in 1956. The cars were not quite as pretty. Chevrolet gave up its Ferrari-like grille for the more traditional full-front chrome. Ford took its slim chrome spear of 1955 and fattened it, then on the two-passenger Thunderbird put a Continental tire that looked out of place. Three-tone paint became common and four-tone jobs appeared.

The great production rush of 1955 took its toll on quality. Squeaks and rattles were practically mandatory in the "sprawling, sloppily built" cars—as *Consumer Reports* called the '56s—that Detroit was rolling out. They were getting bigger, more powerful, and faster, but steering and braking were not keeping up with the straightahead power gains. "People want a Lincoln at Ford prices and we have to give it to them," said George Walker, the top Ford stylist then. Strangely, the customers began to stay away, with production falling to 27 percent from 1955 to 5.8 million.

The 1956s were a relatively clean, finless group of cars with improving acceleration and mileage that would be impressive today. (Plymouth's V-8 ran 0–60 m.p.h. in 12 seconds and got 14 miles a gallon, and the Olds Super 88 ran it in 11.6 seconds and got 12 m.p.g., highway and heavy

Find oil in Libya. Dulles says he takes U.S. to brink of war to keep peace. Khrushchev i
Rioters keep Negro Autherine Lucy from Alabama campus; she's expelled. South defies U.S.

traffic combined.) There was a new Lincoln and a new Continental for the buyer with $10,000, a new Corvette, and more options.

Then there was safety. The issue had been bubbling up in recent years as the number of cars and the death toll increased and the horsepower race accelerated. In 1956 "the auto industry has taken its first toddling but well-advertised steps" in safety, *Consumer Reports* noted. All cars had improved door latches. Older doors had been popping open in accidents and bouncing the riders over the concrete; earlier safety theories mistakenly considered this a plus because it got the rider out of the car. The theory was wrong because hitting the concrete was a lot worse than hitting a thin metal dash.

1.
Axle trouble cost the 1956 Packard its reputation for quality.

n Cyprus; 201 killed in year, Archbishop Makarious exiled. Arab Fedayeen kill Israelis daily along bor
itizens councils spreading. Ike to run for second term with Nixon. Stevenson beats Kefauver for Democ

2.
Three tones, continental tire and the headlights inside the grille made the Rambler one of the great uglies of the decade.

Ford was having trouble selling against Chevrolet's super car, and while Chevy received a mild face-lift for '56 Ford received much less. "Would you marry Mrs. Duffy again just because she had her face lifted?" Archie of Duffy's Tavern (a well-known radio comedy show) asked in a Ford radio commercial dig at Chevy. So Ford decided to push safety and announced its cars had "Life Guard" design and actually advertised safety: the better door locks, the deep-dish steering wheel on all its cars, the "safety" rear-view mirror (if you banged into it the mirror was willing to move a bit; if you banged into the other kind they stubbornly stayed in place and took up room in the skull). The padded dash and factory-installed seat belts were optional.

Chevy's motto was "The Hot One's Even Hotter."

Guess who ate the porridge in 1956?

By spring Ford abandoned its safety campaign and "safety doesn't sell"

. Israelis retaliate. Mid-East arms embargo but Communists feed arms to Egypt. Dulles threatens to
c nomination. Southern Congressmen issue manifesto attacking integration rules. 6 Marines drown in n

3.
The Ferrari grille was gone on the 1956 Chevrolet, but the hot one was even hotter.

became a gospel in Detroit. Robert McNamara was then heading the Ford division and it was said "McNamara's selling safety and Chevy's selling cars."

Chevrolet was a better automobile than the Ford—faster, lighter, better fuel economy (15 m.p.g. versus 13.5), cheaper and by most standards better looking too. Ford let its safety campaign take the rap for its poor sales, which was easier than admitting that Chevrolet had a better car.

There had been some safety controversy earlier—some complaints about the steering column as a threat (Chevy even put a neat point on the hub of its column); about pointed, chromed, skull-penetrating knobs across the dash; about the lack of good padding on the dash. Ford enraged the other

am aid. French call reserves for Algerian rebellion. Jailed communists in satellite nations like Gomu
raining attacked, reformed. Journalist Victor Riesel blinded by labor thugs. M.I.T. bans frat hazing

auto makers by advertising safety (the unwritten law was that to imply that safety had anything to do with vehicles would hurt everybody's sales), and Ford's sales failure buried safety in Detroit.

A bit of serious safety design then might have defused the entire issue. Instead, Detroit's strategy was to criticize the critics. "If we made a car that was completely safe to ride in I wonder if it would sell," said one unnamed G.M. official quoted by *Fortune* magazine. There was a letter unearthed by Ralph Nader and put in his book *Unsafe at Any Speed*. A New York

MOTOR VEHICLE DEATHS

Year	*Deaths**
1946	33,411
1948	32,259
1950	34,763
1952	37,794
1954	35,586
1956	39,628
1958	36,981
1960	38,137
1962	40,804
1964	47,700
1974	46,200

** Includes pedestrian deaths running 8,000–11,000 a year*

4.
The Lincoln, a clean design for its day, 223″ in length, was long on the outside but not particulurly roomy on the inside.

of Poland freed in thaw. U.S. rejects China talk offer. Workers revolt in Poznan, 55 killed. U.S. s
r death. Steel workers strike 30 days. 15,400 polio cases in year, half 1955 total. Prices up 2.9%

5.
Four-door hardtops like this Buick Super were popular in 1956.

banker had written to General Motors in the mid-1950s suggesting that the dashboards could be dangerous. His eight-year-old son had been thrown against the dash in a sudden stop and broken a tooth. G.M.'s vehicle safety engineer, Howard Gandelot had answered thusly:

"As soon as the youngsters get large enough to be able to see out when standing up, that's what they want to do—and I don't blame them. When this time arrived with both our boys I made it a practice to train them so that at the command 'Hands!' they would immediately place their hands on the instrument panel if standing in the front compartment, or on the back of the front seat if in the rear, to protect themselves against sudden stops. This took a little effort and on a couple of occasions I purposely

am aid; Egypt seizes Suez Canal. England-France mobilize. Dulles warns against force. Gomulka takes
ourt curbs security risk firings for nonsensitive jobs. $33 billion, 41,000 mile interstate highway bi

pumped them a trifle when they didn't respond immediately to the command so that they learned quickly. Even now when either one of them is on the front seat, at the command of 'Hands!' they brace themselves. I frequently give these commands even when there is no occasion to do so, just so we all keep in practice."

With safety efforts like that General Motors didn't need enemies; it just needed time for the word to get around. It's not that auto men were uncaring. After all, they drove cars themselves, as did their wives, sons,

6.
Chrysler was just feeling its way into fins on cars like this Coronet. Next year they would have fins designed to conquer the world.

Polish Communists, Khrushchev in Warsaw threatens invasion; Polish army, workers ready to fight, USSR
passed. Orville Hodge, Illinois auditor arrested, stole $1 million. Italian Andrea Doria sinks. U.S.

7.
Chrysler's Imperial (foreground), and New Yorker (background). Don't those wide white walls look better?

daughters, mothers, and mistresses. They just were not willing to admit that accidents were a natural part of traffic and that car interiors had to be made safe for when accidents occurred. Instead of going to work on the engineering to do the job, they thought up excuses, earning the condemnation they would receive a decade later.

By 1954 reports were creeping back to Detroit: a California scientist, Dr. Arie Haagen-Smit, had shown that Los Angeles smog actually was

own. Revolt in Hungary. Imre Nagy to power, promises democracy. Israel invades Egypt, win, drive to
st airborne H-bomb. School integration riots in Kentucky, Texas. Tennessee guard stops mobs in Clint

caused by a photochemical reaction involving sunlight and auto emissions. Detroiters aware of the studies laughed. "What Los Angeles needs," went a Detroit joke, "is filter-tipped people."

Detroit, though, was beginning to pay attention to the motivational researchers. Cars were extensions of personality, they said, and thus to sell cars search not for engineering improvements but for the secrets of the personality. "There is a link between sexual prowess and horsepower in the minds of most men," Dr. Jean Rosenbaum, a psychiatrist, wrote later, and this, he said, is "largely responsible for the sale and success of the big cars."

8.
Safety wouldn't sell these '56 Fords. Note the paint work around the hooded headlights.

l. British-French invade, too. U.S. demands peace, forces Israel, others to withdraw. Russians brea
Ike wins big, carrying 41 states. Average hospital room cost: $15.10 a day double. Convictions of Co

The words "see what a big car I have," said the doctor, can be translated as "see what a big penis I have (or wish I had)" and "see what a great lover I am." There were some who believed these things. A big rear end might be criticized as "anal compulsive." When James Nance, who headed Packard and took over Studebaker in the merger, saw Loewy's pretty coupe, restyled and renamed the Hawk for 1956, one Studebaker stylist remembered bitterly, "he said he didn't like the slant of the hood line. He said, 'That car's penis is falling, what's the matter with you guys?'"

Almost all 1956 cars had wraparound windshields, creating a safety issue because the wipers did not reach far enough to prevent a big blind spot on the sides in rain or snow. Horsepower was up and the four-door hardtop became common, with even Ford and Chevy having them. At G.M. the Corvette was new with wind-up windows and a three-speed manual trans-

9.
Farewell spiked heels . . . farewell 1956 Holiday Oldsmobile. We will not forget you.

nder Smith Act overturned on appeal. Bus segregation ends in Montgomery, demands to end bus bias in B
rothers ends tent circus performances. Movies: The Ten Commandments, Around the World in 80 Days, Bus

mission as standard. The basic Chevrolet was still drawing raves. "Top-notch road handling" and "quick and sure footed" said *Consumer Reports*. Cadillac's engine went up to 285 h.p. on the standard model, and 305 h.p. on the Eldorado as the engine received its first major change since 1949. Cadillac also brought out a vinyl-roof hardtop and put long, sharp fins on the Eldorado, a warning of the coming fin war.

At Chrysler each division created a high-powered, good-handling model copied from 1955's Chrysler 300 (which became the 300B in 1956). At Plymouth it was the Fury, Dodge the D-500, DeSoto the Adventurer. These cars carried the equipment to give them speed and acceleration: four-barrel carburetors, special manifolds, hotter crankshafts, but also racing tires, stiffer springs, and suspension systems to produce the handling the buffs sought.

Chrysler also had a pushbutton automatic transmission with the buttons on the left-hand side of the dash. Packard and American Motors had them too. At the end of 1956 Packard called back its new models for axle repairs, helping to cement the image of troubled cars. At the end of 1956 the Detroit Packard plant was closed and future Packards were modified Studebakers. "It took Nance something like a year and a half to go through $64 million, and at the end of that he had a couple of warmed-over versions of nothing," said Robert Bourke, the Studebaker designer.

Ford's Lincoln and Mark Continental were all new. The Lincoln was a surprisingly clean and handsome design, and one critic said Ford deserved the medal of honor for cutting down on the chrome. It was big, though—223 inches long, 7 inches longer than the '55 Lincoln and 8 inches longer than the 1956 Cadillac 62 model. Despite that length (and a 46-foot turning circle, poorest in the industry) there was no more room on the inside, a symbol of Detroit's growing interest in form and disinterest in content.

1956

Production

General Motors	3,062,400
Ford	1,669,200
Chrysler	870,300
American Motors	104,200
Studebaker-Packard	95,800
Total	5,801,900

gham trigger arrests of Negroes. Oklahoma 20, Maryland 6 in Orange Bowl. Brink's robbery solved. H.L.
. New York Giants 47, Chicago Bears 7 for NFL title. Russia wins winter, summer Olympics. Plays: My F

10.
The Pontiac Star Chief hardtop with its massive mouthlike grille.

The trunk was big too, but so deep that you needed a boat hook to get anything out that was way up front.

The Continental Mark II was Ford's major effort to create a new market and break Cadillac's hold. The aim was a luxury car of magnificent design—the best—with price no concern. The Mark II was even shipped to dealers in a fleece-lined bag.

Henry Ford II put his younger brother William Clay Ford in charge of the Mark II project. When Henry saw their first prototype he said, "I wouldn't give you a dime for that." He should have saved the criticism for the next version. All the Ford folks loved the long, low Mark II (the trouble was, some said, that if you were old enough to have the $10,000 to buy it then you weren't young enough to bend over and get into the

ıa Magnani (The Rose Tatoo). San Francisco (Bill Russell, K.C. Jones) over Seattle 83-71 for NCAA titl
ınd Dog, Love Me Tender. Also Tennessee Ernie Ford: 16 Tons. Also The Yellow Rose of Texas, Che Sera

56-inch high car). The Mark had absolutely no character, and in just a few months they were being discounted. Ford had 2,200 orders when the car went on sale and went downhill from there. It was in production only two years.

Ironically, General Motors would duplicate Ford's disaster in 1957, but there is some question even to this day on whether they learned the lesson: that fleece-lined bags and gadgets do not a great car make.

ılitzer to MacKinley Kantor (Andersonville). Needles wins Kentucky Derby. Pop: Elvis with Blue Suede
Poor People of Paris. Rocky Marciano retires as champion. Floyd Patterson beats Archie Moore in 5th

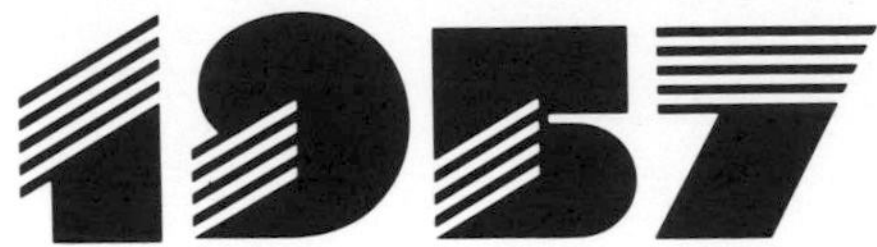

"This was the age of 'gorp.'"
—Richard Teague, American Motors vice-president

Even now it is difficult to speak of the Mercury Turnpike Cruiser of 1957 without giggling. That car seemed to come from some other world and to see it was not necessarily to believe it. No doubt it was an automobile ahead of its time—and with any luck, its time will never come. For the first time Mercury was given a body of its own, more than just a hand-me-down Ford, and after the Turnpike Cruiser it was the last time.

The medium-priced cars had boomed in 1955, which was when the Cruiser was planned. Mercury men hoped to grab the industry's styling leadership with the Cruiser, and it is likely that they were also planning to sandbag a new highly publicized medium-priced car that would come from Ford the next year—Edsel.

The Cruiser had dual headlights, a weird hood over them, and a 368-cubic-inch-displacement, 290-horsepower V-8 under a huge hood. There was a magnificent dog leg caused by the wraparound windshield, strange tortured sheetmetal along the rear (called "sculpturing" then and now) and the space-age Seat-O-Matic with controls 1–7 and A–E to put the driver's seat automatically into the desired position. Reverse rear windows could be lowered. Strangest of all were the two antenna-like steel rods extending

Anthony Eden resigns after Suez defeat. MIG Jets to Syria. Strikes, unrest in Hungary
Filibuster curb beaten in Senate; George Metesky, NY's mad bomber, caught. Massive unic

1.
The Hudson Hornet in four tones. See if you can count the V's in the body trim.

horizontally from the upper corners of the windshield, and behind them devices that looked like microphones. "It looked like you could keep the windows closed at the drive-in and order your hamburgers through them," said one Detroiter. Actually, they were vents that leaked in rain.

The Turnpike Cruiser and the cars of the next few years marked another age. "This," said Richard Teague, American Motors styling vice-president, "was the age of 'gorp.'" The Turnpike Cruiser was put out of its misery in two years (only 23,000 were built) but the age of gorp was to run to 1960.

Ford also invented the Skyliner in 1957, the steel-topped convertible that was to be the answer for all those people who said they would buy a convertible if only it had a steel top. It took 6 roof mechanisms, 13 switches,

own, arrests, executions. UN force to Gaza; U.S., others guarantee Israeli ship passage in Gulf of Aqa
ruption exposed. Teamsters tied to Oregon vice rackets; Dave Beck, president, convicted of embezzling

10 solenoids, 9 circuit breakers, 5 motors, and 610 feet of wire to make it work, which wasn't always. Of course, when the top was in the trunk there was no room for luggage. It was a grand idea whose time hadn't come, and still hasn't. The Skyliner was put out of its misery in three years.

Yet it was a Ford year. The '57 Ford was longer than Chevy by 2 inches (at 202 inches), wider by 3 inches, lower by nearly 3 inches, and its standard V-8 was rated at 190 h.p. to 162 h.p. for Chevy (both had higher horsepower options, of course). "Ah, those '57s," said Gene Bordinat, Ford's styling boss, "with those great thrusting fenders. G.M. pulls back its fenders. Ours reach."

2.
Ford's Mark II, a $10,000 car which was abandoned after just a couple of years of production.

ina relaxation; seizes passports of visitors to China. Moslem leaders murdered in France by Algerian r
ffa elected new Teamster boss; Teamsters, Bakers, Laundry workers ousted from AFL-CIO. Washington, D.C

3.
Cadillac Eldorado Brougham, at $13,500, was another effort to crack the super high priced market. It had every gadget but an automatic dishwasher, and flopped, too.

"Beat Chevy" came true as Robert McNamara's team produced 1,494,000 sales to 1,456,000 for Ed Cole's Chevrolet—the first Ford win since 1935.

If that wasn't bad enough for G.M., Chrysler was shouting, "Suddenly it's 1960." Chrysler had rushed ahead and pushed out Virgil Exner's high-finned cars, the highest fins in the world, and Plymouth pushed Buick out of third place. That Plymouth at 207 inches long was 5 inches longer than the Ford. Its basic V-8 at 197 h.p. was bigger than Ford's or Chevy's, and the engine on the Chrysler 300C was rated at 390 h.p. The Chrysler-built cars had torsion-bar suspension using specially treated steel bars instead of coil springs, and a rear-facing seat on the mammoth nine-passenger wagon.

One problem was that they sold faster than Chrysler could build them, and it's been reliably reported that plant managers, looking at rows of cars in the repair bank, said, "ship them." The '57s became noted for not

s; French ban newspapers revealing Algerian torture. NY Times calls Castro idealistic, not Communist.
hool integration called great success. KKK bombs homes, churches in Montgomery. Sen. Joseph McCarthy

4.
The King of Gorp: The Mercury Turnpike Cruiser. Notice the futuristic pods at the windshield corners. They let in the rain.

1957

Production

General Motors	2,816,400
Ford	1,889,700
Chrysler	1,222,300
American Motors	114,100
Studebaker-Packard	72,900
Total	6,115,400

only good looks—because the Chrysler fin was the finest-looking fin in autodom despite its size—but for leaks and electrical breakdowns.

Just for more bad news, people were buying Ramblers and imports, and George Romney, the American Motors president, was beginning to break the code: He was critcizing other automobiles, calling them gas-guzzlers.

In all it was a lively year, with dual headlights appearing on more cars: The fourteen-inch wheel became standard in the industry, which raised an eyebrow or two because, although they helped cars look lower, they also left less room for brakes, and with horsepower and weight going up, brakes were pretty important. There was a spreading of advancements such as six-way power seats, electric door locks, and fuel injection.

rms Common Market; Russians call it peace threat. India sets up state in disputed Kashimir; riots in F
urt rules Dupont's 23% ownership of G.M. violates law. 64 Mafia leaders caught in Appalacian, NY, raid

Business perked up a bit with 6.1 million cars built, up 300,000 from 1956. G.M.'s output was down, with Ford and Chrysler making the big gains. When the General Motors brass saw those big-finned Chryslers, "we panicked," admits Bill Mitchell, the styling vice-president. From that panic came the crash program that produced the gull-wing Chevrolet of '59, the flying Buick and the stab-in-the-back Cadillac fins, the stars of the age of gorp. For 1958 G.M. poured on more chrome.

The Corvette got fuel injection, which made it more potent on the tracks. For Cadillac there were black-rubber tips on the Cadillac Dagmars, which helped to hold down the puncture marks from those bumpers. G.M. also introduced the X frame that year, a frame without side members, allowing

5.
The Studebaker President. Studebaker was fading fast as the merger with Packard produced a weaker, not stronger company.

tan. USSR-Yugoslavia make up; quarrel again. Hussein of Jordan ousts reds, pro-Egyptians; U.S. fleet
ıssian spy Rudolf Abel caught, jailed. Hurricane kills 550 around Cameron, La. Congress passes voting

6.
Rambler, with its stationwagon, was beginning to show signs of sales strength but the big boom was two years away.

7.
With models like this DeSoto Firesweep, an all new design for 1957, Chrysler triggered the great fin war.

support. Mao says let 100 flowers blossom, criticism erupts; pull out poisonous weeds, says Mao. U.S
ll, first civil rights law since Reconstruction. Seven southern states defy courts, no integration. N

8.
This Ford, longer, lower and wider than Chevrolet, outsold its sales rival; the first Ford victory since 1935.

lower car heights. Privately some other car makers called the X frame dangerous (even some G.M. divisions would not use it), not sturdy enough in accidents. It was difficult to document that the frame really was a safety hazard, it must be admitted, although G.M. abandoned it a few years later.

The strangest vehicle in G.M.'s lineup for '57 was its answer to Ford's '56 Continental Mark II (which was continued in '57), the $13,500 Eldorado Brougham. The Brougham was a four-door hardtop with a brushed stainless-steel roof, quadruple headlights, and every gadget known to man. There

nts $95 million aid to Poland. Polish student riots put down hard. Khrushchev ousts Molotov, others i
lle school blown up. Gov. Faubus sends national guard to keep 9 Negroes from Little Rock Central High

9.
The Chevy two-tone hardtop, a clean looking car but still much like the '55 and smaller than the Fords and Plymouths that year.

was the automatic headlight dimmer, polarized sun visors, individual front and rear heating, a trunk that raised and lowered electrically from the dash, automatic speed setting (Cruise Control), an automatic signal-seeking, two-speaker radio, and rear side windows that went back automatically when the door opened and closed automatically when the door closed to make entry easier. It was said of the Brougham that you had to be a dealer to keep it running.

Its biggest innovation was air suspension, which involved using air bags instead of springs or torsion bars to keep the car level and the ride smooth—theoretically very clever. "Those levelers make for an eerie sensation when you sit down in the driver's seat," one car magazine reported. "Suddenly the car begins to moan quietly and to gently lift you up half an inch or so."

arty fight. Pro-Reds take over Syria, Turkish-Syrian tension, U.S. arms to Jordan, Iraq. USSR fires I
gnores courts; Ike sends in army, takes over guard, troops under Gen. Edwin Walker break up mobs, enfor

But most of the bags leaked, and when they leaked the car just settled down on its axles, flat on the ground, like a sick elephant. Fortunately, that could not happen often because only 704 Broughams were turned out in the two years the car was made here (another 200 were built with Italian-made bodies later, but the '57 and '58 Detroit-built Broughams are considered the prime models).

G.M. was developing one winner in 1957, though: the car was Pontiac and the division was directed by Semon "Bunkie" Knudsen. Bunkie took over Pontiac in 1956 and as he recalled it "the average Pontiac buyer was sixty-five years old then." He saw the '57s and did not like them. There was very little time to make changes, but he changed what he could—the chrome. "They had those suspenders running over the hood," he recalled, twin chrome strips, the Silver Streaks, a Pontiac trademark along with the Indian head. He pulled them off. "Some dealers even had those old wooden Indians, six feet tall, outside their showrooms. We even found some in our own storerooms" (Pontiac was an Indian chief from the Detroit area). Out they all went.

Then Bunkie put together a first-rate engineering and styling team and took Pontiac racing. Racing had grown dramatically in the few years since Ed Cole of Chevrolet had built his V-8 and loosed it on the Fords at the ovals. Pierre Ollier recalled the scene then in *Special Interest Autos*: "At the big Southeastern ovals, when the action really got hot, the announcer would break in and ask, 'Who's for Forrrrrrrrrd?' and half the crowd would leap up and roar, 'Forrrrrrrrrd.' Then the announcer would ask, 'And who's for Chevvvvvvvy?' and the other half would try to out-roar the first."

The racing promotions tied to Detroit's speed and horsepower race caused a safety uproar, and in 1957 the car makers decided to back away, banning, through the Automobile Manufacturers Association, factory participation

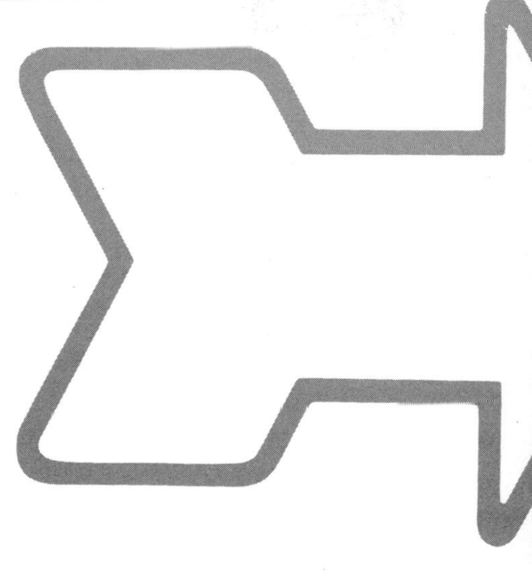

U.S. has none. USSR puts Sputnik satellite in orbit, launches another with dog Laika. Uproar in U.S.
esegregation. Senate probes missile-science gap, defense-research spending lifted. Navy satellite roc

10.
The Pontiac Star Chief with everything.

ssile, space lag. Western prestige falls. Air force on constant alert, planes always in air. U.S. pu
, world ridicule. Dow-Jones slumps to 417.79 Oct 22, recession on. Ike has mild stroke, ok; proposes

11.
The Buick Century hardtop. The multi-color exterior, the heavy use of chrome, and the exaggerated front and rear ends were coming together in 1957.

in the sport. Some pulled out and some—particularly the young G.M. division leaders—fed money and parts to the stock car heroes secretly. It was always officially denied as the company's highest officials piously talked of abandoning racing and winked at the participation.

"I still remember our first win," said Bunkie. "It was 1957 and they still were racing on the beach at Daytona. Cotten Owens and Banjo Matthews won for us, and I heard someone in the stands say, 'My god, look what's happened to grandpa.' "

Look what happened. Knudsen turned Pontiac into the hot car and the

issiles in Europe. Fighting in Cuba. TCU 28, Syracuse 27 in Cotton Bowl. TV Quiz Booms: Charles Van
illion science school aid. NY has 7 day subway strike. Married: Elizabeth Taylor-Mike Todd; Howard Hu

big seller in the medium-priced field, kept racing and used the track names to decorate his models—Grand Prix, Grand Am, and GTO.

In a strange twist of fate Pontiac's success enabled a Ford to fire a Knudsen for the second time in history. Bunkie was the son of William "Big Bill" Knudsen. That Knudsen had been a high Ford executive until Henry Ford I fired him in the early 1920s (Henry, sooner or later, always fired his best men). Big Bill was hired by G.M., took over Chevrolet and made Chevy number one. Then he became president of General Motors and headed America's massive war production effort in World War II for the government. Bunkie's success at Pontiac made him Ed Cole's successor at Chevrolet and a candidate for the G.M. presidency. Cole won the job. Bunkie was not happy, and in 1968 Henry Ford II hired him as president of Ford. Bunkie ruled Ford with a firm hand, as G.M. men do, and offended some of the established princes there. (G.M.'s management system might be called domestic centralism, like Russia. Ford is a monarchy with a king, Henry II, who says "My name is on the building" when the arguments get tough. But it's a kingdom with strong princes and dukes ruling their provinces such as styling or sales.) Henry II fired Bunkie in September 1969, just nineteen months after having hired him and just as his grandfather fired Bunkie's father.

"Things just didn't work out," Henry II said. Bunkie, a millionaire in his own right, later took over White Motors, a big truck maker in Cleveland, and the firing opened the road to the top for Lee Iacocca, who fathered Ford's first Mustang.

munist Party. Oscars to Yul Brenner (The King & I), Ingrid Bergman (Anastasia), Around the World in 8
ove Lucy, $64,000 Question, Lawrence Welk. Video tape first used. Iron Liege wins Derby. Confidenti

ĕdsĕl (ed·sul,n., mid Amer from Edsel, an automobile of the mid-20th century) 1. (often cap) A failure of massive proportions. 2. A project of great promise with a commonplace result, sometimes amusing. 3. A financial disaster. Syn.: Calamity, debacle, catastrophe, joke.

—Webster's Dictionary, 23 Edition

"Someone hopped on that front end and called it a toilet seat, and it was dead from that minute." That's how Ernie Breech, the chairman of Ford, explained the Edsel disaster. Of course, they called it much worse than that.

"OK, they called it a big vagina," said Gene Bordinat, Ford's styling vice-president. "The physical appearance of the Edsel was displeasing from a psychological and emotional point of view and because the front grille looked like a huge open mouth," theorized Dr. Jean Rosenbaum, the psychiatrist who believes automobiles are sexual symbols.

"Look, I don't think we've sold one car because of any Freudian motivations," said Bordinat. "It just wasn't a good design. God, the one off the Mercury was a basket case." And once an entire nation starts laughing at your product and making off-color jokes about its styling, well, it doesn't help.

How did it happen? How did the grandest effort of the brilliant team that had pulled Ford back from the brink after World War II, that had

1.
The last Edsel looked a bit like a Pontiac and wasn't too bad a car.

actually *beat* Chevy, fail? How did $350 million get thrown away? How did Henry II let them put his father's name (Edsel) on a car like that? Why didn't someone just get up and say "Stop! That's awful!"

Ford had a problem, and it became strikingly evident in the mid-1950s. Sales were booming, but the medium-priced cars were growing fast—the Buicks (which were nudging Plymouth from third place), the Oldsmobiles, the Dodges, and the Chryslers. In 1954 those cars took 35 percent of the market. In 1955 it was nearly 41 percent. Detroit's theory was that folks tended to trade up from a Chevrolet to a Pontiac or Olds, from a Plymouth to a Dodge or Chrysler. At Ford all they could trade up to was Mercury, a car that seemed to have "Born to Lose" tattooed across its grille.

From the days of the Model T, Ford knew and understood the folks at the bottom of the car market, while G.M. somehow had the best feeling for the middle class. Now the market was swinging away from the bottom. "We have been growing customers for General Motors," complained Lewis Crusoe, a Ford executive.

The Ford team agreed that they needed a new middle car. Most of the young executives wanted to go flat-out and create an all-new car with an all-new dealer force and an all-new division to sell it—instant Buick, all-out

2.
Somehow it all came together in Edsel. This was a '58 Ranger.

war against General Motors on G.M.'s turf. Breech said he was one of the doubters (the doubters wanted a go-slow approach, slipping a new top-line model in, then expanding it). But Ford decided to build a complete line of new cars, two series, one priced above the lower-priced Fords (and built from the basic Ford body shell), and the second, *la crème*, priced above the high-priced Mercury models and built from that shell. "The new Ford team had not failed in anything it had undertaken yet," Breech said, and they were "great salesmen." The all-out war faction had won.

Roy Brown, named chief Edsel stylist, compared all the medium-priced cars and decided he had to create a car that "would be readily recognizable," distinct from all the others. Since the grille was the first thing everyone saw, and since all the others had spreading horizontal grilles (The Great Chrome Fence School of Design), Brown decided on a vertical grille, a throwback to the old Packard.

Bordinat insists the first designs were good, very clean and simple. Changes came after complaints that "the front end isn't powerful enough," with more and more suggestions fed into the design until the horsecollar was created. Still, when it was rolled out before the Ford executives they applauded and even the designers loved it.

It is hard for us now to imagine the enthusiasm that a new car generated in those days. A new car then was bigger than a space rendezvous, bigger than Sonny and/or Cher; not as big as World War III but just about. "You would have been superhuman not to be caught up in the launch," said Bordinat trying to explain why it looked good to its creators. "It was hysterical. You weren't just dancing on a button" for the managers. "You hyped the hell out of yourself."

As a substitute for innovative engineering there were pushbuttons: a

3.
What can you say after you say you're sorry. The 1958 Edsel Citation.

pushbutton automatic in the steering wheel hub, a pushbutton to open the trunk, for the lights, for the radio antenna and the wipers. There was also the biggest engine Ford could cram in—345 h.p.

To name the car, Ford studied thousands of candidates. The high point of the search was the literate but semiserious and then tongue-in-cheek correspondence between David Wallace, the Edsel market research expert, and Marianne Moore, the noted poet, published in *The New Yorker* magazine.

Wallace wrote to her for help in finding a name: "We should like this name to be more than just a label. Specifically, we should like it to have a compelling quality in itself and by itself. To convey, through association or other conjuration, some visceral feeling of elegance, fleetness, advanced features and design."

Miss Moore rose grandly to the occasion, proposing names ranging from Silver Sword to Hurricane Accipter (Hawk) to Impeccable, Resilient Bullet or Arc-en-Ciel (the rainbow) down to Utopian Turtletop.

The letters ended when Wallace wrote that Ford had chosen its name. "It fails somewhat of the resonance, gaiety, and zest we were seeking. But it has a personal dignity and meaning to many of us here. Our name, dear Miss Moore, is—Edsel.

"I hope you will understand."

The more expensive Edsels were the Corsair and Citation; the smaller were Ranger and Pacer. In line with the motivational research of the time (some people complained that too much effort was spent figuring people's motivations and not enough on engineering) the cars were aimed for the "younger executive or professional family on the way up," and advertised: "They'll know you've arrived."

The hoopla was almost unbearable. For two years the press had speculated and dug out details about the cars to come, building up the tension. At the showing for the press before the car went on sale Ford hired stunt drivers to make like the chase scene in "The French Connection." Reporters' wives got a fashion show hosted by a female impersonator, which was not quite *de rigueur* in those days. The wives did not know it wasn't a she, and neither did the top Ford executive who spent the afternoon talking to her —until she bared "her" chest. Gayle Warnock, the publicity man who hired the stunt drivers and "her," had an impish sense of humor that

EDSEL

Model Year	*Output*
1958	63,110
1959	44,891
1960	2,846

4.
By 1959, the Edsel was more of a dolled up Ford than a distinctively different car.

was not always appreciated, but he was right about one thing when he said: "When we introduce this car and people find out it has four wheels and four doors and a steering wheel just like every other one, I'm afraid they're going to be disappointed because the enthusiasm on this thing is just short of fantastic."

Nearly 3 million Americans were said to have seen Edsel on "E Day" in September, 1957. Nobody bought it. In early October, just one month after introduction, sales were running only 300 a day and the sickly smell of failure surrounded Edsel. By November, Wallace said, "there was panic and its concomitant, mob action."

Dealers quit (and failed, too, because many had invested heavily to sell the car). The Manhattan Edsel dealer quit in November and began selling George Romney's Ramblers, a sign of the revolution in the air. In January 1958, just four months after introduction, the separate Edsel division was folded into the Lincoln-Mercury division, where it became an unwanted embarrassment. The speed with which Ford quit on the Edsel was amazing. Executives who had anything to do with the Edsel were exiled or left the company. (The auto business is tough, so there are winners and losers, and the companies protect their losers by making desk jobs for them—except at Ford. There you come back with your shield or get out.)

The 1959 sales stayed low, and the 1960 model abandoned the familiar horsecollar grille (and looked a bit like a Pontiac of later years). Only 2,846 of the 1960 models were built before Ford killed the car. In all, 110,810 Edsels were built.

"We were on the edge of correcting a lot of sins," said Bordinat. *Consumer Reports*, no Edsel lover, called the later '59 "in some ways even a likeable model."

What went wrong?

Certainly the 1958 recession hurt, the worst car year since the recovery after the war, and the slump was particularly hard on medium-priced car sales. The total in that class sagged from 41 percent in 1955 to 28 percent in 1958 as the compacts and imports boomed. (Not much later DeSoto folded, and Dodge became a low rather than a high medium-priced car).

There were defects. All new cars have defects that are ironed out as production goes along because all the testing in the world cannot match the trials a few thousand customers put on a car. Edsel's problems, though, were plentiful and well publicized. *Consumer Reports* said Edsel was the fastest car in the quarter mile it had ever tested but used words like "wallowed," "bounced," and "rocked" in describing the ride, and said the car had a tendency to shake like jelly.

Some say if Edsel had arrived two years before or two years later it would have succeeded. Some say there was too much emphasis on motivational research. S. I. Hayakawa, the noted language master, said the trouble with selling "symbolic gratification" with expensive items like the Edsel "is the competition offered by much cheaper forms of symbolic gratification such as *Playboy*," or *Astounding Science Fiction* magazine, or even television.

Wallace, the market researcher, liked to think the Soviet sputnik which went up a bit before Edsel had something to do with it. America had been beaten in technology and its people were turning against its products in an orgy of self-denial. "Not buying Edsel was their hair shirt," he said.

More likely it was a common-sense reaction against the age of gorp.

"All the guys would stand around looking under each others' hoods."

—Nancy Miller, on the Houston drive-in scene

"Women would drive down the street in their purple Lincolns wearing purple hats and with a poodle on the seat dyed to match," remembers Nancy Miller, who lived in Houston in 1958. "Mink coats and purple Lincolns with big horns on the hood. Of course, my idea of heaven was a mink coat and a Corvette," because what teenager wants a Lincoln. Learning to drive in Texas was easy. "My daddy put me in our gray Oldsmobile on a dirt road and said 'OK kid, drive.' "

Of course, the kids drove older cars. "When I had to drive to LaMar High School my parents gave me a '54 Ford. It had the greatest engine in the world, just terrifyingly loud at the drive-in. Our drive-in was the Buccaneer. It was the kind of place where the waitresses came out chewing gum and said 'hiyuhbub' and all the guys would stand around looking under each others' hoods."

Later, as small cars became acceptable, she owned an old Renault. "The charm of that car was I could leave it in the street with the keys in and no one would take it," she said. The Renault proved, in fact, that being small and foreign was not enough for Americans even if they were tired of Detroit's monsters.

Fighting fierce in Algeria. West rejects European atom free zone as trap. U.S. pledges Democrats attack Ike's low military spending. Major recession on; January jobless at 4.5

1\.
Romney's Rambler was a handsome car by 1958. This compact drove the dinosaur from the driveway.

Import sales began to boom in 1958. Volkswagen was up to 79,000 Beetles and another 25,000 vans or combiwagons that year, and 160,000 Beetles in 1959. The import total in 1959 was 600,000 cars, or 10 percent of the U.S. car market. Coming up fast in second place and closing in on VW was Renault, the French-made car. Once the Renaults began falling apart after a year or two of driving, Renault was never again an important seller in America, even though the company apologized in its later ads for the dogs of 1958 and 1959.

Studebaker-Packard also learned in 1958 that a car had to be more than just cheap to sell. In trouble (Packard was being folded and production was nose-diving from 182,000 in 1955 to 57,000 in 1958), the company stripped a model (out went the interior and exterior trim), cut its price,

s aid. Egypt-Syria form United Arab Republic. Nasser moves to overthrow other Arab governments. Figh
lion. Hoffa runs Teamsters with court-appointed monitors. Charles Starkweather 19, Caril Fugate 14 c

and named it the Scotsman. Nobody bought it. Americans might want a small car or a low-priced car but they did not want a car that said cheap.

Interestingly, the same group that was criticizing Detroit's cars on safety and size was pointing to the VW as the model of what an automobile should be like: simple and utilitarian. The VW, however, as anyone who ever drove one knew, was underpowered (which could mean trouble when you came onto a freeway in traffic) and notoriously unstable in a crosswind.

"My husband was driving well behind a Beetle once," Fran Cerra, the

2.

The Studebaker Hawk with fins added to keep up with the style trend.

nher von Braun rushes army satellite into orbit; other navy, airforceOK. Indonesian revolt against Suk
els open second front. French army bombs Tunisia without government , army rockets fail in moon shots

3. *Last of the Packards: A 1958 wagon, a Studebaker with the Packard name, a sad, sad end.*

consumer news writer for *The New York Times* says. "The road was clear but suddenly the VW just turned over." The person driving was not hurt, though. If the driver was true to form he or she went out and bought another, for Beetle owners loved their cars and even gloried in their deficiencies. To attack the Beetle then was to be labeled as a defender of Detroit's cars. Years later, when Ralph Nader had won his war against Detroit, he turned his attack on the German car, calling it one of the most dangerous on the road, with little affect (although VW did improve power and stability somewhat).

The year was the worst for Detroit in postwar history. There was a major recession and a sizeable revolt against the cars Detroit was building. Only 4.2 million cars were assembled in 1958, just better than half the produc-

put down. Ike proposes US-USSR cultural exchanges. Russia suspends A-tests; none follow. Tito tell
orbits. Regulatory agencies accused of taking payola. Sherman Adams, Ike aide, took gifts from busin

4.
The VW before they even called it the Beetle. Sales sound in the recession.

tion of 1955. G.M.'s output was down a fourth, Ford's down a third, and Chrysler, suffering from its bad-car image earned with the '57s, saw production fall more than 50 percent from 1957. "People no longer think it's just wonderful to go someplace sitting down," Lewis Crusoe of Ford said later.

American Motors was rolling, with the old Nash and Hudson names buried. They were making Ramblers. Only 217,000 were built in 1958 but

nds off, praises U.S. aid. Algerian army, French fleet revolts, De Gaulle takes power, ends threat of
.ts. Blizzard kills 71 in Northeast. Major union corruption in hearings: theft, mob ties. Dave Beck,

that was good for American Motors. It almost doubled the production of the preceding year. Output would almost double again in 1959.

There was even a song ("Beep Beep") about the Cadillac driver trying to stay ahead of the Rambler when, at 120 m.p.h., as fast as the Cadillac could go, a little Rambler pulls alongside and the driver yells across the road asking how he could get the car out of second gear.

No Rambler ever passed any Cadillac at 120 in those days, but the song showed that Rambler was shedding its loser image and winning acceptance. Why not? The car actually was beginning to look good, especially when compared with the '58s and '59s coming from the competition. The ugly grille with the inboard headlights was slimmed out and the lamps moved to the normal position. The lines were straight and clean, there was no

5.
The Cadillac sedan. The whitewalls were getting thinner.

war. VP Nixon attacked by red mobs in Caracus. Imre Nagy, Gen. Pal Maleter, Hungarian revolt leader
eamsters head, jailed. Government antirecession moves in housing, roads, more jobless pay, tax cuts.

6.
The chrome ladened Impala was new and an instant success. Some thought it looked like a little Cadillac.

tortured metal sculpturing, and the fin was not bad as fins go. The wagon—and Rambler was scoring big in the station-wagon trade—was as good-looking a wagon as was made. Mileage was fair, price was low, and the car was getting a reputation for solidness, all while the competition was growing longer. Chevrolet was 209 inches long for 1958 and going up; the medium-priced cars were even longer. Rambler was only 191 inches long.

George Romney was busy then saying that nothing in the world is stronger than an idea whose time has come. He evangelized across the nation, poking fun at "the dinosaur in the driveway" and practically trademarking the word "compact" for the Rambler-size car. If American Motors could not out-advertise its competitors, Romney put the company on the news pages. He was so successful (there was a moment when American Motors was poised to overtake Chrysler) that the automobile business was

eeks, Turks, British fight on Cyprus. Russians shoot down U.S. plane. Marines land in Lebanon, put do
ubs Negro churches, synagogues. Alaska voted statehood. A-subs cruise under North Pole. Court kills

too small for him. He turned to politics, was elected governor of Michigan, and was at one time the leading Republican candidate for the presidential nomination of 1968. But then, instead of being cheered as the underdog as he had been at American Motors, he became hooted as the frontrunner. Finally he stumbled on Vietnam, telling a TV reporter that he had been "brainwashed" on the war. He was trying to say that he had believed the

7.
Remember the strapless evening gown? The car is a DeSoto. The dog is a poodle.

sser-backed rebellion, withdrawn. Chinese reds shell Quemoy, U.S. warns them off. New French constitu
l ban on U.S. $900 million Federal aid to science education. Court orders Little Rock schools desegre

8.
The Chrysler Windsor. The fin craze was fading but Chrysler was stuck with them and sales plummeted.

government's lies, but the word "brainwashed" backfired and his candidacy was destroyed. So Richard Nixon moved forward, captured the nomination, and won the election.

The best news for car buyers in 1958 was a Federal law ordering that the suggested list price be posted on a window of each new car, ending the practice of giving the customer a phony price or exaggerating the cost of options.

The low point might have been the promotion of air suspension. This option was offered on most '58s, at least on paper. Air might be free but the

Gaulle president, offers peace talk to Algerians, they refuse. USSR resumes A-tests. Pope Pius XII d
bama, Virginia rebel, close schools, defy court. Democrats sweep Congress, State House in votes. Nel

system was costly, offered few advantages over conventional springing, and broke down. Air suspension was pulled from the market about as soon as it came out.

Chevy at 209 inches long for 1958 was 9 inches longer than 1957, bigger than Ford. There was a new top-line model, heavy with chrome but handsome anyway, called Impala. The standard V-8 was the 283-cubic-inch, 185-horsepower engine with options running up to 280 h.p. Chevy recap-

9.
The boat, 227″ long, 5,000 pounds heavy. Ford wanted to design a lean and hungry Lincoln Continental and this is what came out.

Pope John XXIII named. Russia to help Egypt build giant Aswan Dam. Russians try pushing Allies from B
ockefeller new NY governor. 87 children, 3 nuns killed in Chicago school fire. Armed forces cut. Ike

tured first place from Ford. Pontiac restyled along Chevrolet lines, Buick dropped its portholes, and dual headlights were common on all lines.

Ford had big changes. The Thunderbird went to a big four-passenger car in two models, hardtop and convertible, and the little two-passenger Bird was gone forever. There was the Edsel, of course, and a modestly dechromed version of the '57 Turnpike Cruiser, although without its awfulness it was nothing. The standard Ford was restyled with a big Thunderbird mouth-like grille, fins were added, and horsepower run up to 300 on the optional engines.

The biggest new model for 1958 was Ford's Lincoln. The stylists said the car was to carry a lean and hungry look, a light and airy perspective, and have dignity and elegance. But the old Lincoln model had some of those traits and still failed to challenge Cadillac. What rolled off the production line was "the boat" as it was called, 227 inches long, 5,000 pounds heavy and capable only of 8 to 10 m.p.g., a worthy successor to the Turnpike Cruiser of '57.

Chrysler had modest styling changes. Although the windshields bent a bit at the top to cut into the roof, the bodies kept the fins of '57, and the hemihead V-8 was finally replaced by a more conventional design.

And criticism was mounting. John Keats hit hard in his book *The Insolent Chariots* that year. "Ah, the Midwest! Land of the simple plowmen!" he wrote. "No doubt it was the Midwesterners' immemorial custom of attending agricultural fairs which led them all to think in terms of the biggest pumpkins, and thus to believe that if it's the biggest, it's the best, no matter whether this means digging the world's deepest sunken garden, or winning the most football games, or building the world's biggest, gaudiest cars."

He was right. Detroit did think bigger was better; the trouble was bigger meant longer hoods and stretched-out rears, not more interior room

1958

Production

General Motors	2,169,200
Ford	1,219,400
Chrysler	581,200
American Motors	217,300
Studebaker-Packard	56,900
Total	4,244,000

10.
By 1958, the Indian head and the suspenders on the hood had disappeared, but the chrome was put on this Chieftain with a trowl.

or comfort. The rear seats were cramped and uncomfortable as cars grew longer. Selling door slams was important, not selling doors that stayed shut in accidents. Mileage was falling as the cars got heavier and the engines bigger. The big burners got less than ten miles to the gallon. When a reporter asked the head of Buick what his division was doing to improve fuel economy, he quipped "We're helping the gas companies, the same as our competitors."

If much of the criticism was valid there was a strong touch of patrician

wman 33, Joanne Woodward 27, married. Mike Todd killed in crash. Kentucky NCAA champs over Seattle 84
l Future King, Dr. Zhivago, Lolita, Only in America, The Affluent Society. Cheryl Crane, 14, Lana Turn

class snobbery, too. "The automobile did not put the adventure of travel within the reach of the common man. Instead it gave him the opportunity to make himself more and more common," Keats wrote.

People with cars no longer had to live and play on their side of the tracks. They could move to the suburbs and crowd their betters. They could buy motor boats, tow them to the water and disturb the sophisticates on their sailboats. They could tow skimobiles to the hills, drink beer, make noise and upset the skiers.

The poor people were buying pianos, and the patricians did not like their music.

ars to Joanne Woodward (The Three Faces of Eve), Alec Guiness (The Bridge over the River Kwai). Yanks
el, The Music Man, Look Back in Anger. Bobby Fischer youngest grandmaster at 15. Tim Tam wins Kentuc

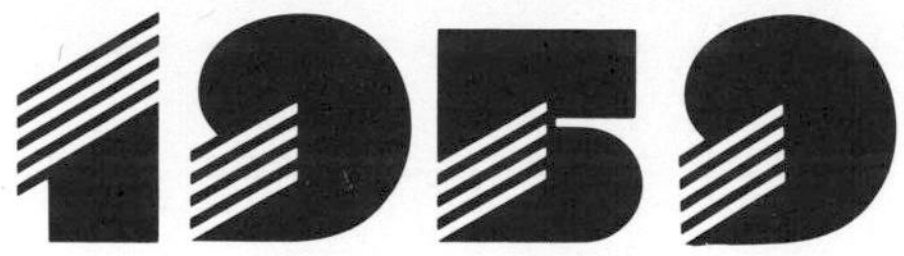

"It was getting your jollies off."

—**Gene Bordinat**

In Hemingway's book *For Whom the Bell Tolls* just as the Republicans are going over the top in the big attack the Red general learns that the Fascists know all about it. They will pull back to escape the bombardment, then ambush the Republicans. But the Republican planes are already in the air and it's just too late to stop. "Golz watched the planes with his hard proud eyes that knew how things could be and how they would be instead," Hemingway wrote, "proud of how they could be, believing in how they could be, even if they never were."

That was 1959. The gaudiest and most fin-bedecked cars ever produced —the gorpiest ever—rolled down the lines with the tide already turned against the stylists. Everyone in Detroit knew they would fail but it was just too late to do anything except cheer them on.

The General Motors cars were the wildest. Chevrolet sprouted giant gull wings dipped in the center to form a potential rust trap. Pontiac offered four fins created by a V at each side of the rear. Buick had a fin so large the car seemed ready to fly away, and new series names: LeSabre, Invicta, Electra. Cadillac carried chest-high killer fins. They were so embarrassing

Batista flees Cuba; stadium trials, executions. Riots in Belgan Congo. De Gaulle preside
Alaska formally a state. Court orders Virginia school integration, 7 desegregate, Ike cal

1.
There never was and never will be another fin like the gull wing on the 1959 Chevrolet.

that Detroit would drag out an engineer every so often to explain how the fins held the cars tight to the road and arrow-straight in cross-winds.

There is always someone to love even the strangest car. "I still think it's gorgeous," says a Detroit sculptor, Elizabeth Hansell, who drove a '59 Chevy as a teenager. "It didn't look like every other car. The sweep of the wing had grace and unity. I cried when my father [a Chevy dealer] took it away from me for a new model."

The car culture continued to flourish. "The block that counts with the chicks nowadays isn't on a guy's sweater," said *Motor Trend*, "but under his hood."

"There's hardly a wheel anywhere that's not decked out with spinners," Mercurys with Corvette engines, steering wheels with hand-knitted booties, and the coaches complaining they were losing their boys to the cars.

er 3 year exile, president. Revolts in Iraq, quits Western Alliance, swings left. Emergency in Rhodes
orts. Teamster Beck guilty of tax evasion, gets five years. Benjamin Davis first Negro major general.

It was Ford's year. The Fords carried Thunderbird styling with flat roofs and the wide Thunderbird "C" pillar at the rear (which helped rear vision and rear-seat headroom). It was the last year Ford was to outsell Chevrolet, barring 1970, when G.M. was closed by strike for months.

At the end of 1960 both Robert McNamara and Ernie Breech left the company—the first for the government, the second for Trans World Airlines because he had finished his re-building job at Ford. And then, while Ford's new compacts outsold Chevrolet's new compacts, the full-size Chev-

2.
General Motors panicked when they saw Chrysler's 1957 fins and came up with wings like this on their Buick.

African nationalist groups banned. Ike agrees to summit; talks with allies. Tibetan revolt against C
bless benefits extended 3 years, economy perks up, unemployment dropping. Dulles has cancer, resigns,

3.
The compact Lark gave Studebaker a few extra years of life.

rolets ran the big Fords to the ground, and Ford was helpless to react without its experienced leaders.

Chrysler had gimmicks, like the optional swivel front seats. The idea was that with the low seats the women could not get out of the cars without their skirts riding up to their navels (1959 was before jeans), so at the touch of a button the seat swung out. (It was a dud; the problem did not bother women. Legs were in then.) There was another first: the electronic rear-view mirror, just what nobody needed.

American Motors' Ramblers won the raves of *Consumer Reports.* The seats were good, the finish was swell and "no other U.S. car has a stauncher body or one more permanently free from squeaks and rattles," said the magazine.

"Our 1959 Rambler wagon, which my father bought used, was a car

ai Lama flees to India. Fierce fighting in Algeria; priests charge French army with Algerian torture.
ter new Secretary of State. St. Lawrence Seaway Open. Negroes try to enter white Birmingham schools,

that was perfect to learn to drive on because with its loose shift linkage and its uncertain clutch and lack of power, if you could learn to drive it you could learn to drive anything," Richard Benyo wrote in the magazine *Small Cars*. "Naturally, when that occasional Saturday night came up when the nerve was worked up to ask Dad for the car and he said 'Yes,' having a Rambler did not mean instant success. No one turned in their seats to see who was pulling up in a hot Rambler station wagon; a Rambler driver never, never got involved in a drag race unless he volunteered to drop the flag for the big-engined cars; and there were certain areas of the parking lot where the hot cars congregated where the Rambler was not allowed to go." The front seats came down and the wagon had enough space to take along a few friends. "What the car lacked in engine power, it easily made up in creature comfort power," Benyo said.

4.
The squared-off Fairlane of 1959 helped carry Ford to a sales victory over Chevrolet.

e asks Reds for limited A-test ban, rejected, then Khrushchev OKs talks. Castro in U.S., on Meet the P
ected. Strontium 90 levels rise in U.S. Payless paydays in Michigan moneysqueeze. 3 segregationists

5.
Compared to most of the offerings in '59, this plain Rambler American was handsome, but only compared to most of the offerings of 1959.

Studebaker had a new compact, its Lark, that a three-man team had engineered in six months, and that gave the South Bend, Ind., company a new life for two years. The Lark was only 175 inches long, the shortest car of '59. The compact weighed about 2,600 pounds (a Plymouth six weighed 3,300 pounds) and carried a basic 90-horsepower six or 180-h.p. V-8. Production bounced up to 154,000. The sporty Hawk cars were still in production, but the Lark carried Studebaker to a rare profitable year. Unfortunately, the next year, before Studebaker could improve the simple Lark, before it could build up its weak dealer force, before it would win the public confidence as American Motors had, the Big Three was swarming over the landscape with its compacts, putting an end to the boomlet. But the 1959 gain pushed up Studebaker's stock and enabled the company to

o Kenyatta, called Mau-Mau leader, freed from prison after 5 years. Belgium promises gradual Congo fr
k school board recalled. Atlanta libraries desegregate. Senate rejects Lewis Straus as Commerce Secr

trade the stock for some nonautomotive firms that continued after the car business folded, saving something for the stock owners.

A striking shift in the market was the swing away from the medium-priced cars. One reason for it was that the ambitious heads of the old "low-priced three," Ford, Chevy, and Plymouth, went after the medium market. They increased the size, power, and optional equipment. A wealthy man might buy an Impala or Fairlane and get as much comfort as he could get in a Buick or Mercury. A "classless" car society had been created and rating services often recommended against spending the extra dollars for a medium-priced car because the others were lower priced, even with the optional gear.

In 1955 a Chevrolet was 196 inches long; by 1959 it was 211 inches long

6.
The Cadillac fins were considered a threat to pedestrians.

n. Big 4 talks on Germany. VP Nixon in USSR, kitchen debate with Khrushchev. France cools on NATO, t
y. Mass murderer Charles Starkweather executed. Steel strike; dock strike, government injunction. At

7.
The market was turning to simpler, cleaner designs. Chrysler, like the others, was caught with its chrome up as on this Dodge.

—an inch longer and a couple of hundred pounds heavier than the Pontiac of 1955. A Ford at 208 inches for 1959 was three inches and hundreds of pounds heavier than the '55 Mercury. All the goodies, power steering, automatics, air conditioning, carpeting, big V-8s, were available on the Impalas and Fairlanes. There was not even much difference in fuel economy between the V-8s and the six-cylinder engines. One tester found the Chevy Bel Air with the 185-h.p. V-8 for 1959 gave 14.3 m.p.g.; the 135-h.p. Bel Air six gave 15.5 m.p.g. The Plymouth Belvedere 230-h.p. V-8 ran at 15.2 m.p.g. and the same model with a six ate more fuel, giving 14 m.p.g., Consumers Union said.

Detroit soon had a slogan: "More car per car." If they couldn't sell more automobiles, they would put more on each car and make it more expensive.

ear weapons. Khrushchev-Ike to exchange visits. K comes to UN, travels U.S. Visits China. Elizabet

ghter Savannah launched. FBI rounds up Mafia leaders. Hawaii becomes 50th state. Gasoline tax raise

Above all, it was the styling of the 1959s that made them unforgettable. "They were obscenities," said Gene Bordinat, Ford's styling vice-president.

"We really went wild," said Bill Mitchell, G.M.'s styling vice-president. "We were mere decorators," hanging ornaments on sheet metal. "They still haunt you."

"After 1955 they were all trying to play can-you-top-this," said Richard

8.
If you like fins, Chrysler's were probably the prettiest, as on this Imperial.

pregnant. Revolt in Laos; U.S. aid asked. Lin Piao Chinese defense minister. USSR rocket hits moon
pay for interstate highways. Congress investigates quiz show rigging; Charles Van Doren admits TV ch

9.
Ford never cared for fins but put them on to keep in style. Notice the strange approach on the Mercury Parklane.

1959

Production

General Motors	2,555,200
Ford	1,745,400
Chrysler	737,800
American Motors	401,400
Studebaker	153,800
Total	5,593,600

Teague, the American Motors stylist. "It could have been a four-wheeled Taj Mahal; it wouldn't have made any difference."

Every stylist has a car that did not work out right. Mitchell, for example, never was happy with the '66 Oldsmobile Toronado, America's first modern front-wheel drive car. The swept-back roof lines looked good in the studio and might have been fine on a smaller car, he says now, but on the street it was "too brutal. In New York in front of 21 it looked like a tank."

Richard Teague still takes a ribbing about the Marlin of 1965, which was to be American Motors' answer to Ford's trim Mustang. It turned into a bulky fastback. The design had been made for a smaller car, yet was put on a big body because of an engine problem and the usual sales argument that a bigger car would appeal to a broader market. "I should have fought harder," says Teague.

The styling problems of the cars of the late 1950s, the '57s, '58s, and '59s were not tied to a particular model. The sickness was common to the breed,

na-India border dispute. DeGaulle delays summit. U.S. moon shots fail. Anti-U.S. riots in Panama. O
estigate disc jockey payola. Hubert Humphrey running for president. ted. Elizabeth Taylor becomes Jew

though there were some exceptional cases—the Edsel, the Turnpike Cruiser, the gull-wing Chevy. Yet the designers themselves are men of good taste, a look at their wives and their clothes confirms it.

"We were the guys that made the cars sell," that was the attitude, said Bordinat. "Oh, it was fun in an uninhibited way. All of a sudden we downtrodden were getting our freedom. That's pretty heady stuff. And there

10.
A neat combination of clean design, chrome and a touch of fin, the '59 Rambler wagon.

oma 21, Syracuse 6 in Orange Bowl. Bobby Fischer, 15, retains U.S. chess title. Oscars: Susan Haywar
marries Eddie. Un-expurgated Lady Chatterly's Lover out, banned from mail. Tomy Lee wins Kentucky D

was an air of mystery about it. It's a simple thing. We could draw. People who don't know how to draw think that's a stroke of magic." The longer, the lower, the wider they got, "the closer they came to looking like your sketches," and then suddenly in 1959 "the cars are looking like our sketches. It wasn't much of a challenge. It was getting your jollies off."

Teague of American Motors says: "It got out of hand. It was like a fire you couldn't put out." In defense of the stylists he says, "Somebody had to say yes. And the styling guy never had the horsepower to say, 'Hey Mr. Chairman, we're going into production on this?' "

Those days are gone forever. In the next few years the number of body styles Detroit produced exploded and the costs of tooling soared, which meant only part of the line could be sharply restyled in any one year. Then the safety and pollution changes required by the government ate up the money and manpower previously set aside for styling change. Today the standard body cycle is six years, and there's talk of stretching that out. There may be a wild model now and then, but design will not leap from extreme to extreme year after year.

"The car will be functionally oriented first and stylists will have to do the best they can with what's left over," Harold MacDonald, Ford's group vice-president for product development, said in 1975. "I am not mad at stylists—styling still sells cars. But there won't be anything extra for stylists to put on the overhang in front or tail fins."

France, calls for Algerian compromise but not independence. Britain, Greece, Turkey create Cypriot rep
civil rights program. John Kennedy, Catholic, presidential candidate, affirms church-state separation

"An Air Force friend of Harley Earl invited him to see some new fighter planes."
—Alfred Sloan Jr., General Motors chairman, on the creation of the tail fin

The tail fin represented the worst in automobile design in the Golden Age, a pretty touch gone absolutely wild—like a fifty-foot woman. To every critic of the automobile the fin was the proof that the industry was unconcerned about safety. Millions for fins, pennies for safety. Detroit explained it could not force side-view mirrors on the public, it could not afford to put a padded dash in every car—yet it could afford without any hesitation to spend millions to redesign, retool, and put on fins that had no purpose. Critics could show that there was nothing being spent on air-pollution research while there was always enough money for new fins.

Ironically, the first little fins looked good, just as a bit of chrome or the right two-tone paint looks good. Alfred Sloan Jr., General Motors' best-known chairman, explained the origin of the fin when he noted that "the rapid movement in styling in the late forties and fifties sometimes seemed to many people to have become too extreme. New styling features were introduced that were far removed from utility, yet they seemed demonstrably effective in capturing public taste.

"One of the most striking of these features of the postwar car was the

1.
The P-38 of World War II days was the inspiration for the automobile fin.

'tail fin' which first appeared on the Cadillac of 1948 and which, though at first it was not easy to sell, has since appeared on almost every major line of cars in one exaggerated form or another. The story of the tail fin began during the war when an Air Force friend of Harley Earl invited him to see some new fighter planes. One of them was the P-38, which had twin G.M. Allison engines, twin fuselages, and twin tail fins. When Mr. Earl saw it, he asked if he could have some of his designers look at it, and after they received clearance, they were allowed to view the plane. They were just as impressed as Mr. Earl, and a few months later their sketches began to show signs of fins."

Earl wanted to put more than fins on the cars. After all, in the days of World War II, airplanes meant excitement, romance, victory—*A Yank in the R.A.F., Thirty Seconds Over Tokyo, Dive Bomber, Test Pilot.* Stylists wanted to catch some of the romance of the air in their cars.

"When you saw those booms, you could see those fenders going back," said Bill Mitchell, who succeeded Earl at G.M. Today the stylists generally believe it was a mistake to think of automobiles as airplanes, but it was hot stuff then.

Earl's designers began developing models with pontoon fenders, airplane-

2.
The first Cadillac fin, the fishtail of 1948 (left), and its descendant, the spear of the 1959 Cadillac.

3.
The strangest fin of all was on the gull wing Chevrolet of 1959.

like cockpits, fins, and pointed noses. Fortunately (for G.M. and probably the rest of us) only the fins stuck. The '50 Studebaker's pointed nose soon faded, and the airplane-like toggle switches that some cars had (Studebaker liked them, and they were neat) are gone now too.

The first fin popped up on the '48 Cadillac, just a cute fishtail at the rear, which was at once controversial. The model caught on but not before a

4.
A history of the fin by Cadillac. The friendly little fishtail didn't get really hysterical until the late 1950s.

5.
Four fins decorated the rear of the 1959 Pontiac Catalina.

nervous Cadillac company prepared a finless model. Before long garages were welding fins to rodders' cars. Somehow the fishtail was just right for Cadillac, a touch of frivolity at the end of that long serious car, the flip of Undine's tail, a wink.

Until 1955 the fins were modest, including Cadillac's. Then suddenly everyone had to have them. The Cadillac Eldorado put on a great shark tail instead of the friendly flipper and others followed. G.M. had half the car market and if anyone did not follow the G.M. lead he looked old and out of step. So Ford stylists reluctantly fell in line. Studebaker had to add glass-fiber fins to its Hawks. Even George Romney added fins to his simple, solid Ramblers.

"It is just like a woman's hat," Romney said. "The automobile business has some of the elements of the millinery industry in it, in that you can make style become the hallmark of modernity."

It was Chrysler, which had ignored styling for a quarter of a century, that turned the fin into a work of art: high, graceful, slanting fins climbing from the middle of the car to the tail. They were big, and if you liked fins, they were beautiful. Stylist Virgil Exner's fantasy fins on the 1957 models sent Chrysler sales soaring.

6.
Ford never liked fins but went along with the crowd reluctantly when the 1959 Fairlane 500 was a big car.

7.
The biggest, yet the best looking of the fins probably were the Chryslers. The 1961 Imperial carried these graceful giants.

That was the same year Ford outsold Chevrolet and General Motors was frightened. "We said, God, we've got to get them," remembers Mitchell of G.M. "We tried to outfin Chrysler. More chrome, more portholes," at first and then the fins that ended fins on the '59s. "We were panicking to Chrysler," Mitchell says regretfully.

If Chrysler's fins were big and beautiful, G.M.'s fins leaned toward the grotesque. On Chevrolet there were the great flat gull wings (which Ford tried modestly to copy later). On Pontiac there was a V at each end—four fins for the connoisseur. On Buick there was an angled wing that started at the front of the hood and wound back. On Cadillac there was a giant airplane tail, pointed, with taillights splitting the fin.

Ralph Nader in *Unsafe at Any Speed* said: "In the year of its greatest height, the Cadillac fin bore an uncanny resemblance to the tail of the stegosaurus, a dinosaur that had two sharp rearward-projecting horns at each side of the tail."

Nader was also able to document accidents. There was a 1964 case involving a California motorcyclist, driving behind a Cadillac that stopped suddenly. The cyclist could not swerve, hit the Cadillac and, wrote Nader, "was hurled into the tail fin which pierced his body below the heart and cut him all the way down to the thigh bone." He survived.

8.
Cadillac began experimenting with unusual fins like this 1957 Eldorado Biarritz.

9.
Even George Romney put fins on his dinosaur-slaying Rambler.

10.
The 1957 Lincoln Premier which doesn't look half bad. Cashmeres were in then.

11.
The 1961 Chrysler Newport. Chrysler planned a line of cars with a big, single, off-center fin, but a new management killed it.

A nine-year-old girl riding her bike in Kensington, Md., bumped into the rear of a '62 Cadillac and its fin "ripped into her body" below the throat.

Nader reported the death of an elderly woman in New York City struck by a fin of a Cadillac rolling backward, and the death of a thirteen-year-old Chicago boy who had run into a '61 Cadillac fin going back after a long fly. It "pierced his heart," Nader said.

General Motors' answer was that there "always is the likelihood of a few unusual types of accidents." The accidents probably were unusual, but the fins, which even looked dangerous, opened the question of whether the company—or the entire industry—even cared if they were dangerous.

But it was probably laughter that got the fins off the cars. G.M. and the other car makers pulled them off after the '59s as soon as their budgets allowed. Cadillac, which does not like sudden style changes, just lowered them until they vanished into the rear fenders. Dodge seemed to take the fin and roll it up, like a metal scroll, and leave it lying on the rear fender on its '62s.

Before the retreat, even greater fins were planned. Chrysler, for example, planned a big single off-center fin for its cars in the '60s, according to the rumor then. But a new president took over after low sales and financial scandals, canceled the single fin and hired a new stylist.

Was there really to be a single fin, a reporter later asked Robert Anderson, who then headed Chrysler's Plymouth division? Yes, he said. The single off-center fin started with a line at the beginning of the hood, ran along the hood, and then continued along the top of the car rising in the fin at the rear.

The reporter whistled, trying to visualize it.

"And if you think that was tough," said Anderson, "you should have tried to get it on the station wagons."

"Prospective buyers need not be unduly concerned."
—*Consumer Reports* rates Corvair's handling

Of the three new compact cars of 1960—Chevrolet's Corvair, Ford's Falcon, and the Plymouth Valiant—Corvair was to have the lasting effect.

The Corvair, in the words of *The New York Times* a decade later, was "a spectacular failure," though the "most innovative American automobile of its day." Indirectly, it led to the government's regulation of the automobile industry.

Ed Cole, the creator of the Chevy V-8 of '55, began pushing for a small car in '55. As U.S. model sales slumped and import sales climbed, he got his OK. Cole, an innovator, wanted no ordinary new car, and the package he put together was a revolution for Detroit: There was a flattened six-cylinder aluminum engine to hold down weight and provide more go than underpowered imports. The engine was air-cooled and placed in the rear, which eliminated the radiator and opened up more room in the passenger compartment. There was a swing axle and independent rear suspension (the rear wheels could swing independently of each other for better handling—a first for a modern American car), and a list price just under $2,000 (options might run the price up a few hundred dollars). The larger cars were now running more than $3,000.

Algerian rightists rebel; DeGaulle puts down, rules by decree, purges army. French explod
U.S. protests Cuban seizure of property, ambassador recalled, tensions rise. Ike to visit

1.
Chevrolet Corvair, with its air cooled, aluminum, rear engine, was the spectacular failure of the decade.

THE COMPACTS

	Production		
Year	*Chevy Corvair*	*Ford Falcon*	*Plymouth Valiant*
1959–1960	338,687	607,956	251,504
1961	316,679	486,079	122,285
1962	296,701	381,559	153,428
1963	251,525	341,870	221,677
1964	195,770	279,114	190,789
1965	204,007	208,970	139,436
1969	3,103	77,265	120,514
1970	—	26,057	279,615

Cole was out to build an American Volkswagen, which Corvair never was. At first Ford's Falcon won the buyers looking for simple transportation and later Plymouth's Valiant filled that role. Corvair discovered a new market with its pretty two-door which came out early in 1960 (only the four-door was ready for production late in '59). Decked out in Chevy's pretty trim, with bucket seats and named Monza, the Corvair was the first sporty car, not quite a sports car but looking a bit like one, and at a relatively low price.

Sharpesville. Riots in Korea; Syngman Rhee quits. Adolf Eichmann captured by Israelis. Khrushchev
S. plane missing over USSR; accidental overflight claimed. Soviets show wrecked U-2, Francis Gary Pow

2.
Plymouth's Valiant compact was last from the starting gate in the small car race.

The car was controversial before the first one was sold. The heart of the dispute was the heavy rear-end weight and the understeer-oversteer argument. American cars generally understeer. When you turn right (around a corner) the car swings out and the faster you're going the wider the swing. Drivers naturally learn to turn the wheel harder to keep the car in a tight path.

An oversteer car tends to swing in, not out, on the turn. The rear end may swing out or around unless the driver eases up on the wheel. Oversteer

ces Ike, summit canceled in U-2 aftermath, USSR quits Geneva talks. New Congo army mutinies. Tribal
IA pilot captured, talks. Khrushchev explodes, Ike cancels USSR visit. Caryl Chessman executed. Vot

3.
The Ford Falcon: Plain but pretty in a plain way, it was the best selling of the new compacts.

is not bad by itself; it's just different if you are used to understeer. In emergency situations the Corvair might react differently from other American cars. General Motors in a last-minute decision to cut costs left off a stabilizer bar that might have helped modify the oversteer. There was another problem: Corvair tried to cover handling problems with its tire inflation—fifteen pounds in the front tires, and twenty-six in the rear when cold, eighteen or thirty when hot—but drivers, dealers, and mechanics were not likely to know or remember the strange tire inflations.

Ford sent anonymous messages to auto writers, old quotations from Maurice Olley, one of G.M.'s top engineers, criticizing rear-engine configurations. Later, Lynn Townsend, who became Chrysler's president after a scandal rocked the company in 1960, was to say "we struggled to do a rear-engined car" at that time "and we couldn't. Our engineers were not willing to go with the weight distribution that it would entail. There was

lgian paratroops back, attack. Katanga province secedes, backed by Belgians. Patrice Lumumba heading
ghts bill passes. Kennedy leads for Democratic nomination. Humphrey quits; Lyndon Johnson campaigns.

no way this management could have even ordered that engineering department to do a rear-engined car."

Consumer Reports, after its first Corvair tests, said this: "As to the Corvair's handling and the sand storm of controversy about understeering vs. oversteering and the advantages and disadvantages in relation to front vs. rear mounting of an engine, CU [Consumers Union, the publisher of the magazine] suggests that prospective buyers need not be unduly concerned."

Those testers also said "it probably is true that Corvair, if driven in ignorance of its oversteering tendency, or with faulty judgment, will get a driver into trouble a little more easily—and into trouble requiring somewhat more skill to get out of—than a car that understeers." They also called Corvair "an engaging car to drive," added that it handled poorly in

4.
Plymouth Fury still stuck with fins although buyers were now rejecting them.

calls for UN troops. Khrushchev threatens US with rockets over Cuba, says Monroe Doctrine dead, sends
ians shoot down U.S. plane over arctic, 4 dead, Khrushchev denounces spying. Kennedy, 43, wins Democra

5.
The Dodge Polara. Do you believe that front end or that rear?

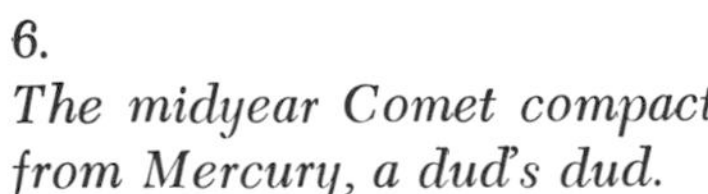

6.
The midyear Comet compact from Mercury, a dud's dud.

Cuba; Ike warns against interfering in Americas. Congo troops fire on refugees, attack missions, rape
ination, Johnson for VP. Dime stores desegregate lunch counters; 94% Negro students still in segregat

crosswinds, and finally said "unless it is recklessly overdriven, no unusual amount of handling skill is required; on the contrary, the Corvair in normal use controls with ease and precision and inspires confidence."

Later there was sharp criticism. Ralph Nader was able to quote Corvair testers who were not so pleased. "The classic Corvair accident is a quick spin in a turn and swoosh!—off the road backwards," wrote one critic. Another said "it was one of the nastiest-handling cars ever built. The tail gave little warning that it was about to let go, and when it did, it let go with a vengeance few drivers could cope with."

Lawyers began making a living on Corvair suits. G.M. paid off on some, and fought and won others. Chevrolet corrected the handling problems on the '64 and '65 models. By then Corvair was less of a car than a cause: Car testers, lawyers, newspaper men, consumer advocates, and businessmen all lined up against each other. Nader in *Unsafe at Any Speed* opened with a well-documented—controversial and debatable, but well-documented—attack on the car, including one major charge that was generally unsupported later: that the rear wheels tended to tuck in when in the air, causing accidents. G.M., upset by all the lawsuits, hired detectives to spy on Nader (they even asked about his sex life). The gumshoes were spotted and soon the word was out that someone was trying to get the consumer activist. The story is that the then-president of General Motors, Jim Roche, gathered his public-relations people together one night to deny that G.M. was trailing Nader, then was stunned to learn that, indeed, G.M. was. He learned that the gumshoes had been ordered by the company lawyer who reported not to Roche but to G.M.'s chairman, Frederic Donner. When the time came later to take the rap and apologize, Donner just happened to be out of the country and Roche had to go before Congress and apologize. When the word spread that G.M. had put detectives on Nader, an important

1960

Production

General Motors	3,193,200
Ford	1,892,000
Chrysler	1,019,300
American Motors	485,800
Studebaker	105,900
Total	6,696,200

laris ICBM fired 1150 miles from sub. Prince Norodom Sihanouk heads Cambodia, seeks peace with red re
asses 6 years after Supreme Court decision. Court orders all Delaware schools integrated by '61. $1

7.
The Chevrolet Bel Air Sport Coupe. It was a year to get away from the wraparound windshield and the gull wing of 1959.

witness before a Congressional committee, G.M. looked as if it were trying to silence a critic. Congress and anyone who could read was enraged and an auto-safety law rolled through, making Detroit a regulated industry. Because of that bill the car makers soon would be spending millions of dollars on items such as five-mile-an-hour bumpers (that added more to the price of a car than they saved in damage insurance) and seat-belt buzzers, let alone the paperwork the government required. The industry never forgave G.M. for the arrogance it showed by hiring the dicks. (G.M. later paid Nader $425,000 for invasion of privacy.)

nese-Tibetan rebels fight. UN's Hammarskjold leads UN troops into rebel Katanga but Lumumba threatens
plus in 1960. Nixon-Henry Cabot Lodge on GOP ticket. Powers convicted, gets 10 years. Medicare passe

How good or bad was the Corvair? After years of investigation the government's own safety agency cleared the car. It was different, which could spell trouble, but not unsafe. G.M. undoubtedly made a mistake in pinching a penny by removing the stabilizer and using trick tire pressures to improve handling. If a car is to be different a responsible manufacturer should drive that extra mile to make sure its customers know about the difference.

The fight also created an aura of play-it-safe in Detroit: try to innovate and you risk a lawsuit. In reality, Ford's Mustang might have done more to kill the Corvair than the safety controversy. Corvair found its niche as

8.
White gloves are passe now. The 1960 Ford was passe in 1960.

-yone. USSR puts two dogs in orbit. Rebellion in Laos, Souvanna flees. Cyprus, Nigeria independent. Khrushchev visits UN, kept in Manhattan by US. JFK-Nixon debate on TV. Negroes in Little Rock High,

a sporty car, and Ford's prettier Mustang captured the market Corvair discovered by accident.

G.M. killed the Corvair in 1969 after 1.7 million had been built. *The New York Times* ran the story on page 1 as an obituary, noting that "the most controversial car of the decade died today after a long illness at the age of ten."

If Corvair represented Cole's dash and innovation, Falcon represented the straightahead, no-nonsense approach of Robert McNamara at Ford. The Falcon was simple—a simple six, a simple transmission, a plain, clean, and even handsome body—solid, well-built, and colorless. While the Falcon outsold the Corvair every year (2.6 million to 1.7 million were the total production runs) it only lasted a year longer.

9.
Pontiac's Catalina. The pointed Pontiac nose was just beginning to develop.

McNamara was named president of Ford in 1960, but quit late the same year to become Defense Secretary. Interestingly, some of his traits visible in Detroit were to show up later in his war policy. McNamara was brilliant, all in the motor world agreed. He could muster facts, weigh them, and make decisions. But as one Ford executive said later, "It didn't matter if he was wrong. He was brilliant enough to make you look bad in the debate."

His last car was the intermediate Fairlane of 1962 (brought out after he departed) which again represented sensible transportation, what he thought would be good for people.

"That Fairlane was his car," a Ford vice-president says. "It looked like it was on stilts and no sex. When he'd made up his mind you couldn't get him to jiggle an eighth of an inch. That's-what-they-should-have was his attitude. He couldn't see any flaws in his own logic. The man had no emotion, and ours is a 50 percent emotion business."

The third of the new '60 compacts was Plymouth's Valiant with a new slant-six engine and sleek Italian styling that finds admirers (not many, but at least a few) even today. The car was rushed out and had troubles—leaks, for example. A driver taking his Valiant out in heavy rain might find puddles—or pools—of water on the floor and in the trunk. Valiant, though, was the little car that could. In a few years the sleek styling was dropped for a boxy look, and was in production years after its better-known rivals went to the boneyard.

Chrysler had other problems that year: a major management scandal. Stockholders were up in arms over falling sales and disappearing profits. The company's executives had the reputation of being the swingers in the rather staid Detroit society (divorce at the top was bad form), and it is true that some of their top men did seem to enjoy a bit of the bubbly and

ngo, expel reds, Lumumba captured. Jordan premier killed. Washington 44, Wisconsin 8 in Rose Bowl. E
torney general. Sit-ins in Atlanta. Planes collide over NYC, 131 dead. Oscars: Charlton Heston (Ben

10.
The Olds Dynamic 88 Holiday 4-door hardtop.

a pretty ankle. Finally Lester Lum Colbert was moved upstairs to chairman and William Newberg named president to shape up the company. In June, just sixty days after being named president, Newberg was fired, charged with conflict of interest, being a partner in a company set up just to do business with Chrysler. Lynn Townsend, an accountant, took over, chopped off heads, killed the fin-mad styling, and got Chrysler rolling again. He rode the Chrysler roller-coaster until 1975, when he quit in another sales slump.

eball league to expand to 10 teams each. Pulitzer to Allan Drury (Advise & Consent). Norman Mailer in
asure Hunt. Charles Van Doren, 13 others arrested for perjury; denied quiz show rigging. Patterson K

The big cars of 1960 were overshadowed by the compacts. (Ford's Mercury dealers got a compact, the plain Comet, in spring. McNamara might have been short on style but he always kept Ford ahead of the competition.) There were other changes, however. Wraparound windshields were fading. Chevrolet flattened out its '59 gull-wing fin while Ford took off its Chevy-beating sharp look of '59 and tried the flat fin and dipped hood. Chevy whipped Ford in '60 and was never seriously challenged again. Edsel was killed. A sliding roof panel, later called a sun roof, was offered on the Thunderbird. Chrysler took its Plymouth models away from Dodge dealers and gave Dodge a Plymouth-like model called the Dart instead. The stylists were back-peddling from the extremes of '59 as fast as they could retool. The modern age was beginning. "We began to get some sense," says Bill Mitchell, G.M.'s top designer.

llevue after stabbing wife. Books: Rise & Fall of Third Reich (Shirer), To Kill a Mockingbird (Lee).
Johansson in 5, retakes title. University of Illinois fires prof for OKing pre-marital sex for adult

"No wives and no girl friends."
—Designer Raymond Loewy on Studebaker's last stand

Studebaker was going down. Smaller cars pouring out of the Big Three's plants in 1960 and 1961 outclassed the little Lark. The Hawk, as stylish as ever, still was the descendent of the '53 Starliner coupe and old hat. Production slumped from 154,000 in 1959 to 79,000 in '61.

Headhunters found a new boss for Studebaker in 1961, Sherwoid Egbert, six feet, four inches of Southern California rah-rah. A few years later Egbert was to fail, giving it all but his life and maybe a little of that, but before she went down Studebaker had one more try. In March 1961, after just a month on the job and while flying from Chicago to Los Angeles "somewhere between Omaha and Denver, I began to sketch the kind of car I would like Studebaker to build," Egbert said. On March 9 he called Raymond Loewy, who had given Studebaker its postwar breakthrough cars and the '53s. He told the designer that he wanted a new sports car, with the design and a finished clay model in six weeks.

A big car maker has hundreds of stylists and modelers. Loewy took three assistants to Palm Springs. There he would keep away from well-meant advice. Detroit stylists under pressure can end up "as nervous wrecks or with peptic ulcers," he said. "We had nothing but fun in the sun and we

War Tension. U.S. breaks relations with Cuba. Minute-man ICBM fired 4200 miles in test. Ike warns military-industrial complex threatens liberty. Georgia repeals school segregat

1.
Checker of Kalamazoo built taxi cabs and sold a few as roomy automobiles.

drank a lot of champagne and the end result is Avanti. I resented very much the Detroit look, as they called it. I've been fighting for more than twenty-five years for more graceful, slender automobiles."

To his comrades "I said no wives and no girl friends. Well, they didn't like that so much but they followed instructions," Loewy said. "We were four together" and in just forty days they designed a plastic-bodied, pinched-waist Coke-bottle-look car with a flat front end, no grille, and an off-center gunsight line down the hood. When it was designed there was another fight because the financial men opposed its construction. In a year

m, the chimp, rockets 115 miles up, down in preorbital test. Kennedy warns U.S. won't allow Laos to f
laws. 7 electrical company executives jailed for price fixing. February unemployment 5.7%. Supreme

and a half, though, the Avanti was on sale. It won for Studebaker all the publicity Egbert had counted on, and it was the first modern American car with disc brakes. It is still in production today, more than a decade after Studebaker folded. A South Bend, Ind., car dealer turns them out and finds buyers willng to pay more than $10,000 for the car.

The Avanti obviously did not save Studebaker. Flashy sports cars that draw onlookers just are not a substitute for handsome, well-engineered sedans and hardtops that people buy, or a substitute for good dealers, or a reputation for quality. The money spent on the Avanti kept Studebaker from producing a sharply restyled line of regular cars. Time just ran out on Studebaker. Money was always short, and getting it meant going to Wall Street and having "some one of those pompous bankers ask me where's South Bend or some dumb thing" as one company man said.

The day came late in 1963 when they knew where South Bend was and said no. Studebaker had some odd-ball acquisitions—firms making floor-

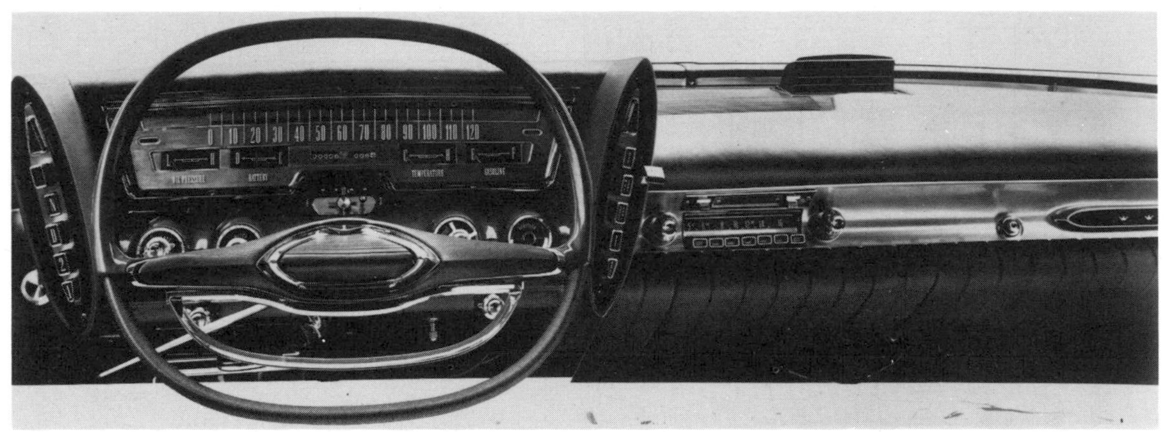

2.
Chrysler's pushbutton automatic transmission (left), on airplane-type Imperial dashboard, popular in the day.

dges U.S. won't invade Cuba. Cuba bombed. U.S.-backed refugee invaders land near Bay of Pigs, beaten
taurants on public land. Alan-Shepard makes up-down preorbital flight. Minimum wage to $1.15 now, $1.

3.
Designing a good looking small car was always a problem. The Rambler American stationwagon exemplifies the problem.

cleaning machines, STP oil additive, and the like—and the money men decided to stop losing money on cars and save what they could. Egbert was sick those last months at Studebaker (he died in 1969). Avanti was Egbert and Loewy's last try to save the car business by catching the imagination of the public with styling and performance. They failed; beau geste.

The biggest car news in 1961 was the new generation of larger, luxury compacts. It was the pattern Detroit was to follow more than once: Bring out a small, low-priced economy model, then follow it up not with smaller, even more fuel-stingy cars, but go in the opposite direction—introduce second-generation cars that are larger, carry bigger engines, offer more optional equipment, destroy the idea of low price and high mileage—and

days; Kennedy takes blame. DeGaulle takes dictatorial power to crush Algerian army revolt. Civil wa
ater. Freedom Riders bus south to test segregation laws, attacked in Anniston, Birmingham, Montgomery

4.
Ford trimmed the size and squared off the style of its handsome big car, but was not to challenge Chevrolet in sales ever again.

help profits. There was also a boom in aluminum engines (to save weight) which lasted a year or two before fading away.

General Motors led the way with three new compacts—the Buick Special (before the year was over there was a bucket-seat version called the Skylark), the Oldsmobile F-85, and the Pontiac Tempest. They were about 188 inches long, a half-foot longer than the first-wave compacts of 1960. The Oldsmobile and Buick models carried a new aluminum V-8 of 155 horsepower, a smooth engine with enough power to move up the hills without flagging. (Chrysler offered an aluminum version of its new six, too, and American Motors offered one. Only Ford, which is conservative on

o, UN intervenes. 3400 Portuguese troops to Angola to quell revolt. Rafael Trujillo assassinated in
U.S. marshalls sent. Court orders Dupont to sell General Motors stock, forbids illegally seized evide

engine design, stayed away from the light metal.) Mileage was in the 16–18-m.p.g. range against the 20–23-m.p.g. range of the Corvair-Falcon-Valiant group.

The Pontiac crew under Bunkie Knudsen tried a more adventuresome route. Instead of trying to design a completely new four-cylinder engine, Pontiac's engineers took an iron V-8 and, in effect, sliced it in half lengthwise, making the half-V a big four-cylinder engine. They also created a new rear-axle system which they called the transaxle; its effect was independent rear suspension and a flatter floor, opening up interior room. Like the Corvair, the radical Tempest engineering effort did not quite click.

5.
Chevy's Corvair Greenbrier. The vans of this era were aimed at families unlike the "sin-bins" of today.

.nican Republic. Kennedy-Khrushchev meet in Vienna; Khrushchev decides Kennedy is soft. Chinese deny
in state criminal trials. James Hoffa re-elected Teamster president. Gen. Edwin Walker accused of sp

6.
Chevrolet's pretty 700 Club Coupe which was the beginning of the sporty car market.

Within a few years the four and the transaxle were gone and Pontiac was pushing the biggest eight that would fit into the Tempest, creating GTO, a new breed of "supercar."

Chrysler moved in 1961 too, bringing out the Dodge Lancer, which was a Plymouth Valiant with five extra inches tacked on. Ford already had its Comet, a larger version of the Falcon being sold by Mercury dealers, and offered a larger 101-h.p. engine for the Falcon in 1961.

American Motors brought out a completely restyled Rambler American, the small car that dated to 1950 and was resurrected in 1958. Even the new version was homely. Dick Teague, now styling vice-president of American Motors, recalled that when he joined the company the first car he saw

n Russia. Kennedy calls for more defense spending, air raid shelters. Congress calls up 250,000 reser
n Birch propaganda, quits army. Smoking-heart disease connected. Miami-Tampa airline hijacked to Cuba

being worked on was that American: "I saw it and I almost kept on walking." He stayed on and lived through mistakes like the '65 Marlin to create the curvey Javelin sporty car, the unique Gremlin (Teague created the Gremlin for only $6 million by chopping off the rear end of the compact Hornet), and the still-debated Pacer small car.

There was an all-new Lincoln, too, and this one a chrome-clean model 212 inches long replacing the bulbous 227-inch boat of past years. This was the third all-new Lincoln in five years, as Ford vainly tried to come up with something that could compete with Cadillac. Cadillac, on the other hand, had discovered that the high rollers do not like constant change; even when they had a poor design they worked out of it slowly. The new Lincoln came in just two models, a four-door hardtop and a four-door convertible, the second four-door soft top in the postwar era (Kaiser had made a handful). Lincoln would not catch or even challenge Cadillac with these either, but was moving in the right direction with its '61s.

7.
There are some who still don't believe the torpedo tube tail of the 1961 Dodge Polara.

ts in crisis. Russia's Yuri Gagarin orbits earth. U.S. stunned. East Germans close Berlin border, bu
ICC bans racial bias in interstate bus travel. Nixon says he won't run for president in '64, will run

8.
Compact sized cars spread into middle priced divisions like the Pontiac Tempest with its 4-cylinder engine.

Some believed that the compact revolution and the return to styling functionalism was final. George Romney said that "appearance is no longer the prime factor in selling," and that car making was in "an era of functionalism."

Not quite. The designers were sweating from their systems the last drops of that age of awfulness. Grotesque designs were out; pouring on chrome was out. Chevrolet removed the last vestige of its gull wings on the 1961s and Buick was finless at last. (A new Buick management was working to

. Russia tests giant A-bomb, U.S. tests resumed. UN's Dag Hammarskjold killed in Africa, Kennedy plec
rnor of California in '62. Living costs up only 0.5% in all '61. University of Georgia integrated aft

9.
Not a fin to be seen on the Chevrolet Bel Air.

build quality automobiles, struggling to regain a lost reputation.) Cadillac kept its big pointy fin, moving slowly so as not to shock its customers.

Ford went back to the sharp squared-off corner look, abandoning its rounded look of 1960, and the big Ford was chopped to 210 inches from 213 inches in 1960. Mercury got an economy model with a six-cylinder engine, and was shortened 4.5 inches. What really happened is that the Mercury-only body was abandoned and the car again became a dolled-up Ford. The Thunderbird received a new skin for 1961 with the slanted

aid to South Vietnam, Maxwell Taylor sent to Saigon. U.S. denies secret decision to send troops. Khr
·iot, court order. John Tower to Senate from Texas, first GOP win there since 1877. Sam Yorty elected

droop-snoot nose. Plymouth dumped its fins for a rounded and chrome-heavy model (to be abandoned the next year) and one of the stranger fins around was on the big Dodge. It was high at the beginning, not at the end at the rear, and tapered down in a roll, with the taillights looking a bit like torpedoes poking out of their tubes. "Science fiction had come true," said one critical stylist looking at the Dodge. "The atomic bomb has worked a mutation."

10.
Last of the DeSotos: The line was killed soon after 1961 production started.

eals Stalin terror, de-Stalinizes. U.S. helicopters to Vietnam. China-Russia splitting. Patterson KOs
eles Mayor. Railroads, airports desegregate. Dow-Jones high 734.9 on Dec. 13. Newton Minow calls TV

11.
The big Buick Invicta.

DeSoto, high-finned to the last, was killed soon after 1961 production started, another victim of the swing from the big medium-priced cars. Until that swing Chrysler had been heavy in the medium-priced market—Dodge, DeSoto, Chrysler, and Imperial at the top. After the swing most of the Dodge cars were at the lower price end with Plymouth.

By 1961 the trend to unitized bodies had swept the industry. In unitized construction (pioneered by American Motors) there was no separate body and frame (or steel skeleton). Rather, the body had the supporting and

emar Johansson in 6th retaining title. Oscars to Elizabeth Taylor (Butterfield 8), Burt Lancaster (El
t wasteland, attacks its violence, mediocrity. Carry Back wins Kentucky Derby. Tony awards for Becke

strengthening steel members built in or welded onto it, with the running parts—wheels and axles—attached. The unitized body was tight and strong, stiff and rattle-free, at least on smaller cars. The car companies later learned that on full-sized cars it lost its advantages and dropped it. Unfortunately it also developed marvelous water traps under the skin, which meant the cars would rust from the inside and fairly quickly, too. To fight that problem car makers were dipping the bodies completely in vats of primer paint or using galvanized panels. Another problem was the tailpipe and muffler system, which was beginning to rust out after a year, bringing on aluminized mufflers, ceramic-coated parts and heavier gauge steel.

New Ford and Chevy vans were appearing on the streets, copied from the original Volkswagen van. The VW van was really underpowered and eventually fell victim to the chicken war—the Germans kept out our cheap frozen chickens to protect their farmers so we raised the duty on their van trucks. The vans were used as delivery trucks or small buses, and big families took to them as station wagons, and later as recreation vehicles for campers.

Strangely the camper van market faded as more ornate campers, mounted on trucks, won the buyers. But a new use for the vans developed, first in California, then spreading east. Youngsters began buying the windowless models, painting murals on the sides, stuffing mattresses on the floor or carpeting them (with three inches of foam rubber under the carpeting), and installing an occasional mirrored ceiling to imitate the fantasy life fashioned by *Playboy*. By 1975 the camper's family van had turned into the X-rated recreation vehicle, the Southern California Sin Bin.

Vantastic, they called it.

1961

Production

General Motors	2,726,600
Ford	1,689,900
Chrysler	648,700
American Motors	372,500
Studebaker	78,700
Total	5,516,400

t Cincinnati in series in 5. Pop hits: Ruby, Wheels, Don't Be Cruel, Never on Sunday, Elvis, Paul Anka
e Alyson-Dick Powell divorced. Syphilis reported up 50% in year. Coronet magazine folds. James Thurb

"Stand on a new Tempest LeMans . . . it bites."
—A Pontiac advertisement

Schizophrenia was Detroit's theme in 1962. The car makers were drifting back into power and luxury, and the hot-car era was just around the corner. The Beach Boys made it in 1962 and over the next few years would be scoring with their car song *I Get Around*, with lyrics and music by Brian Wilson: "She's got a competition clutch with four on the floor yeah, She purrs like a kitten till the lake pipes roar" or "We always take my car 'cause she's never been beat, and we never missed yet with the gurrrlls we meet."* At the same time most of the cars coming out were models planned three years before, in the recession, and were aimed at economy lovers. Detroit tried to make it up with special engine options, power packs and hot ads. Olds with its Jetfire offered a turbocharged V-8 (0–60 m.p.h. in 9.2 seconds). Chevy bored out (widened the cylinders to increase power) its V-8 to 327 cubic inches displacement (250 horsepower) and offered a 409 c.i.d. which the Beach Boys sang about. Plymouth offered up to 420 h.p. Chrysler's 300 H was advertised as the "Beautiful Brute" and Chrysler warned, "you know when you trigger the H! Three-hundred eighty hot-blooded horses under its hood for a whiplash getaway." Dodge warned that its "takeoff will sock you back in your seat."

* *I Get Around.* Words and Music by Brian Wilson. © 1964, Irving Music, Inc. Used by permission of the author and publisher.

Cuba-Russia sign trade pact. Francis Powers traded for Soviet spy. Nuclear ban talks col
KKK bombers of Freedom bus get probation. John Glenn orbits earth. Memphis lunch counter

1.
Notice that the door openings on the Lincoln face each other, a rare design.

"Stand on a new Tempest LeMans . . . it bites," Pontiac whispered, and Chevrolet warned the Corvette gang: "Don't sit down unless you mean business." Chevrolet also introduced its Monza Spyder hotrod option, and Ford moved openly into automobile racing.

The auto companies, through their association, pledged a voluntary withdrawal from stock-car racing in 1957 because of the public uproar over racing, the horsepower race, and the growing numbers of highway deaths. Regardless, Detroit, particularly the young division leaders at Chevrolet, Pontiac, and Ford, kept pumping money to the race garages and drivers secretly. Finally Henry Ford II tired of the charade—and the beatings by General Motors cars—and said his company would openly race.

The manufacturers said winning meant sales, which was really hard to prove by the sales figures. They claimed that racing improved the quality

Vietnam despite Kennedy denials. Khrushchev refuses A-ban with inspection, U.S. resumes tests in air.
ked, Kennedy enraged, sics agents on leaders, hike rescinded. Court bans school prayer. Billie Sol Es

of cars, and that was impossible to prove. There's no doubt it was a big sport, particularly in the South.

"To a great many good old boys a hot car was a symbol of heating up life itself," Tom Wolfe wrote in "The Last American Hero." Not only could a country boy make money racing, but, Wolfe said, "to millions of good old boys, and girls, the automobile represented not only liberation from what was still pretty much a land-bound form of social organization but also a great leap forward into twentieth-century glamor, an idea that was being dinned in on the South like everywhere else."

2.
Chrysler's 300 H, 380 horsepower and whiplash getaway.

na-India border war; China wins easily. Fighting in Laos; 5,000 U.S. troops to Thailand. Dutch surre
ndicted in fertilizer fraud. Ex-Judge George Wallace elected governor of Alabama. Ike warns against

3.
Studebaker's Hawk, the descendant of the famous 1953 Loewy coupe. The Hawks were handsome, but a tired idea in 1962.

4.
Chrysler's Plymouth Fury, all new and the shortest car in its class. Unfortunately, people were beginning to look at bigger cars again.

f New Guinea to Indonesia. Adolph Eichmann. 14 nations guanantee Laos. Rebels take over Algeria, spl
president's power, big defense spending. Court upsets Freedom Rider convictions. Nixon beaten in Cali

5.
Dodge Dart which was a new Plymouth-like car for Dodge.

Detroit's young pushers liked speed—they liked to win—and being in racing meant warring on a competitor (that was fun). Racing meant a chance to get out of the office (more fun), and making a new class of friend (the tracks always attracted the prettiest women, and that was fun, too)—all on the company's money. Ford spent millions of dollars to build special racers to win European runs that were not well known in America. "The biggest thing about it is the internal enthusiasm," said one Ford vice-president. "I don't know how you handle that in dollars, but it's worth something. People in the house need a shot in the arm." That is probably the real reason Detroit went racing: not to improve sales or improve the breed, but because it was fun, and winning the big ones gave the boys and girls in the office a shot in the arm. Detroit finally quit when profits got tight and Congressmen got a little tired of the explanation that dollars spent on safety raised prices but dollars spent on racing were different.

set up dictatorship. Berliners riot against Reds after killing at wall. Thousands of Russians, arms m
ia governor's race, vows to quit politics. Thalidomide tied to birth defects. Sherri Finkbine abortio

6.
Rambler called its standard cars the Classic and built over 450,000 in a year.

NUMBER OF MODELS	
Year	*Quantity*
1949	205
1951	243
1953	210
1955	216
1957	245
1959	239
1961	260
1963	336
1965	348

The killing of the Cardinal was another sign that the economy trend was in retreat. Ford planned the Cardinal as a new type of small car, a world car made of some imported components. The Cardinal was tinier than the Falcon and would have a new European-built V-4 engine and front-wheel drive (the power of the engine would go to the front wheels and pull the car, rather than to the rear wheels as usual to push it). This would have been an engineering sensation for the United States and opened up interior room as well.

Sixty days before job number one was to roll down the line at Louisville the car was canceled. The market was swinging away from gasoline-stingy models, Ford figured, and the radical engineering was running up the production bill—something that means trouble for a low-priced car. General Motors always had this trouble, using radical engineering approaches to small cars like the Corvair and Vega—and running up the cost and price.

Cuba. Senators warn of missiles. Fighting again in Congo. China-Soviet split widens. Russians putti
er drug's use, opens abortion debate. Drug safety bill passed. Black Muslim-police shootout in Los An

Next time we try to build a small car, Lee Iacocca, the Ford executive said, "it will be something we know how to build." Sure enough, when the compact-size Mustang came out in mid-1964 it was conventional with the old six and V-8 engines, and later the small Maverick was completely conventional. The small Pinto that came out in the early 1970s carried a standard transmission, and while it did use an imported V-4, the engine was the well-tested descendant of the engine planned for the Cardinal almost a decade earlier.

7.
The Oldsmobile Starfire hardtop. Flash was not exactly out of fashion.

-missiles in Cuba. Kennedy orders blockade, readies invasion, Khrushchev blinks, Soviet ships turn ba

s. Demonstrations north-south against housing, school, pool bias. KKK cross burnings in Louisiana, c

Economy models were still coming out in 1962. Buick offered a new iron V-6 engine as a cheaper substitute (by ninety dollars) for the aluminum V-8 in the compact Special. The V-6 was dropped a few years later and the tooling sold to American Motors for its Jeeps. When the energy crisis came in the early 1970s, G.M. bought the tooling back and offered the V-6 again in some 1975 models.

Chrysler brought out completely restyled Plymouth and Dodge models, planned when the great retreat from size and power was underway. The

8.
The Chevy II 300 aimed at combating Ford's compact Falcon since the Corvair wasn't doing the job.

siles, bombers withdrawn from Cuba. U.S. proposes hot line to Russia. 1100 Bay of Pigs prisoners ran
Georgia. Ted Kennedy, 30, wins senate seat. James Meredith, negro, enters University of Mississippi.

9.
Exposed taillights had their moment on the Imperial LeBaron.

new Plymouth was 202 inches long, 7.5 inches shorter than the Chevrolet and Ford cars and even the '61 Plymouth. At 3,140 pounds the new Plymouth was 300–400 pounds lighter than the '61 Plymouth.

Dodge was now building three sizes of cars: the compact Lancer which was the Dodge version of the Plymouth Valiant, the Dodge Dart which was the Dodge version of the new smaller Plymouth, and the old full-size Dodge now known as the Custom 880. In fact, Dodge dropped the big 880 in the middle of the 1961 model year, then started building it again in the middle of 1962—an example of how confused the car makers were. Later, to add to the confusion, the Dodge Lancer name was to be killed and the Dart name affixed to the Dodge compact. Chrysler has often found it easier to change names than cars. Today General Motors and Ford are

for $53 million in food, medicine. U.S. pdeges not to invade Cuba, blockade lifted. Vatican II. McN
, ex-Gen. Edwin Walker arrested after leading charge against marshalls, 2 killed, federal troops sent.

supposed to be spending hundreds of millions of dollars to redesign their big cars down to the size of their intermediates. Chrysler appears to be solving the problem by planning to get rid of its big Plymouth and put that big-model name—Fury—on its intermediate, not an unreasonable approach.

American Motors cut down the size of its Ambassador by nine inches, making it just a high-horsepower version of its compact Rambler, and there were complaints that the Ambassador didn't have the handling a 270-h.p. car needs.

Ford had a brand-new size car for 1962, its Fairlane (the name that started out as the top-line model years before). Fairlane was the last of Robert McNamara's practical cars, 197 inches long (against 181 inches for the Falcon), and about the size of the full-size car of seven years earlier. This is the size the car designers of today expect to be the standard of tomorrow. Ford, which beat G.M. with a compact for its medium-priced division (the Mercury Comet), was two years out in front of the competition with this new intermediate-size car. Chevrolet played catchup with its Chevelle, and Plymouth with its Belvedere (and eventually the Fairlane name was dropped for Torino). These moves proved that Ford had not lost its nerve because of the Edsel disaster. "We are like Chinese bandits," said one Ford official. "We hit them and run." For all the innovation (including the Mustang) Ford had a tough time gaining on G.M. and at times looked more like mice on a treadmill than the Chinese bandits.

Chevrolet, realizing its Corvair was no sales match for the Falcon in the small-car market, threw a new model into the fight in 1962—the Chevy II (which lives today as the Nova). The II was 183 inches long, about as plain a car as G.M. had made since 1955, and with new four- and six-cylinder engines. The four, like the Pontiac Tempest four, eventually failed

1962

Production

General Motors	3,741,500
Ford	1,935,200
Chrysler	716,800
American Motors	454,700
Studebaker	87,000
Total	6,935,200

ays South Vietnam winning people over. Poison fog kills 106 in London. Minnesota 21, UCLA 3 in Rose B
omney elected Michigan governor. Kennedy bans bias in federally aided housing. Books: Letting Go (Phi

10.
The intermediate sized car first appeared in 1962 crowding the sales of big cars like this Mercury.

and was killed; it just did not have the guts a 2,600-pound car needed in America.

"I was driving down 12th Street in Detroit the day after Martin Luther King Jr. was murdered," a Detroit reporter recalled, "in a Chevy II with that four-cylinder motor. I was looking for signs of trouble. Then about two blocks in front of me right where the 1967 riot started I saw a mob go after a taxi and the rocks were flying. I floored that car and spun the wheel left to get off 12th. All of a sudden I knew what was wrong with that four.

rnie Kovacs killed in Corvair crash. Mrs. Kennedy makes White House TV tour. Push for New Math start
oth), Ship of Fools (Katherine Porter), Seven Days in May (Knebel-Baily), Another Country (James Baldw

That was the slowest charge and turn I ever made and I can still hear that engine coughing as I pushed the pedal through the floor."

The new Fairlane and Chevy II were major steps in the model proliferation that was to sweep the industry over the next few years. Instead of one type of Ford, there soon were five distinct lines all with a variety of models, engines, and trim packages. The number of models jumped from 216 in 1955 to 296 in 1962 to 370 by 1967. The cost of this variety was enormous and by 1975 Detroit decided the price was too high. E. M. "Pete" Estes, G.M.'s president in 1975, told a reporter that G.M. should halve its five dozen body styles and cut its eight distinct engines to only four (one four-cylinder, two sixes, and one basic V-8, he said).

A major safety development was Detroit's decision to put seat-belt anchors in all cars at the factory. When seat belts were installed at the dealer it was a major operation costing a buyer twenty-five to thirty-five dollars for just the front seat belts. When the anchors were put in at the factories the belts could be hooked up for a few dollars. That move opened the way for factory installation of seat belts on all cars, which came a couple of years later, a voluntary move pushed by safety campaigners.

In the '62s wraparound windshields had about vanished. Detroit was putting cheaper two-ply tires on most models as standard equipment, and with heavier cars and bigger engines, tires were beginning to go at 15,000 miles. This meant customers had to take expensive optional tires or replace the new ones soon, another complaint that eventually helped insure a Federal safety law. The tire problem was finally solved when Detroit gave in and began putting excellent radial tires on cars in the 1970s.

. Cuban embargo tightened. France, Algerian rebels sign truce; right wing terror erupts. Press repor
egregated. Supreme Court moves to redistrict state legislatures. New Orleans segregationists excommur

THE WAGONS

"A station wagon makes me feel . . . kinda married."
—A teenager in 1960.

B. F.'s daughter, John Marquand's famous fictional heiress, certainly would have been driven back to the estate in one. If she had lived in the 1930s instead of the 1920s, Daisy would have driven around in one to see Jay Gatsby before he met that unseemly end in the pool.

That's what the specially built, wood-bodied station wagon was, even for the first few years after World War II. The emphasis was on the word "station," as in meeting the train at the station in Darien for the run to the country place. Of course, the wood always was beautifully varnished; the gardener took care of it. There even were some wood-bodied cars, sedans and convertibles, matching the monied look of the wagons. They also died just a few years after the war, too expensive to build, too costly to buy and too much trouble to take care of in the age of mass production and mass markets. (The surfers of the 1950s discovered the last of the old woodies and made them part of the beach scene until they disintegrated.)

The wagons were the cars most clearly identified with the Golden Age of American automobiles. They were not glamorous; they were the workhorses, the cars that symbolized the society we were building.

Just right for the new house in suburban Primrose Park, the house that wasn't quite finished. Just right to carry the sheet rock for the attic and the plywood panels for the basement. Just right for dragging around the three kids who came one two three (the ice cream stains wiped right off the seats). Just right for the three bags of fertilizer, the sod bought from the discount lawn store because the lawn was being put in from scratch, and for the young cherry trees for the yard. Just right for Shady Hollow Lane because the street wasn't paved yet and it wouldn't be for two years and that wagon could take it. Just right for the once-a-week load-up at the new A&P, because it was three miles away and who wanted that run every day.

They were not quite as good as a car, and they were not quite as good as a truck. They were cold in the winter, rattled all the time, cost $300–500

1.
The Plymouth Suburban of 1949 started the wagon revolution. All metal, low priced, and a fold-down seat, just the thing for the growing suburbs.

2.
The 1952 Ranch Wagon was Ford's move into the market that Plymouth discovered.

more than a car, and were weak on handling, performance and mileage. They were perfect.

Later the wagon became so identified with the unswinging suburban set that dating in Dad's became a handicap. "If my date showed up in a station wagon, I wouldn't go out with him," a teenager told *Motor Trend* in 1960. "I don't know why, but a station wagon makes me feel . . . kinda married."

Some credit Willys with the first modern all-metal wagon. True, Willys

3.
This '48 Ford Woodie was typical of the wagons of the period. The wood panels kept the price up and maintenance was a problem.

did have a metal vehicle they called a wagon, but it looked like a Jeep. The new suburbanite had his fill of Jeeps. He wanted something, but that wasn't it.

Plymouth deserves the credit. After World War II General Motors and Ford threatened to bring out small cars. They killed them. Meanwhile, Chrysler had readied some short-wheelbase models to be competitive and brought them out in 1949. The sedan and coupe never amounted to much. The low-priced (for a wagon), all-metal Plymouth Suburban did—with a fold-down second seat, a real cargo hold, and passenger-car steering.

Compared to today's long, low, sleekly slanted, air-cooled and carpeted wagons, that '49 Suburban looked like a panel truck. But it was a revolution. No more would the wagon be the second or third car of the patrician class: the woodie was off to "a deserved doom," said one magazine.

The next metal wagon was the small Rambler of 1950, sturdy, good on gas, and easy to handle, though too small to carry much cargo.

4.
The Rambler wagon was the first effort to make a small but useful station-wagon. This is a '53, but the first models were out in 1950.

5.
Chevrolet's Nomad wagon, like this 1957 model, was the first station-wagon to be designed with flashy auto styling.

Ford's 1952 Ranch Wagon was dead on. "Old turtle top," Gene Bordinat, Ford's styling director, called it. Today, like the Suburban, it looks like a panel truck: thick roof, sliding glass on the rear side windows. It was Ford's first all-metal wagon, a low-priced two-door with the fold-down back seat. The four-door Ford Country Squires were more expensive and carried decorative wood-like trim. Chevy followed with a wagon on a truck chassis, the Carryall, which looked like a hearse, and Ford had a lead in the wagon field it never relinquished. Somehow Ford understood better what wagon customers wanted. They built a wagon to carry things; G.M. built them to carry Cinderella to the ball or to take the patricians across the country in style (the patricians always flew). In 1966 Ford devised the Dual-Action tailgate: it came down like an ordinary tailgate for loading; or it opened like a door for easy climbing into the back. G.M. answered in 1973 with the clamshell tailgate. It looked great on that slanted-roof wagon, but the owner had to stand patiently out in the rain while the glass slid slowly up into the roof and then the gate slid down slowly under the car.

"We never abandon the traditional thought of what a wagon should be," says Bordinat of Ford. "And we've got no pride." If Ford sees a good idea, it will copy. "G.M. has a lot of pride," he said, noting the tailgate. "They can't bring themselves to copy us."

In 1960 Ford had 32 percent of the wagon production; all G.M. had 31 percent (G.M. always outsells Ford roughly two to one overall in the United States), little American Motors had 19 percent, and Chrysler 16

6.
American Motors came back from the brink of extinction with wagons like this '58 Rambler Rebel.

7.
In the late '50s, the car makers began making wagons longer, fancier and costlier like this 1959 Pontiac Bonneville Safari.

percent. In 1974 Ford took 43 percent of the wagon sales, G.M. 36 percent, Chrysler 14 percent, and American Motors 7 percent. (One of American Motors' problems is the failure to realize that its success was built on station wagons. American Motors put its development dollars into bigger cars, smaller cars, and sportier cars, not wagons).

Ford's '52 Ranch Wagon was 198 inches long to 186 inches for the Plymouth; Plymouth got the message and lengthened the next year. For 1954 Chrysler developed the rear window that rolled into the tailgate before it dropped (before that the glass flipped up while the tailgate flipped down).

Ford put hot engines in its wagons to goose performance. Chevy brought out the first high-style wagon in 1955, the Nomad (and its sister, the Pontiac Safari), a heavily chromed model with the first wraparound rear windows. It was a two-door—two doors look sportier to G.M.—and since four-door wagons are more practical, only 23,000 Nomads were sold in three years. At least the styling message was not lost; the box on wheels was out. Chrysler developed the answer to the third seat in 1957 with the backward-facing seat. This got the third seat off the hump and made it easier to get into the rear.

Volume went from 174,000 in the 1951 model year, or 3 percent of the industry, to 580,000 or 8 percent in 1955, to nearly a million or 17 percent

The compact 1960 Plymouth Valiant wagon.

9.
Wood was out of fashion, but imitation wood became a popular wagon option. The 1961 Ford Country Squire.

STATION WAGON OUTPUT		
Model Year	*Number*	*Percent of Total Production*
1951	175,000	3.3
1953	303,000	4.9
1955	580,000	8.2
1957	844,000	13.6
1959	937,000	16.9
1961	867,000	16.
1963	964,000	13.1
1965	969,000	10.9

by 1959. By 1965 the total was working down to 11 percent as the suburban boom leveled.

In the late 1950s and early 1960s the wagons were long and low with plenty of window glass, with roof racks and with rear ends canting forward to get away from the boxy look. They had chrome and fins, and by the 1960s they were luxury vehicles, carpeted (even the cargo deck) and air-conditioned with stereo, with the biggest engines, and all the power accessories (steering, brakes, seats). A '58 Country Squire carried a 265-h.p. V-8 and would run 0–60 m.p.h. in a neat 12 seconds.

"Almost all of the wagon has been bred out of it," lamented *Consumer Reports* of the new breed. Testers forgot the suburbs had been completed in the decade and a half since Plymouth discovered the Suburban. The basement was paneled, the attic room was finished. The sod was put in long ago and the cherry trees had been flowering for a dozen years. Shady

Hollow was paved in 1954 and the wagons did not go anywhere off-road. The babies were in high school and they did not drip ice cream. And when the folks went out they wanted comfort and good looks.

Handsome, of course, does not mean silly. In 1964 G.M. had another of its station-wagon ideas, the Vista Cruiser Olds and Buick with the raised roof to give them the touring-bus look. Of course, all they raised was the price; you could not see much out of those windows and they let the heat

10.
Plymouth developed the rear facing third seat. This is a 1964 9-passenger Fury.

11.
The raised roof on the 1964 Buick (left), really didn't add much to the wagon's charm. The Buick Special (right), was the smaller, intermediate size wagon.

in. Like the clamshell tailgate, it was an idea that looked better than it worked.

As the wagon market slowed with the aging of the suburbs, two sister markets grew. In the West the high-powered and fancy-looking pickup truck became popular. These had the ruggedness to run off the roads and carry a big load, and with bucket seats, automatic and air, the passenger compartments were as comfortable as any car's.

Next came the van market which grew first as a vacation or recreation vehicle as the suburban folks grew older and wanted more comfortable traveling. Then their children picked the van up, decorated it on the outside with the wild murals and color of the high-times 1970s and on the inside with beds, stereo, and mirrors that would make the old wagons of Primrose Park blush. No carrying fertilizer, sod, or lumber in these offspring of the station wagon. And no worry about feeling married in them, either.

"I never saw too much chrome on those high-class cars."

—Bunkie Knudsen makes a Grand Prix

"It was in London, a foggy night. I was in front of the Claridge," remembers Bill Mitchell, the General Motors styling chief, "and out of the fog comes this Rolls." He still remembers the impression of the sharp edged corners coming up through the mist. When he got back to the drawing board the outline of a new car was implanted in his mind: the Buick Riviera.

The Riviera with its semifastback lines and sharp edges was G.M.'s belated answer to Ford's Thunderbird. Later, as G.M. does, it would swamp the competition with models—the front-wheel drive Oldsmobile Toronado, which was too bulky, Mitchell admitted, and the Pontiac Grand Prix which came out in 1963, too. Then came the Chevrolet Monte Carlo, the Ford Torino Elite and finally the Chrysler Cordoba, all competing in the big personal-car market the big Bird developed. The early Rivieras were the prettiest of them all.

A *Car & Driver* writer said of the Riviera: "It isn't long, and it won't get to a hundred in ten seconds, and it'll never be what you might call one of the low-priced three. But then neither is Sophia Loren."

"That '63 was the peer of all the Rivieras," says Richard Teague, the

Katanga in Congo surrenders to UN. Cuban crisis eases, Russian troops pulling out; Castr
Clemson, Tulane desegregate. New drug test regulations after thalidomide. Senate attack

1.
Studebaker's plastic bodied Avanti, the last, lovely throw of the dice: snake eyes.

admiring designer from American Motors. Mitchell still is proud of it, but not what happened to it later. The sharp lines deteriorated, the car got wider and longer. The '63 was 208 inches long and 76.6 inches wide. The '75 was 15 inches longer, 3 inches wider, and about 650 pounds heavier. It's not a new story. "The marketing people told us we lost a lot of sales because it only had four seats, so we widened it," Mitchell said with a shrug.

A similar fate befell the '65 Mustang. "We started off with a rather concise Mustang," said Gene Bordinat, the Ford stylist. But someone wanted bigger engines. After all, the Mustang was to be "boss," and bigger engines

a; they unite with Nasser, form UAR, then separate again. Five U.S. copters shot down in Vietnam. Ke
ols, churches. Court orders free lawyers for indigents. Alcatraz closed. Draft extended 4 years. T

meant heavier supports and bigger tires. "The demise of the little compromise sports car," said Bordinat, more in sorrow.

Rarely do the second- or third-year versions of a model mean styling improvement. If the first-year car looks good, someone wants to add something. "It's like rewriting a piece of music; you bastardize it. Or like Hollywood with a book," says Mitchell. Still, there is occasional improvement: the '56 Ramblers were almost weird; by 1959 the changes had produced an acceptable sedan and a handsome station wagon.

In general, the '63 cars were a handsome lot. The chrome was being stripped away and Pontiac's Grand Prix was a winner for it. "They wanted a Riviera," said Mitchell, but could not get the new body. So Pontiac took one of the standard bodies and cleaned it up. "I give them credit. They had the guts to leave the chrome off," Mitchell said.

2.
The '63 Rambler with its simpler, squared off design might be in style today.

independent; Jomo Kenyatta prime minister. Strategic Hamlits in Vietnam. Christine Keeler-John Profu
l killer Nathan Leopold paroled. Atomic sub Thresher sinks, 129 lost. Thousands arrested in Birmingh

3.
A foggy night in London town; when the mist cleared, Bill Mitchell had the Buick Riviera.

Bunkie Knudsen, the Pontiac division manager, said he always "had a great deal of respect" for cars such as the Rolls-Royce and Bentley. "I never saw too much chrome on those high-class cars," he says. They leave the chrome off. "The cheapest car is the one with all the chrome." So Bunkie pulled the brightwork off his Grand Prix and produced a handsome auto.

Even American Motors, flush with the profits of the compact revolution, produced a simple and genuinely good-looking '63 (Rambler was *Motor Trend's* Car of the Year). If you slapped a Mercedes-type grille on the '63 or '64 Rambler and pulled off a bit of body chrome the car would look much like Detroit's planned cars of the late 1970s. American Motors, which built 480,365 cars that year, went downhill from then on. Ford's Fairlane, Chevy's Chevelle, and Plymouth's Belvedere were competing against

ernment sex scandal. Ben-Gurion quits in Israel, Pope John XXIII dies. Russian man, woman in space.
test; court upsets sit-in convictions; Medgar Evers murdered in Mississippi, Byron de la Beckwith charg

the Rambler soon, with newer models and bigger dealer groups, and the trend was to size and power, not American Motors' strong points. The new president was Roy Abernethy (Romney had turned to politics) and he was competent. "But Roy was a big man and he liked big cars," Jim Dunne, an editor of *Popular Science* said. When he tried to compete against the Big Three on their ground the Ramblers were flattened. Only when buyers swung again toward economy did American Motors, flashing Teague's pretty Hornets, Gremlins, and Pacers, bounce back.

Chrysler made a startling recovery in 1963 too. The short Plymouths and Dodges of 1962 were lengthened three inches. The hemihead engine, killed years before, was pushed into hot '64 models, and Chrysler-built cars began crowding into the winning circles of the stock car ovals. The small Plymouth Valiant and Dodge Dart were restyled; gone was the Italian look,

4.
Designers were taking off the chrome and beginning to push up the power and Pontiac, with cars like the Bonneville Vista hardtop, were scoring in the market.

lists demonstrate in Vietnam, priest immolates self, Diem attacks pagodas, 15,000 U.S. troops there, st
acquitted. Massive Freedom Marches, Detroit (100,000), Washington (200,000). Court bars school praye

5.
Chrysler junked its short car approach, brought back its big engines, and made a startling recovery with cars like this Dodge Polara.

in was a simple, squarish design, and the two compacts began creeping up on the competition. Those two models kept Chrysler in business in the lean years later on.

Chrysler's 1963 production shot up to 1,047,722 from 716,809 in 1962, almost a 50-percent gain. By 1964 Chrysler was building 1.5 million cars. "We styled them for aerodynamics and we were doing just great," said Lynn Townsend, the clean-broom president who took over in 1960. "That racing image brought youth to us"—particularly with the intermediate-size cars like the Road Runner—"but when we hit the environmental years, our business in the intermediates just fell right on the floor."

The first antipollution device, a small blow-by valve to control crankcase fumes, was put on all the '63s. Later public pressure and the Clean Air Act of 1970 called for much more dramatic improvements. Detroit had a problem because many of the people calling for cleaner cars just did not like cars, so any answer short of an outright ban would not satisfy them. Then the government felt the best way to improve the air was to make the

ts. Test ban treaty with USSR. Ben Bella elected first Algerian president. Pope Paul VI; Vatican II
eralized guard forces integration at University of Alabama. Equal work, equal pay bill. Valachi revea

pollution standards a little tougher each year. This meant the car makers were constantly working for an improvement, then changing the system again after one year—before they even got it working right, like cutting off the dog's tail an inch at a time so it wouldn't hurt as much.

To meet the tough rules of the 1970 law Detroit began de-tuning its engines—modifying them for emission control rather than for power and economy—while cars were getting heavier and using bigger engines. This brought mileage down to the 10-m.p.g. range on ordinary Fords and Chevrolets—and station wagons were giving 7 or 8 miles a gallon. This low mileage came just as the oil crisis hit, triggered by the 1973 Mideast War, and as gasoline prices began to soar. The money and manpower tied up in emission controls plus the spending on safety cut ordinary design spending drastically.

6.
Chrysler's compacts like this Dodge Dart were restyled and the simple design proved popular for years.

mes. Caribbean hurricane kills 6,000. Adenauer quits in Germany. Military coupe in South Vietnam.
osa Nostra. Birth Pill Enovid called safe. Kennedy baby Patrick dies. 4 girls killed in Birmingham

7.
Ford's intermediate Mercury Meteor was just too plain to succeed and didn't.

"You have a fantastic car," said Harold Sperlich, a Ford vice-president, in 1974. "It's lighter, more environmental, a better car. It costs $400 million. The finance guy sits at the end of the table and says, 'We don't have $400 million. We've got $380 million and the government says we've got to spend $300 million for bumpers.'" With the press on to produce high-mileage cars, however, G.M. says it will spend $15 billion in the middle and late 1970s, with the bulk of it going to redesign smaller, fuel-stingier cars.

In 1963, though, it was upward and onward. The recession was over and production zoomed to 7.6 million, the best year since 1955. Only Studebaker did not share the prosperity. The plastic-bodied Avanti was brought out early in the year, although like any rush job, Studebaker had trouble getting it into production. The company set its '64 model preview in late summer of 1963 at Utah's Salt Flats. There Studebaker sent its Larks and

ther murdered; report U.S. OKed coupe. US-USSR hotline. French farmers riot against government. JFK
oing. Sabin Polio vaccine. John Kennedy assassinated in Dallas. LBJ takes oath in plane. Dallas pol

Avantis whipping across the sands at 120 to 150 miles an hour to prove its cars were up-to-date. The Avanti had already won raves, but one sporty car could not save Studebaker, and in December production was stopped in the United States. Studebakers were built in Canada for a while, a corporate gimmick to have some cars to offer dealers so the dealers could not sue. As the dealers died the Canadian output was folded.

The car makers also were deep into the warranty war in 1963. The problem was that car quality was slumping. The engines and gadgets were more complicated, meaning there was more to break down. Power steering, automatics, power windows, seats, and air conditioning, for example, un-

8.
The Ford Galaxie, with its Thunderbird-like roof line, was as big as a medium priced model.

wheat sale to Russia. Greeks, Turks fight in Cyprus, truce. LBJ plans to carry on war in Vietnam. C
arrest Lee Harvey Oswald. Oswald murdered by night club owner Jack Ruby. Warren Commission to invest

9.
Air-conditioning was becoming common in cars like the Oldsmobile Starfire Coupe in 1963, a symbol of the swing to luxury.

1963

Production

General Motors	4,077,300
Ford	1,963,900
Chrysler	1,047,700
American Motors	480,400
Studebaker	67,900
Total	7,637,200

known on a low-priced car a decade before, were common and liable to break down. Production was getting sloppy, too. If five screws were needed to keep a pad on the side of the door, one would be missing from the start and another would fall off within a week of purchase. Detroit's idea was to increase the warranty, which was cheaper than improving the car. First they were increased to one full year or 12,000 miles. Then Chrysler went to a five-year or 50,000-mile warranty for its engine and drive-train parts (all the parts that drive the car), and then other car makers went to two years or 24,000 miles instead of following Chrysler.

Buyers found it easy to get a warranty but hard to get their cars fixed. The warranties were in small type and lawyers' language aimed at disqualifying car owners. Finally Ralph Nader and his crew attacked the industry, the Federal Trade Commission investigated, and Congress outlawed the wild but dishonest guarantee claims. The car makers went back to the one-year warranty, promising that this time they meant it.

Perhaps the strongest symbol of the move to luxury was the dramatic

:es U.S. Embassy; U.S. stops Cuban trade. America condems apartiad in South Africa. Newspaper strikes
vows to carry Kennedy programs. Studebaker quits US auto making. Washington predicts war end by 1965

growth of air conditioning. In 1955 only 129,000 cars took the then-new coolers. By 1960 the figure was 414,000 or 7 percent of the total; by 1963 the figure topped 1 million, 14 percent of production; by 1965 it was 2 million, nearly a quarter of the output; and by 1973 three-fourths of the model run carried air conditioning despite the $300–400 price and the lower mileage.

10.
The Chevrolet Biscayne and the sedans were losing out to higher priced Impalas and hardtops by 1963.

New York, Cleveland. Oscars: Lawrence of Arabia, Gregory Peck (To Kill a Mockingbird), Anne Bancroft (
ex Karras suspended for betting. Who's Afraid of Virginia Woolf wins critics award. Chateaugay takes

Just listing features offered on the '63s showed Detroit's direction. The four-speed stick shift was in as an extra-cost option to give a little more takeoff at the top light, not as an economy accessory. Ford had the industry's first fully synchronized three-speed shifter, too, good for the same crowd.

Chevrolet brought out its super-sleek Stingray Corvette, and Chevy offered V-8s ranging from 195 to 425 h.p. Ford put a V-8 in its small Falcon (for the Sprint hardtop and convertible models). Pontiac junked its aluminum V-8 (and offered an iron-block V-8) and Chrysler junked its aluminum sixes. Aluminum did not catch on with customers and there were improved thin-wall casting techniques for iron.

G.M. offered the tilt-way steering wheel to allow the pudgy to get in their big cars a bit easier.

G.M.'s Buick Special, Olds F-85, and Pontiac Tempest compact models grew four inches longer and the items in demand were bucket seats and floor consoles.

Studebaker tried something else, making seat belts standard on its cars in February of 1963. We know what happened to them.

AIR-CONDITIONING INSTALLATIONS

Model Year	*Number*	*Percent of Total Production*
1955	129,000	1
1956	176,000	3
1957	228,000	4
1958	195,000	5
1959	345,000	6
1960	414,000	7
1961	438,000	8
1962	757,000	11
1963	1,032,000	14
1964	1,412,000	18
1965	2,061,000	23
1975	4,500,000	70

hrushchev chickened. France vetoes Britain for Common Market. Quebec separatists form; bombings foll
buster fails. 413 arrested protesting moviehouse bias in Baltimore; Maryland archbishop bars discrimi

"How far, how soon, Daddy?"

—Pontiac's GTO

Gran Turismo Omologato. In America that became a single word—GTO. The Pontiac gang did not bring the GTO out with a big splash; just a small announcement to an unwaiting world that Pontiac had a new model. "GTO appeared on the American scene like a Methodist minister leaving a massage parlor," wrote David Davis Jr., who ran *Car & Driver* magazine then. There was a story that Pontiac was trying to slip the car past the General Motors brass and the other jealous G.M. divisions. Some of the top executives did not know about the car until they saw Pontiac's little announcement, then challenged the division's right to push out a new model without upstairs OK, especially with the growing safety ruckus. Pontiac found a subclause under the G.M. constitution allowing the variation, and anyway it was done.

"My first ride in a GTO left me with a feeling like losing my virginity, going into combat, and tasting my first draft beer all in about seven seconds," Davis wrote later (*Car & Driver's* cover for its '64 GTO test showed the Pontiac bearing down on a Ferrari and the headline read "Tempest GTO: 0–100 in 11.8 sec.").

What Pontiac had done was to jam its big V-8 engine into its smaller

Riots in Canal Zone, 23 dead; Panama ousts U.S. diplomats. LBJ pledges aid to South Vietn LBJ calls for war on poverty, a great society. Barry Goldwater seeks GOP nomination. Mi

1.
Pontiac's GTO, the first of the muscle cars. Not the thing to drive to a Sierra Club meeting.

and lighter compact-intermediate, the Tempest. Until then the biggest engines had been reserved for the big cars. Pontiac loaded the model with hotrod gear. It was super; it was muscle.

"I remember that the GTO slammed out of the hole like it was being fired from a catapult," Davis wrote, "that the tach needle flung itself across the dial like a windshield wiper, that the noise from those three two-throat carburetors on that heavy old 389-cubic-inch Pontiac V-8 sounded like some awful doomsday Hoover-God sucking up sinners."

"It was not," Davis wrote, "a car that anyone would drive to a meeting

Germany. Vietcong on attack. McNamara sees U.S. troops out of Vietnam by end of '65, visits Saigon,
son, Macomb, Miss. Malcolm X breaks with Black Muslims. 8 steel companies charged with price fixing.

of the Sierra Club." Pontiac had created a new species, the supercar, the muscle cars that were to quiver and roar at the stop lights for the next half decade, tearing forward and out of sight at the first hint of green, super street rods, fresh from the factory with special treatment from the dealer. They were cheaper and more reliable than the big cars with the super engines that required a crew of mechanics to assemble and keep together.

The GTO, not a super handler, offered raw power, American style. Davis said the GTO was a car that "let you climb inside and then asked you, 'how far, how soon, Daddy?' " When you floored it, "suddenly the trees were all

2.
The Studebaker Commander. The South Bend, Indiana company folded its U.S. production at the end of 1963.

e aid pledged, Westmoreland named U.S. commander. Fighting in Cyprus, UN troops in. Rightest revolt
w civil rights bill passed. 3 civil rights workers missing in Mississippi, FBI enters, finds bodies,

3.
Chevrolet finally had an intermediate, the Chevelle.

blurred and you were looking good—if a little pale." The first GTO was a plain car: no special chrome bath, no wall-to-wall decals, no spoilers, no joke names like "Boss" or "The Judge" or "Roadrunner." Just straight-ahead power.

"Gas was cheap, we had lots of it, and power was king. The guy who could go fastest was the hero; the guy who went slowest was the chump; and the guy who had to walk to the dairy mart we won't even talk about," wrote Richard Benyo describing life when he graduated from Jim Thorpe High School in Pennsylvania in 1964. They were, he recalled, the days of cherry cokes, 25-cent-a-gallon gasoline, black pants with pink piping down the sides, and "the Original Dick Clark American Bandstand every afternoon from Philadelphia, 'Silhouettes' by the Rays, 'Sixteen Candles' by the

---

het Lao attack; U.S. arms rightists. Khrushchev visits USSR. UN quits Congo after four years, Moise T
ed quickly. Mob of 800 whites attacks integrationist parade in St. Augustine, Fla. Escobedo decision

Crests, Frankie Avalon, Annette, rate-a-record, *77 Sunset Strip, Route 66, Maverick*, and . . . cars."

It was another boom year for automobiles, the second in a row, with 1964 production up to 7.7 million. Only American Motors was not sharing in the good times. Number four had a newly styled Rambler American, the first real redo for the little car since 1950. It was neat and slim, four inches longer, with curved side windows (the coming thing), but Rambler was on the way down. "Ramblers were, you see, sort of the bottom of the barrel. Like out of the Top Pop 40 and all that," Benyo wrote.

The big news was the arrival of Chevrolet's Chevelle, the intermediate or middle-size car a couple of years behind Ford's Fairlane (just as G.M.'s Riviera was a few years behind Ford's Thunderbird, just as Chevy's Camaro was a few years behind Ford's Mustang). G.M. came on like the thundering herd. The wheelbases of three compacts—Pontiac's Tempest,

4.
Restyled Chrysler Valiant compact which was more of a sales success than the earlier, more dramatically styled small car

e on top; New Congo rebellion, U.S. aids suppression. Mexico refuses to break Cuban ties. Riots in S
t rules police may not question suspect without rights warning. Antipoverty bill passed. Goldwater d

5.
The Rambler American was a remarkably clean design for a small car, but the buyers were looking for power and prestige again.

Buick's Special, and the Olds F-85—went up three inches, in effect making them intermediates and part of the Chevelle family.

Cadillac's fins went down quite a bit but the engine went up to 429 c.i.d. from 390, which meant the best could run past 120 m.p.h. That was much like the industry trend: power was up (even the Corvair got a boost to 164 c.i.d. from 145); interior trim was aimed to look luxurious; and the outside styling was conservative—chrome was pulled off, the metal sculpturing was at a minimum, windows and windshields were bigger, and the big-car look was in.

As evidence that the Age of Hedonism was flowering, Cadillac was developing its mink test: girls in mink coats would get in and get out of test Cadillacs, sit up and lie back, all to make sure that the minks and the Cadillac's upholstery went together, that the mink coats did not catch or

bodian rioters attack U.S. embassy; LBJ says U.S. will stand firm in Vietnam, U.S. charges ships attac
remism in defense of liberty is no wrong; wins GOP nomination with Miller for VP. Race riots in NYC,

discolor on Cadillac seats. All this at the same time G.M. was explaining that it could not force safety down the car buyers' throats. Had Ralph Nader known about the mink-test program Detroit might have been laughed into regulation. G.M. also brought out its vistavision station wagons in mid-1964, imitating the look of the big Greyhound touring buses.

At Ford the small Falcon received a major redo and the emphasis was on the luxury options and engines. The standard two-door Falcon without options still had a list price of $1,985, but for the Futura Hardtop, listed at $2,315 and loaded with options, the price was close to $3,000 before discount. Thunderbird's strange roadster effort appeared for the last time in 1964—this was the standard T-Bird with a removable section fitted over the rear seats of the convertible aimed at turning it into a two-seater. The Mercury Meteor, a short-lived Mercury version of the Fairlane, was killed. Some of the technical experiments of the past years were fading in the 1964 swing to conservative styling and engineering; developments such as

1964

Production

General Motors	3,956,600
Ford	2,145,900
Chrysler	1,242,200
American Motors	393,900
Studebaker	500
Total	7,739,100

6.
The big Buick Wildcat.

Gulf of Tonkin; U.S. planes attack North Vietnam; Congress OKs any retribution. USSR orbits 3-man sp
ter, Jersey City, N. Philadelphia. Hoffa convicted of jury tampering, gets 8 years. LBJ wins Democra

7.
Compacts have grown in size. By 1964, the Olds F-85 Cutlass was really an intermediate like the Chevelle.

the Pontiac transaxle and the aluminum engines were disappearing. Car makers had developed thin-wall casting techniques that allowed them to make the iron blocks lighter, lessening the advantage of the more expensive aluminum.

With all the emphasis on luxury and power the number of car buyers opting out of Detroit's dream machines began to grow again. Import sales were up to 484,000 in 1964, a gain of 100,000 from 1963. By 1968 import sales pushed to 1 million, fought off the challenge in the early 1970s of Detroit's subcompact cars, the Ford Pinto, Chevy Vega, and American Motors' Gremlin, jumped to 1.7 million by 1973, and surged even in the recession year of 1975, taking one of every five new-car sales here. They sold well even though the imported car at $4,000 was more expensive than a small stripped American model.

In 1964 the Volkswagen took better than 60 percent of the import sales in the United States. During the next decade the Japanese mounted a major assault on the U.S. market as Toyota and Datsun sold small cars just above

ip. Riots in Saigon. Khrushchev ousted, allowed to live in Moscow; Brezhnev, Kosygin rule. China tes
nination; Humphrey for Veep. 24 Negro churches burned in Mississippi. Warren report out; find no cons

the Volkswagen class. Subaru was in the same range, while Mazda sold the first really popular rotary-engine car and Honda developed a successful tiny car that sold well in the gasoline crisis with its boast of 39 m.p.g. Detroit decided to join with the Japanese instead of fighting them. Ford and Chevrolet began selling Japanese-made pickup trucks and Chrysler sold a Mitsubishi-built model (from the folks who gave you the Zero, one reporter quipped) named the Dodge Colt. For 1976 G.M. decided to bring in a Japanese car instead of its German Opel. The imports began picking up in 1964 and probably could have been stopped then, but Detroit, concentrating on power and size instead, was not interested. And American quality was slipping.

The safety war escalated in 1964, too. Threatened with national legislation and action by individual states, Detroit made seat belts standard equipment on January 1, 1964. Even this was too late to stop the consumer safety movement. In summer the Congress told the government's General Services Administration to work up a set of safety standards for the cars the government buys. Once the Federal government was insisting on changes for safety, Detroit knew it would have to make them on all cars. Detroit also was finding itself hard pressed to explain why all cars did not have padded dashes and visors, impact-absorbing steering columns, or dual-brake systems. Detroit executives could no longer brush off the demands with jokes; they were forced to try to explain from the witness chairs of congressional committees, and the legislators had the habit of talking back to the auto men.

Frederic Donner, the G.M. chairman under whose stewardship gumshoes were sent after Ralph Nader, told the Senate that "if we were to force on people things they are not prepared to buy (like safety equipment), we would face a consumer revolt."

IMPORTS

Year	*Sales*	*Percent of Total U.S. Car Market*
1954	33,000	negligible
1955	58,000	negligible
1956	98,000	1.7
1957	207,000	3.5
1958	379,000	8.1
1959	614,000	10.2
1960	499,000	7.6
1961	379,000	6.5
1962	339,000	4.9
1963	386,000	5.1
1964	484,000	6.0
1965	569,000	6.1
1974	1,369,000	15.7

device. Fighting on Cambodian border. Whites rescued in Congo. U.S. base near Saigon attacked. Fais
r in JFK murder. Walter Jenkins, LBJ aide, quits after morals arrest. 2 Negroes in University of Miss

8.
The Mercury Marauder. Whatever it was, it wasn't the Turnpike Cruiser.

That, as Ralph Nader noted in *Unsafe at Any Speed*, caused the *Medical Tribune* to raise the image of "sans-culotte consumers, waving red flags, attacking the castles of General Motors dealers, determined to rip seat belts, dual-braking systems, left-hand mirrors, safety tires, padded dashboards, etc., out of every car or die in the attempt."

After the safety law was passed the car makers were able to come up with major improvements, and on their own. The collapsing steering column developed by G.M. was a major safety improvement, and the glass manufacturers developed safer windshields. The price the car makers and car owners paid for Detroit's early resistance was a flood of government proposals and orders that did little to further the cause of real safety and pushed up the cost of new cars. A reaction finally set in when the government ordered the interlock system on all cars: The car would not start unless seat and shoulder belts were buckled on. Stung by voter anger, Congress itself voted those off cars in the mid-1970s.

oses Saud in Arabia. More aid pledged to Saigon. LBJ plans new Panama Canal. Sugar bowl: Alabama 12,
cefully. LBJ carries 44 states, wins presidency. Married: Liz & Richard Burton; Anne Bancroft-Mel Br

9.
The intermediate Fairlane from Ford, once a no-sex plain car, was getting the full trim treatment by 1964.

10.
Chrysler had come back strong in the market by 1964 with models like this big Dodge Polara hardtop.

issippi 7. Surgeon general calls smoking health hazard. Russia wins winter Olympics, U.S. wins in su
NY World's Fair opens to civil rights demonstrations. Oscars to Tom Jones; Sidney Portier (Lilies of

THE CONVERTIBLE

"In the age of air-conditioning, real air has lost its value."

—A front-page story in *The New York Times*

No more will the kid with the DA throw that look at your girl from his top-down convertible. No more will you see a rag top pull away and have that pang, knowing it could be you if only, if only. The convertible is dead.

The station wagon was for suburbanites, all lumber and children. The hardtop was for the upwardly mobile, all gray flannel and brief cases. The convertible—ah, that was the glamour car in the Golden Age, that was for lovers.

Its image was the open road, the wind in your face, her hair blowing back, and then parking at night to look at the stars. There certainly was a sex image. "Not only is it a sex symbol, but it signifies freedom, lack of restraint, and a fun attitude toward life," said Dr. Jean Rosenbaum in his book *Is Your Volkswagen a Sex Symbol?* It may even represent bisexuality, he figured. "In envy of women, men may wish to have an opening of their own," he said. If that's a little heavy, just remember that owning a convertible set you just a bit apart from the pattern of life developing across postwar America. If you were filthy rich, your soft top said you made it your way and didn't care what everyone else thought. If you were young and even raggedy, your soft top said you just didn't care. And, as important

CONVERTIBLES		
Year	*Number*	*Percent of Total Production*
1949	201,000	4
1951	140,000	3
1953	155,000	3
1955	212,000	3
1957	266,000	4
1959	258,000	5
1961	264,000	5
1963	489,000	7
1965	507,000	6
1974	28,000	negligible

1.
The 1957 Ford steeltop convertible. After one good year, sales went to nothing.

2.
A man and his dog and the '48 Ford. Ford, more than other auto makers, tried to keep the convertible going.

as the symbolism, they were pretty, pretty cars, at least at first. Everyone wanted one.

They're finished now. American Motors stopped building ragtops after 1968, Chrysler built its last in the '71 model run, then Ford dropped out and General Motors began eliminating them, until by 1976 only one, the $13,000 Eldorado, was in production. They peaked in the Golden Age: In 1950 some 206,000 were built, in 1960 more than 283,000, and 507,000 in 1965. Never had so many convertibles been built in a single year and never again were—or will—so many be built.

Some say it was air-conditioning that killed the soft top. But the answer is more complicated. There just was no room in modern America for a car that represented the free spirit. Twentieth-century reality kept butting in. The star of the Golden Age died of culture shock.

"I got behind a sand-and-gravel truck on the freeway. Nearly blasted me out of the car and took my skin off," Kenneth Spenser, a Ford car designer once told a reporter who asked why they vanished. "In the age of air-conditioning, real air has lost its value," *The New York Times* said in its front-page farewell tribute to them.

In the age of the freeway, speed of 70 m.p.h. turned a breeze into a hurricane, and the soot and dirt of the big ditch peppered a rider's face.

3.
The '51 Ford convertible was one of the prettiest softtops. Convertibles accounted for 3 percent of production that year.

4.
By 1963, convertibles accounted for 7 percent of the production with compacts like this popular Ford Falcon helping sales.

"I love my convertible," a Detroit secretary said, but she would not drive with her top down on a freeway. "It's too dirty."

"When I came out here from the East I had a convertible," Frank Wylie, a Detroiter, reminisced. "You could drive up through the hills and down through the valleys, top down, and you felt like you owned the world. But you can't look at much at 70 miles an hour."

In the age of imitation the hardtop and vinyl-covered roof stole the sharp look of the convertible. Even the word "hardtop" came from the expression "hardtop convertible" which is what G.M. called its style-setting, flat-roof, no-center-pillar body style of the 1950s and 1960s (which, like the convertible, is gone now).

In the age of Ralph Nader and consumerism the dangers of a rollover became an issue, and rattles and leaks that were part of the convertible became unacceptable. In the age of crime, protection of the soft top was impossible. Tops were slashed for the fun of it. In the age of untrained mechanics, service was a headache and replacing a top was a major enterprise. And in the age of bored workers and efficiency-minded managers the convertible was just a big nuisance on the assembly line.

"After you designed a car, you tried to fit a convertible onto it," one stylist explained, and as the rear panels began flowing into the roof of the 1950s this became a harder job. Without the steel roof, the convertible needed tougher sides and floors to hold it together, which meant extra design in manufacturing and then extra repair costs.

"You've got to put up with some problems with convertibles," a Ford product planner said. There are the birds and the tree drippings, the wind noise and the tops that flapped and bellowed. The rear seating was tight

5.
The wet look was in. The car is a 1963 Chevy Impala ragtop.

6.
The 1959 Biarritz. And who could ask for anything more.

because of the space needed for the top. The rear window always was trouble; plastic scratched and the glass broke if the top did not fit correctly. Sometimes the rain leaked in, and it gets pretty cold in winter, fall, or even spring in much of America.

"You're almost grateful for some warm fumes," said Joe Strum, a Chrysler official. "It took the strength of 10,000 men to lock the top down," remembered Fred Taylor, managing editor of the *Wall Street Journal*.

Yet the love was there, too. "That top was down all the time," said Gene Bordinat, a Ford vice-president. "The sun burned the hell out of me in the summer, and in the winter I kept the top down till water froze in my hair. And my wife always complained that it ruined her hair. So why did I have it? It was a great car for watching polo."

The first automobiles built were actually open—roadsters, they were

7.
The Pontiac Bonneville. Big engines, leather bucket seats, consoles and the like may have pushed the convertible price too high.

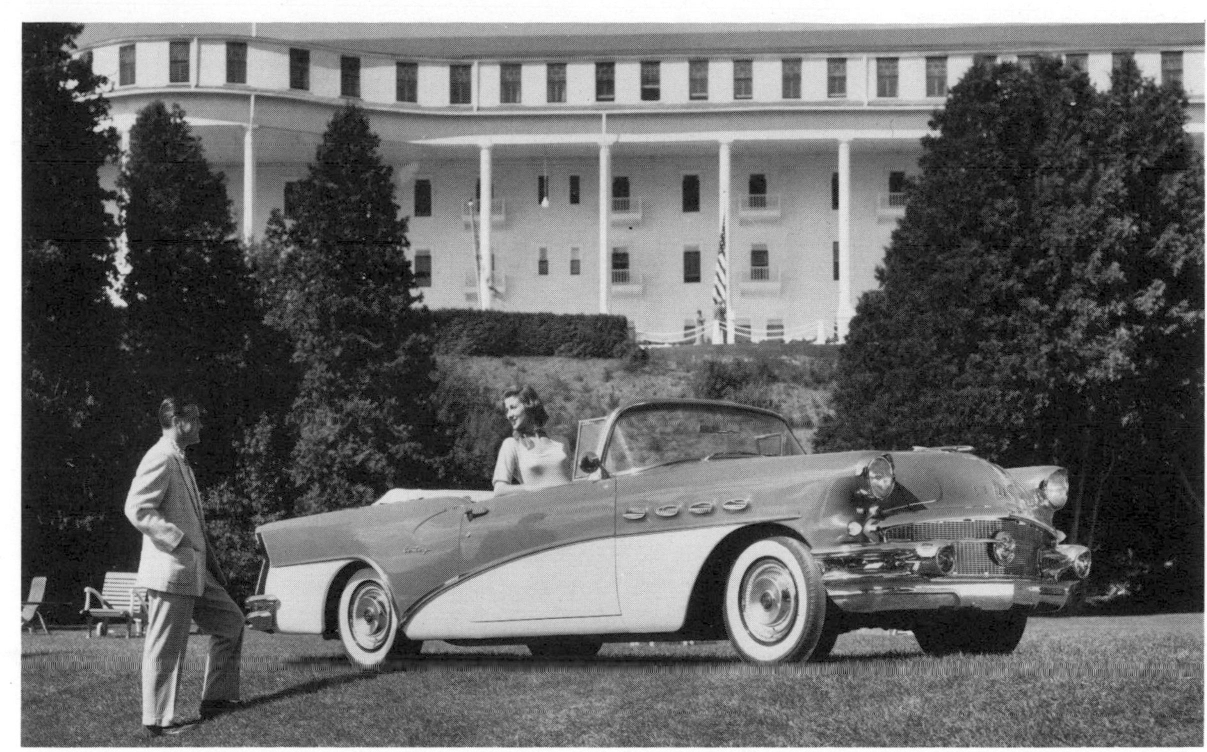

8.
The Buick Century. The convertible did have a sexy image, but dig that 1956 suit.

9.
The small 1948 Nash Ambassador. Notice how high the riders sit.

called, not convertibles. Then the techniques for building cars with enclosed roofs were developed in the 1920s, opening the way for the widespread use of the automobile.

Ford worked hardest in the Golden Age to develop new convertibles, all of which failed: the four-door Lincoln convertibles that were introduced in 1961, the '60 Thunderbird with the disappearing top, and the steel-roof convertible of 1957. That model, the Skyliner, with its motors, switches, solenoids and circuit breakers, "was like launching a rocket," its designer said. The Skyliner was killed before the second-stage version—with fewer motors—went into production.

"That's a good one to learn a lesson from about what people say and what people mean," Bordinat said. "People told us 'I'd buy one if it had a steel roof.' After one good year sales went to nothing. There were always people who wanted a convertible. Then they put the top down and they didn't like it at all."

Some believe that the convertible did not have to die and that Detroit gave it a push towards oblivion. After all, millions of Americans ride

10.
The '49 Hudson. Before freeways, driving speeds were lower, and riding with the top down was a pleasure.

11.
The 1959 Plymouth Fury. Air-conditioning and the fast driving speed of the highway helped kill the convertible.

motorcycles and others bounce in open dune buggies proving that some wind in the face is acceptable. One theory is that when the inexpensive (around $1,500) early postwar ragtops grew in popularity the manufacturers loaded them with expensive optional equipment, possibly pricing them beyond the range of the natural buyers, the young. But that's only theory. "You run and run after some things and you just run out of breath," said Strum of Chrysler, who loved them.

The sliding sun roof, a European innovation, now appears on American cars, but it's not the same. Still, the Granny dress came back; so did the suit jacket with the belt in the back, and so did the Tiffany lamp. Will the convertible come back? Not likely.

"What's the cause and effect when something's dying?" said one auto man in Detroit. "We had other fish to fry."

"MUSTANG! MUSTANG! MUSTANG!"
—*Time* magazine

"The trim white car rolled restlessly through the winding roads of Bloomfield Hills, like a high-strung pony dancing to get started on its morning run. In that auto-conscious Detroit suburb, where people can spend whole evenings talking about the virtues of a taillight, it did not go long unnoticed despite its lack of identifying insignia. Groups of children on their way to school turned to stare at it and point. The driver of a Volkswagen raised his fingers in a V-for-victory sign. As the car picked up speed and headed southward toward Detroit, a flickering trace of satisfaction crossed its driver's hawklike face. He carefully knocked the ash from his Ignacio Haya Gold Label cigar into the shiny new dashboard tray. At each traffic light, his dark eyes surveyed the car's interior and his fingers roamed over every piece of metal and fabric within reach. At one light, the driver of a Chevrolet Impala pulled alongside and mouthed through his closed window: 'Is that it?' He was left behind in the exhaust. As the white car approached a school bus and slowed again, the windows flew up and the children inside chanted: 'Mustang! Mustang! Mustang!' "

That improbable prose was the opening of *Time* magazine's cover story on Lee Iacocca and his Mustang, the car that propelled him to the presi-

U.S. bombs Ho Chi Minh Trail in Laos. Indonesia quits UN. U.S. planes bomb North Vietnam
LBJ calls for Great Society. Gerald Ford House minority leader. 18 charged with '64 civi

1.

The American Motors Marlin. The effort to create a sporty car by putting a fastback roof on a big body produced a whale-like look.

dency of Ford Motor Company. *Newsweek* put Iacocca and Mustang on its cover that same spring week in 1964 (the Mustang, called a '65, was shown in April of 1964), the first time the two news magazines ever carried the same cover story in the same week. That's how important automobiles were a decade ago, and what excitement the little pony stirred.

The Mustang was born of Ford's desire to create a poor man's T-Bird, something they had been thinking of since the two-passenger Bird was killed. Ford also aimed to catch up with the bucket-seat pizzaz market Chevrolet's Monza had uncovered, and was bidding to break out of unselling, dull-looking cars, a heritage from 1960. When the car market began to boom early in the 1960s the big sleek Chevys showed their tailpipes to Ford. Work on the Mustang project began in 1961 and in September 1962 the final go-ahead was given. Just eighteen months later the car was in production. Iacocca rejected a proposal for a two-seater, figuring correctly that the market would not be big enough. From the beginning the styling team under Joseph Oros knew it had a winner. It also had a

down leftists. Red cosmonaut walks in space. U.S. Gemini missions aloft, in orbit, space walking mat
Alabama, arrested; police attack Selma rights march, mass protests across nation. Federal troops prote

2.
Pontiac held chrome to a minimum on its Grand Prix and produced a handsome automobile. Floor console and bucket seats made it a competitor for Thunderbird.

1965

BUCKET SEATS

Model Year	Number	Percent of Total Production
1961	313,000	6
1962	959,000	14
1963	1,227,000	17
1964	1,465,000	19
1965	2,053,000	23

3.
Plymouth put a fastback roof with a gigantic rear window on its Valiant compact, but the Barracuda was never a serious challenger to Mustang.

g Reds. Camera landed on moon. W. Germany-Israel establish relations. Vietnam buildup: 21,000 in Ju
elma-Montgomery march; white Detroiter Viola Liuzzo murdered in Alabama, KKK men arrested, acquitted.

4.
The Corvair Corsa was close to a sports car in handling, but the car looked tired compared to the new Mustang.

long hood, short trunk, and tight back seat, but with looks like Mustang's who cared. The car, with an Italian front end, was 182 inches long and only 51 inches high. "All the $25,000 cars I'd seen at Torino [the Italian auto show] had that pointed, mouthy appearance," Iacocca said.

"I liked T-Bird II for the name," Henry Ford II complained, "but nobody else seemed to." Henry did not insist, and because of that a generation of pony names was born for Ford: Mustang, Maverick, Pinto, Mustang II.

The Mustang was an instant success when shown at the 1964 New York World's Fair. (A couple of reporters, remembering Ford's habit of getting rid of executives who slip, left a phony newspaper with the headline "Mustang Killed, Iacocca Out" at the rostrum were Lee Iacocca was to introduce the car. He did not laugh. Years later, on another stage, when Henry Ford II told the press he had fired Bunkie Knudsen as Ford's

e to 75,000, marines in Danang. Force upped to 125,000 and in combat. Ho vows to fight 20 years. In
s for new voting rights bill, Congress passes. U.S. orders all school districts desegregated by fall,

5.
The long hood and short trunk of the Mustang set a styling trend that lasted a decade. These first Mustangs were probably the prettiest.

'akistan fighting. UN cease fire. Castro permits Cubans with U.S. relatives to leave; airlift begun. LBJ calls for billboard, junkyard-free highways. NY bars death penalty. Negro riot in Watts, 34 ki

6.
The top of the line, Chevrolet Caprice. Conservative styling on the outside, fancy trim on the inside and a big engine made the car a big success.

president, clearing the way to the top for Lee, there are those who swear he slyly rubbed his nose and made an obscene gesture to those reporters.) "Lee said the American public doesn't like a sports car. It wants one that looks like a sports car," said Gene Bordinat, Ford's styling vice-president.

The base price was $2,368, which bought bucket seats and a three-speed stick on the floor. The options were plentiful and the car begged to be dolled up. Even when dressed to the roofline it was only $3,000. A 210-horsepower V-8 added $182, automatic transmission was $189 (the console, $52) and a four-speed stick $188. A rally-pac (clock and tachometer) was $76, simulated wire-wheel covers $46. There were 50 options. "Start putting in the extras," Iacocca had told his engineers when the low-priced version was costed out. "Put in class for the mass. If we're right, this will make the Model A look like nothing."

The Mustang was a fine automobile, despite critics' complaints that it was nothing but a prettied-up Falcon. Even *Consumer Reports*, which tried to sniff at Mustang, calling it "a nonutilitarian vehicle" with a "not inspired

ombe ousted in Congo (Zaire), Gen. Mobutu takes power. Communist rebellion spreads in Indonesia. Whi
g hot summers begin. Antiwar rally in NY draws 17,000, huge peace march in Washington. Vivian Malone

look" having just a "fillip of prestige" and only "a little of the aura" of T-Bird and Riviera, broke down. The variety of four engine options, three clutches, seven transmissions, two drive shafts, three wheel and tire sizes, three suspensions, four steering systems and four brake options, the magazine said, allowed the car to go "from a tame little filly all the way to a hot charger." The Mustang was quiet, well put together and good riding—which is rare for a new car. Chevrolet's Corvair "really handles like a sports car," the magazine said after its tests, but Mustang was good for a light car. She accelerated 0–60 m.p.h. in 17 seconds for the 101-h.p. six, in 10.5 seconds for the V-8, and under 10 seconds for the hottest packages, yet ran at 21 m.p.g. for the six and 15 m.p.g. for the V-8.

"I never think of the car laying an egg. If I did, I think I'd go nuts,"

7.
The Plymouth Belvedere Satellite intermediate. The full size Plymouth of '64 was cut down 3 inches to become this '65 car.

et up independent Rhodesia, overcome sanctions. Winston Churchill dead. Nguyen Van Thieu, Nguyen Cao
t Negro graduate of University of Alabama. Court kills Connecticut antibirth control law. Health war

8.
The luxury Imperial, which never was a serious challenger to Cadillac, was recently abandoned.

Iacocca said. In the first six months 420,000 Mustangs were sold, breaking the old mark for first-year sales held by Robert McNamara's Falcon.

There was a mistake or two. The rear bumpers were laid close up to the sheet metal. "When the gap between bumper and sheet metal becomes an inch greater, the resultant effect detracts from the appearance of the entire vehicle," Bordinat said. Ford led the industry in violating sound engineering by laying bumpers against sheet metal. It looked good, but any parking lot knock would crumple sheet metal. This enraged the owners,

nt for power in Vietnam. U.S. intensifies air war, hits missile sites, Haiphong. Boumedienne ousts Be
on cigarettes. Silver eliminated from dimes, quarters. Medicare passes. Henry Cabot Lodge new ambas

the insurance companies that paid the bill (and they became an important lobby against Detroit), and any Congressman who ever parked a car. This brought on the government-ordered five-mile-an-hour bumper, cost hundreds of millions of dollars in engineering and tooling, added $50–100 to the price of every car, added 100 pounds of weight, and made the cars nose heavy. All that came later, though.

The great tragedy is that Ford took its slim Mustang of 1965 and fed it. Seven years later the Mustang was 8 inches longer, 6 inches wider, nearly 600 pounds heavier, and $1,500 costlier. Sales nosedived.

"What happened to the Mustang market?" said Iacocca later. "It didn't go anywhere. It's still there. Tastes don't change that fast. We changed the

9.
Ford's Galaxie 500 XL.

lla to rule Algeria. DeGaulle wins runoff election in France. Vatican II: massive reforms, priest to
r in Saigon. U.S. immigration quotas liberalized. NYC papers closed by strike. Dow-Jones average to

10.
The Mercury Monterey was distinct from the Ford line and another unsuccessful attempt to cut into GM's dominance.

car. The market never left us. The original Mustang buyer is still there, still waiting for a good little car. We walked away from the market."

In 1965, however, everybody tried to play catch-up with Ford's Mustang. Chevy bravely came out with a new version of its Corvair, the first real restyling, and it was a gem. All the handling faults were gone, and there was a lovely hop-up fender and sports-car handling. Pretty as the Corvair looked, the Mustang was better; the little pancake six in the rear just could not run with Mustang's V-8. Later Chevy brought out the Camaro to match Mustang. Bill Mitchell, G.M.'s styling vice-president, still is irked by that model. "That first Camaro was committeed to death," he said. (Later models with the Z emblem rated high with the buffs and the Camaro was still in production years after the original Mustang was killed.)

gregation, kiss of peace, Latin mass ends. Chinese-India border crisis. Vietnam war going our way, M
942.64 Oct. 11. John Lindsay elected mayor of NYC. Abe Fortas named to Supreme Court. Power failur

Plymouth tried to stay in the game with the Barracuda, a Valiant with a new fastback roof and the biggest rear window ever. The car heated up inside so Chrysler invented flow-through ventilation for it: air came in the front and out the back without the wind noise from opening the window just a crack. Flow-through caught on around Detroit. Then G.M. figured it could save money by getting rid of the side vent windows and did so; the remainder of the car makers followed suit because G.M. made the vents seem old-fashioned, even though everyone but G.M. liked them. The Barracuda was a $5 million tooling job—peanuts, but it could not compete with Mustang. Later Chrysler brought out other sports versions, a new Barracuda and the Dodge Challenger, which never sold well. Eventually Chrysler gave up.

American Motors put a fastback roof on its Rambler and named the resulting whale the Marlin, again proof that fastbacks only look good on small cars. Richard Teague, the styling vice-president of American Motors, used to say that when times were tough "for three years they paid me in Marlin deck lids." He made up for it with his sporty, curvy Javelin car a few years later.

The sporty cars ignited an explosion, with production bursting to a record 9.3 million. All but American Motors shared the boom; they lamely called their '65s "The Sensible Spectaculars." All three big companies had new cars. Chevrolet had the new top-line Caprice with its vinyl roof, 120 pounds more weight, 3 inches more length, and 2 inches more width than the '64s. It had curved side glass and a replacement for the X-frame which some said was not protective in a side crash. Oldsmobile had its 4-4-2 (four-speed transmission, four-barrel carburetor, and two tailpipes) and Cadillac got rid of its fins at last.

1965

Production

General Motors	4,949,400
Ford	2,565,800
Chrysler	1,467,600
American Motors	346,400
Total	9,329,200

ge Bundy says; more troops requested. Michigan 34, Oregon State 7 in Rose Bowl: Pop: Folk at peak; Bob
cks out New York, entire northeast. Joan Baez (We Shall Overcome, It's All Over Now), Donovan (To Catch

11.
The Cadillac Calais Sedan. The fins are finally gone.

Ford introduced the LTD and flow-through ventilation, had a much-improved six, and developed Ford's quietness as a selling point. Mercury was all new and did not look like a Ford. A fastback Mustang, the 2+2, was added to the line in 1965 to supplement the notchback and convertible brought out in April.

·k (Downtown); Motown's Sound, the Supremes. Beatles are big, sell 140 million records in U.S. in '65,
.s for everyday wear, body stockings, fishnet bathing suit, see-through undies and the granny dress. O

Plymouth had an all-new big car, 209 inches long (Dodge was new, too) and the short '64 Plymouth was chopped 3 inches to a 203-inch length and became the intermediate Belvedere. Chrysler's compact Valiant and Dart were becoming acknowledged as the best of the compacts by 1965 as Corvair and Falcon went for power and pizzaz. Chrysler dropped its push-button automatic transmission for the conventional automatic shifter.

Disc brakes were put on ten cars, vinyl tops were becoming popular, and everything was coming up roses. Except quality.

"The condition of the 1965 cars," *Consumer Reports* said, "is about the worst, so far as sloppiness in production goes" in the decade, just "incredibly sloppy." Ignition switches failed, wires were loose, windows were not in right, transmission fluid and heaters leaked, seat adjusters jammed, engines would not start in park (often still don't), doors did not fit, turn signals did not work.

And a pollster said that the public rated car dealers less honest and trustworthy than undertakers, plumbers, and gas station managers. That said something. But nobody was listening.

0 hear them at Yankee Stadium; Paul McCartney (Yesterday). Clothes: Courreges' revolution; mini skirt
Rex Harrison (My Fair Lady), Julie Andrews (Mary Poppins). Cassius Clay destroys Sonny Liston in 1st

AFTERWORD

Long nights cryin' by the record machine,
Dreamin' of my Chevy and my old blue jeans.
—Crocodile Rock © 1972 Dick James Music Limited

Nineteen-hundred-sixty-five was the peak, and the cars—even the country—seemed to go downhill from then. The engines got bigger, not better, the paint became wilder, and the knobs fell off the dash. An army went to Vietnam and body counts became as important as horsepower, and the summers became long and hot.

There will be automobiles, and in just a few years more the mileage may be up to what it was a couple of decades ago. With some engineering they might run as well as they did in the past. They will be nonpolluting and roomy and safe, too, but they will never be as cheap, and the variety and choice will go.

Something will be missing, that wildness, the willingness to take a risk, the absolute awfulness when they were bad, and the thrill they gave when they were good.

They'll be cars—but they won't be quite as much fun.